THE
COMPLETE
WINE
COURSE

AUTHOR'S ACKNOWLEDGMENTS

My thanks for help with this book go to the numerous winemakers and friends that I have met and cracked open a bottle or two with over the years; to the late Hamish Cobban who inspired me to teach and Mike Grubb who taught me to drink better wine. Once again I dedicate this book to Rebecca and Chlöe and to the memory of Mum and Dad, to Eric who could never get over the fact that I could write a book and to Jill for seeing me through dark days.

Finally, I would like to thank Martin and the team at Carlton Books for their understanding over my loose interpretation of the word 'deadline'.

ABOUT THE AUTHOR

Tom Forrest was born in Edinburgh, since when he has been cursed with having to support the Scottish football and rugby teams. He first fell in love with wine, especially Pinot Noir, at the age of 18 when he was given a bottle of Nuits-St-Georges by a hotel manager. Following a career in hotel management, he began teaching wine & spirits to hospitality students in 1982 and is currently the Executive Manager – Wine Experience and Education at Vinopolis, where he has been working since 1999.

Tom is a member of the Institute of Wines and Spirits and a Certified WSET Wine Educator. He oversees the WSET education programme and the calendar of master classes at Vinopolis, which includes the "Meet the Experts" series, where Oz Clarke regularly features. His travels around the world invariably end up at a vineyard or two, and Tom has judged at various international wine competitions since 1997. In 2007 he won the UK Champagne Ambassador competition and was a European finalist. Tom has appeared on television shows, including *This Morning*, *The Daily Politics*, *Fake Britain* and *Come Date With Me*, as well as various local radio stations in London and south-east England, including BBC Radio 4's *Today* programme, *You and Yours* and the BBC World Service.

First published in 2003
Second edition 2013
Carlton Books Limited
20 Mortimer Street
London
W1T 3JW

10 9 8 7 6 5 4 3 2 1

A CIP catalogue record for this book is available from the British Library.

ISBN 978-1-78097-389-0

Printed in China

THE
COMPLETE
WINE
COURSE

TOM FORREST

CARLTON
BOOKS

CONTENTS

Silvaner/Sylvaner   67
Colombard   67
Palomino Fino   67
Cross-bred Whites:
Müller-Thurgau   68

Introduction   **7**   Bacchus   68
                                          Scheurebe   68

How Wine is Made   **10**   Ortega   68
                                          Pinot Blanc   69

How to Taste   **28**   Pinot Gris   69
                                          Aromatic White Varieties:

Know Your Grapes   **36**   Muscat   70
                                          Viognier   71

Main Grape Varieties   **52**   Gewürtztraminer   72
Principal Whites: Principal Reds:
Chardonnay   54   Cabernet Sauvignon   74
Sauvignon Blanc   56   Merlot   81
Sémillon   58   Pinot Noir   84
Chenin Blanc   61   Syrah/Shiraz   89
Riesling   62   Lesser-known Reds:
Lesser-known Whites: Petit Verdot   91
Aligoté   64   Cabernet Franc   91
Grüner Veltliner   64   Carmenère   93
Marsanne   64   Gamay   94
Rousanne   64   Grenache   95
Verdelho   66   Sangiovese   96

Nebbiolo	98
Barbera	101
Zinfandel	102
Tempranillo	103

Wine Styles 104
Red Bordeaux 108
Red Burgundy 114
White Burgundy 116
Sancerre and Pouilly-Fumé 120
Riesling 122
Champagne 127
Crémant 136
Sauternes 137
Sherry 140
Port 142

Wine Around the World 148
France 150
Germany 200
Italy 216
Spain 236
Portugal 250
USA & Canada 256
South America 268
Australia 278

New Zealand 292
South Africa 296
Austria 304
The Rest of the World 308

Wine Labels 318

Serving Wine 326

Wine and Food 338

Storing Wine 346

New World vs Old World 358

Wine and Health 364

**Organic/Biodynamic/
Natural Winemaking** 370

Vintages 376

Glossary 384

Further Information 394

Index 395

Picture Credits 400

WINE: A BASIC COURSE

INTRODUCTION

When I wrote the introduction to the first edition of this book, more than ten years ago – how time flies! – I was excited about the changes that had happened in the world of wine since I had first stumbled upon it, Narnia like, as a young chef in a hotel in North Berwick.

As I sit here writing this introduction I am still excited and passionate about wine and explaining its wonders in a no-nonsense manner, removing as much of the pretence that can surround this subject. Wine is a beverage after all, don't get me wrong, it is a great beverage that gives us a lot of pleasure, but at its heart it is something that we drink. Like most things however, some wines are better than others and I hope that with my help you can drink better wines.

But that got me thinking, what has changed over the past ten years? Well, one thing that has changed us all in the past few years has been the economic crash of 2008, the heady Champagne days of the early 'noughties' has been replaced by the harsh reality of the Prosecco 'teens' an analogy that perfectly represents our drinking habits in these times. We can't afford to celebrate in the old manner (or don't want to be seen spending to excess) so we choose a lower key wine. We still enjoy it but we spend our money more carefully.

So, in New Zealand and Australia, wineries whose business plan was based on rising consumption and prices are going bankrupt, even first growth 'Clarets' from Bordeaux are struggling to sell all their wines at the price they think they

Previous pages: Vines near Carcassonne in the Languedoc, France. **Left:** A sunset over vineyards in the Napa Valley.

Above: The finished product – a good glass of wine!
Right: The author, Tom Forrest.

deserve. Whilst at the lower end of the market, tax increases and currency fluctuations mean that cheap wine has to be made even more cheaply to keep the price down. The result seems to be that we are drinking less wine, but by spending a bit more a bottle, we are drinking better wine. We might not dine out as much, but we are entertaining, eating and drinking more at home and are willing to trade up the wines we drink.

However everything is not bad, the Chinese economy especially is still holding up and they have discovered wine in a big way. Not only are they (with government support) undertaking a massive vine planting programme, they are buying up vineyards right, left and centre in Bordeaux,

Burgundy , Australia and New Zealand, with the idea that they will directly supply the growing Chinese market.

As wine gets harder to sell, winemakers are trying to find new ways to make their wines look unique. This has seen a rise the number of Organic and Biodynamically produced wines appearing on the market as winemakers, and consumers, begin to understand the impact of 'heavy duty' winemaking on the environment and there is a growing interest in 'natural' winemaking, which I talk about in some detail.

Another thing that seems to have changed is my taste in wines. When I was drawing up my 'Top Tastes' for this edition I found that my tasting notes were much more European focussed than in the past. Perhaps this is partly because of the changes in the Australian wine industry that I talk about in the book, perhaps I have changed as I get older. Who knows? But at the moment there seem to be some really passionate and exciting winemakers stamping their individuality on the wines of Europe.

And English wines (once a joke or at best a cottage industry), from a standing start just over 50 years ago, the sparkling wines of England and Wales are recognised as being up there with the best. Our white table wines aren't bad either. In fact I am drinking a glass of a Blanc de Blancs English sparkling wine from the Sussex vineyards of Nyetimber as I write this.

New(ish) grape varieties have made a name for themselves in the past few years, Albarino from Galicia in northern Spain and Falanghina from Campania in Southern Italy to name but two. These traditional grape varieties have been "re-invented" by young winemakers who are producing fresh, crisp wines in a modern style.

Speaking of European wines, the E.U. has recently brought in legislation to try to harmonise the legislation that protects the names of wines (and foods) produced in the E.U. The terms PDO and PGI will, I hope, become more commonplace in the next few years and I have tried to use the new terms, where appropriate, in this book. For example, A.C .will become A.P. (Controlée to Protègée, Vin de Pays becomes IGP etc.) however at the moment this does not appear to be mandatory so you might still see the old terms being used.

I haven't begun to look at any effects of global warming on wine. The scare stories tell us that the South of France might be too hot to produce wine in the next 20 or so years and that wine regions will have to move further North. Who knows, a future edition might be raving about the new vineyards of Southern Scotland, however Liisa, I think that Finland will have to wait a while.

So, there are still lots of things happening to keep the wine drinker happy and I hope that this book will help you through the minefield of wine buying and that by understanding the terms on wine labels and the styles of wines to look out for, drink better and enjoy the experience to tasting fine wines.

Finally, and this hasn't changed, I hope that reading this book gives you the confidence to try new, different and interesting wines from old and new regions of production. Remember the only way to work out if you like a wine or not, is to try it for yourself. So …

Happy quaffing!

Tom Forrest

CHAPTER 1

HOW WINE IS MADE

At first glance, this is relatively easy: wine is just fermented grape juice, after all. However, if it were that simple, we would make our own wine from a few bunches of supermarket grapes instead of having to rely on the winemaker for it. In reality, wine is like many other simple ideas, where a number of straightforward practices combine to produce a complex process. And yet it is the very complexity of this process that makes wine such a fascinating subject; it makes each wine taste different from the next, even though they may share similar grape varieties, soil structures, and climates.

THE INGREDIENTS FOR MAKING WINE

It may be stating the obvious, but wine is made with the best quality grapes available. Nowadays, winemakers can have as much influence on the way in

which grapes are grown as the grape growers, or viticulturists, themselves.

THE FRUIT

The grape is virtually the perfect home-brew kit, containing all the necessary ingredients for the fermentation and production of wine:

• The pulp contains water, sugars (glucose and fructose), acids, and flavouring compounds.

Previous pages: A view of the cellars at Château Lafite in France.

Below: Wine is drawn off from the bottom of the vat prior to pumping over the 'cap' to help colour extraction.

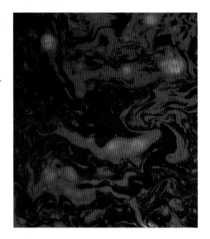

Right: Fermenting grape juice, which will need to be stirred occasionally to allow the skins to release their colour and tannins.
Far right: Stainless-steel vats, unlike oak barrels, do not add anything to the wine during fermentation or maturation.

• The skin contains flavouring compounds and colouring pigments – in particular, anthocyanins for making red wines. (It is because the grape pulp is virtually colourless that white wines can be made from red grapes; Champagne, for example, is normally made with a blend of grapes, including the reds Pinot Noir and Pinot Meunier as well as the white Chardonnay.)

• The skin is covered with a waxy substance, called the "bloom," which contains nutrients that the yeasts stick to and use during the fermentation process.

THE YEAST

Yeast is a marvellous, single-celled plant, which lives off sugar and, as a by-product during fermentation, produces alcohol and carbon dioxide (CO_2). This process also makes small quantities of other volatile compounds, such as esters, ketones, and aldehydes, all of which add to the aromas and flavours of a wine. Once the wine has reached about 15 per cent alcohol by volume, or all the sugar has been consumed, the yeasts will die and settle on the bottom of the vessel as sediment or "lees."

A further by-product of the fermentation process is heat. This has to be controlled, since too much heat will not only kill the yeasts in extreme cases but also affect the flavour of the wine. White wines especially have to be fermented at relatively low temperatures – somewhere between 12 and 19°C (54 –66˚F) – in order to keep the main aromas intact. Different flavours develop in the wine at different temperatures and times of the fermentation, and this is where temperature control becomes vitally important to the winemaking process. Red wines tend to be fermented at slightly higher temperatures, to aid the extraction of more colour from the skins.

WINEMAKING EQUIPMENT

The size and material of the fermentation vessel will have an effect upon the heat produced. Barrels, because they are

small, do not naturally reach the high temperatures that large vats do, and so rarely need help controlling the temperature. Vats can be made from epoxy-lined concrete, wood, or stainless steel. The latter is now the most common, because refrigeration can be used easily to control the temperature and to develop the flavours that winemakers desire in the final wine blend.

The material that the vessel is made from can influence the flavour of a wine, depending on the style of wine the wine-maker wants to produce. Stainless steel, an inert metal, neither adds nor removes flavours, but leaves wine with a clean,

The wooden staves of oak barrels are formed into shape by heating them up so that they become malleable. Iron rings are then put round them to hold the wood together.

sharp taste. New and old oak barrels, or a combination of both, can be used for adding flavour to the fermenting or maturing wine. Coopers have made barrels in the same manner for thousands of years. The staves of the barrel start straight and are placed in a frame over a wood-chip fire, where the heat makes the wood pliable. By forcing hoops down the staves, the cooper can shape them into a barrel shape. Heat not only softens the wood but also draws the extracts in the wood out to the surface and caramelises them. This is known as toasting, and winemakers can specify the level of 'toast' they want for their barrels.

The main extract in oak is the sweetly flavoured vanillin, but there are additional substances, such as lactones, which give a coconut flavour, and phenols, which add spicy characters. The influence of such flavours diminishes each time the barrel is used, and after about five times the influence is almost zero. This means that the winemaker can add complexity to the final wine by blending wines from barrels of different ages, thereby introducing a combination of wood flavours.

MAKING THE WINE

On the face of it, the winemaking process has hardly changed since time began. Grapes are picked at the desired stage of ripeness. They can be collected by hand, which allows for a selection of the best grapes in the field, with rotten or underripe bunches or berries being discarded before they reach the winery. The bunches can either be placed in small baskets, thus preventing any damage to the fruit before it is pressed, or

Below: These traditional vertical presses are used for extracting the juice from the grapes because they are less expensive than doing it by foot.
Below right: Grape pickers take some of the harvest down to the collecting point.

'slapping' the vine with fibreglass rods to remove the bunches, which are then collected by conveyor belts, transported to trucks, and taken to the winery.

PRESSING THE GRAPES
Once at the winery, the grapes are pressed. Treading grapes by foot is one of the best

transferred into a large truck for transport to the winery. The costs of hand harvesting are high, so it is normally reserved for better quality wines, although there are some vineyards that are too steep for any other method.

Many vineyards now use mechanical harvesters to keep costs down. These have the advantage of being available for work twenty-four hours a day if necessary, and many hot-climate wineries deliberately pick their fruit at night to keep it cooler. The machines work by ways to do this, although it is very rarely used today. The foot is hard enough to split the skins of the grapes but soft enough to prevent damage to the seeds, which would release bitter oils into the wine, or to the stalks, which would add unwanted tannins. However, costs and the sheer volume of grapes that need to be pressed quickly in order to avoid oxidation damage mean that mechanical presses have become the norm.

Wine presses come in two forms: the more traditional vertical or basket press, where a horizontal disc is pushed down into a wooden basket and the juice escapes through gaps in the sides; or the more modern horizontal press, which basically turns the vertical press on its side.

These presses have perforated skins against which the grapes are forced, either by an air bag or by two vertical disks moving toward each other. Another form of horizontal press uses a screw to push the grapes through a perforated base. This has a higher output and is used in the larger commercial wineries.

The volume of juice pressed from the grapes will depend on the variety, but on average 1.13 kilograms of grapes will produce enough juice to make an average bottle of wine (750ml). Red wines have to be pressed during or after fermentation, so that the skins stay in contact with the juice and release their colour. Red-wine grapes, therefore, have to be split or crushed and destemmed rather than pressed.

Once the grapes have been pressed, the skins, seeds, and stalks are removed and the juice is placed directly in the fermentation vessel. (In the case of red wine, the skins are kept with the juice in the vessel.) At this point, sulphur dioxide (SO_2) is added to prevent any bacterial contamination and to kill any 'wild' yeasts that could affect the flavour. If the fruit does not contain enough natural sugars, chaptalisation may be carried out. This is the addition of a small amount of sugar to the juice or grape must – a process discovered by a Dr Jean-Antoine Chaptal, which is strictly controlled in the areas of

Sometimes pressing grapes can be a real group effort, as these winery workers show in Portugal.

'Press wine' being extracted from red grape skins after fermentation using a horizontal press. This stronger flavoured wine can then be blended with the 'free run' wines if needed.

the world where it is permitted because, if overdone, it can ruin a wine.

At this point, a cultured yeast might also be added. Research has discovered that different strains of yeast can bring different qualities to a wine. Some produce higher levels of alcohol, whereas

others may enhance certain flavours in the final wine. One such strain is popular in Beaujolais, for example, where it brings out a banana flavour in the wine. The acid level of the grape juice can also be adjusted at this point.

FERMENTATION

Once the yeasts have been added, fermentation will start quickly. A controlled fermentation will normally last for anywhere between one and three weeks, depending on the grape variety and the style of wine. Once fermentation has begun, however, red wines still need a lot of attention.

First, if left alone, the skins in the vat will float to the surface and form a cap. This reduces the amount of skin contact with the wine and will prevent the maximum extraction of colour from the skins. To overcome this, the cap must be broken up and mixed with the wine on a regular basis. This 'maceration' can be done using a process known as 'pumping over', where wine is taken from the bottom of the vat and pumped over the cap to break it up. Alternative methods include suspending someone over the vat, who then stamps down on the cap to break it up, or reaching into the vat with hydraulic rams or paddles.

Some modern wineries overcome this problem by using rotary fermenters – stainless-steel vats on their sides, which use motors to rotate the contents, working much in the way as a washing machine does. These machines can be computer-controlled to time the amount and duration of the turns, maximising the colour extraction while minimising any damage to the wine.

Another factor to take into account when making a red wine is the length of time the skins stay in contact with the wine. This will depend on the thickness of the grape skins – thick skins contain more colouring pigment – and the style of the

When the fermentaion of the wine is complete, it is transferred to vats or barrels for maturation. These old oak vats will contribute to the development of the wine's flavours, unlike stainless steel.

wine that is being made. Rosé wines, for example, may need only two or three days' maceration before the still fermenting juice is drawn off, whereas full-bodied reds may require twelve or more.

MATURATION

Once fermentation is over, the maturation process begins. Again, the winemaker has a choice of vessels. Stainless steel will impart nothing to the wine, but will allow it to be efficiently stabilised. Products such as tartrates need to be removed from the wine at this stage and any proteins that would make the wine hazy. Tartrates are a natural product, that form sugarlike crystals and, although harmless, many winemakers remove them before bottling, to keep their wines looking pristine.

Oak barrels will again add those desirable, smoky vanilla notes, depending on the age of the barrel. Top quality red wines that are meant to age well in the bottle will normally spend 18 months to two years in barrels before being bottled, because, in addition to the flavours, wood tannins are also absorbed by the wine. These help preserve the wine during its long 'sleep' in the cellared bottle.

During this maturation period, the wine will be 'racked' – that is, the wine will be drawn off any sediment lying at the bottom of the vessel and pumped into a new vat. In some cases, a second, bacterial 'fermentation' will take place. Called a malolactic fermentation, this converts the harsh malic acid (also common to apples) to a softer lactic acid (as found in dairy products). This is most easily detected in white Chardonnays, which develop a creamy note on the nose and palate. Malolactic fermentation is not encouraged in white wines, such as those made with Sauvignon Blanc grapes, where a tart, refreshing acidity is desired in the final wine.

THE FINAL STAGES

Before bottling, the wine can be 'fined', or filtered, to remove any last unwanted particles. Finer wines will receive gentler treatments, because it is easy to filter out some of their character at the same time. Such methods tend to use natural products, mixed with a little wine, which

are added to the vessel and allowed to fall through the wine, collecting particles on the way down. These include, egg white and bentonite, a form of earth.

Eventually the wine is bottled. White wines tend to be bottled earlier than reds, in some cases just six months after the harvest. It is important that the bottling machinery and the bottles are sterile, so the wine is uncontaminated and will not spoil before it is opened. If the wine is sweet, winemakers may add some extra SO_2 to prevent a second fermentation.

The bottling process is extremely important, as it could still all go wrong at this stage if the machinery and the bottles are not kept scrupulously clean.

CHAPTER 2

HOW TO TASTE

If you really want to understand wine and know how to choose the best, then being able to assess its characteristics properly can be a great help.

Tasting wine can be as simple as it sounds: swill some round in your mouth and see if you like it. It can also be a serious analysis of the contents of the glass. For most people, it will be a combination of the two. There are only a few occasions on which you may be called upon to taste wine. First, you may be buying it – either a bottle with a meal or a case at the cellar door – and want to check that it is not faulty, or wish to keep accurate records of the wines that you have bought and drunk, perhaps to note how the wine has changed over the years.

Second, you may be judging it against other wines that you know, or third, as a party game, you may be trying to identify

a wine 'blind' – in other words, someone is asking you to identify a wine purely by tasting it. In all of these cases the process is the same. You look at the wine, smell it and then taste it. Peculiarly, the last stage actually tells you very little, it simply confirms things that your senses of sight and smell have told you already.

BREAKING THE PROCESS DOWN

The first items that you need are a glass, a white background, and a well-lit space, with no distracting aromas. (Incidentally, don't wear perfume or cologne at a wine-tasting event because the aroma will put off other tasters, even if you have got used to the smell yourself.)

The glass should be clear, of even thickness, and narrower at the top than at the bottom. This allows the aromas to be concentrated and directed towards your nose when you smell the wine. The glass should also be of a generous size, so that you can swirl the wine around without spilling it. This releases the volatile elements, making it easier to smell them. The International Standards Organisation has a glass design that is used all over the world in competitions and in wineries. The important thing, if you are a serious wine taster, is to keep the glasses that you use scrupulously clean. Always wash them separately, without detergent, and dry them with a cloth that is not used for any other purpose. This prevents them from becoming contaminated with smells such as detergent fragrance and cooking fat.

Swilling the wine around in the glass helps to reveal its aromas and its alcohol content.

WHAT TO LOOK FOR IN A WINE

After placing a small amount of wine in the glass, tip it to a 45° angle and look through the wine to the white background. This makes it easier to see any nuances of shade in colour. The wine should be clear and bright: if it is hazy or dull looking, it is showing signs of faulty fermentation or filtering. There should not be any bubbles moving through the wine (unless it is sparkling), which could be a sign that it has begun to ferment again. Don't be put off if there are some bubbles sticking to the glass, however. Sometimes, winemakers add a dash of carbon dioxide gas to help keep the wine fresh, and this can cause such bubbles. A quick swirl should get rid of them.

Now look at the colour of the wine. You will notice that its shade will fade between the middle, or core, of the wine and the rim of the glass. In fact, some wines will have a transparent ring round the rim. The size of this ring will tell you something about the intensity of flavour in the wine – the larger the transparent ring, the more dilute the flavours tend to be. You may note, in red wines, that the colour will actually change as you look toward the rim. As red wine ages, the colour goes from a youthful purple to a mature tawny or brick colour and you can first detect this colour change on the rim of the wine.

Swirl the wine around the glass, coating as much of the glass as possible, without spilling any. As the wine falls back down the glass, you will note that it does not fall down as a sheet, but forms 'beads' and lines as it drops. The technical term for these beads is 'legs'. The legs show the alcohol content of the wine, and, put simply, the more legs the wine has, the more alcohol there is in the wine. And alcohol is a good thing. Bear in mind that in cool climates it can be difficult to get the grapes to the correct stage of ripeness before harvesting, in which case, the more alcohol in the wine, the better the wine should be. The French *Appellation* system recognises this by laying down minimum alcohol levels that the wine has to achieve before it can be awarded the *Appellation Protégée (A.P.)*.

WHAT THE NOSE CAN TELL YOU

So far, simply by looking at the wine, you can begin to comment on its condition, age, alcohol content, and quality.

Now smell the wine. Swill it around the glass again, to release its volatile elements, before sticking your nose in and taking a good sniff. Think about the aromas: does the wine smell like wine? Most faults show up on the nose of the wine.

COMMON FAULTS DETECTED BY THE NOSE OF A WINE

These are the main faults that you will find by the nose of the wine. There are others, but good winemakers will spot them in the winery and take measures to correct them before bottling the wines.

• Excess sulphur: SO_2 is a preservative, but if too much is used, it leaves an aroma similar to a burnt match on the wine. This can normally be removed by mixing some air with the wine – either by decanting or giving it a good swirl in the glass.

• Oxidation: this is caused when oxygen comes into contact with wine. White wines, especially, may take on a brownish colour but, more importantly, the wine – red or white – will have a 'sherrylike' aroma as the oxygen reacts with the alcohol. It can also smell dull and flat.

• Cork or corked: it is important to note that a corked wine is not one that has bits of cork floating in it. That may be unattractive, but will not affect the taste. Corked wine has been contaminated, via the cork, by a substance called 2-4-6 Trichloroanisole (TCA). The cork can become contaminated during the sterilisation process, by coming into contact with chlorine.

We are very sensitive to TCA; recent estimates state that a teaspoon of TCA would be sufficient to spoil all the wine made in Australia in a year. The result of this contact is a distinctive musty aroma, similar to damp cardboard or stale, sweaty sneakers.

Professional wine tasters will make notes during a tasting session to remind themselves of what they thought about a wine and if it is one to remember.

• Vinegar: this is an extension of contact with oxygen. Sometimes, in addition to oxygen, bacteria, and especially acetobacter, come into contact with the wine. The effect of these bacteria on the alcohol is to produce acetic acid and start the process of turning the wine to vinegar.

• Hydrogen sulphide or reduction: mainly found in red wines, this is an aroma, reminiscent of rotten eggs, which is formed during the fermentation process when yeasts react with sulphur dioxide. This aroma can be easily removed from the wine by adding air to it through decanting.

Having decided that the wine is 'clean', or not faulty, you can examine the fruit characters of the aromas. Consider the intensity of the fruit aromas: are they strong or weak? Weak aromas may indicate a dilute or thinly flavoured wine, whereas more intense aromas are normally signs of a better-quality wine.

Strangely enough, looking at and then smelling a wine will tell you more about a wine than tasting it.

WINE AROMA CATEGORIES

• Fruity: oddly enough, very few wines smell or taste of grapes. Common fruity aromas are of black or red fruits, such as blackcurrants, raspberries, cherries, strawberries, or plums; tropical fruits such as pineapples, melons, and mangoes; stone fruits, such as peaches and apricots; and citrus fruits such as lemons, limes, grapefruit, and oranges.

• Floral: aromas such as honeysuckle and elderflower are common on some white wines. Red wines can have violet or rose aromas.

• Vegetal: pale-coloured white wines tend to have grassy or leafy aromas, such as nettle, asparagus, or freshly cut grass and garden peas. Some red wines can have bell pepper or brassica (cabbage) aromas, and some mature reds even go as far as 'farmy', compost aromas.

• Spicy: white and black pepper, cedarwood, and spice aromas appear on some aromatic white wines, but mainly on red wines.

• Savoury: these mainly appear on red wines, and aromas such as black coffee, soy sauce, and beef extract are not uncommon.

• Other aromas: depending on the wines and their ages, you might also find that, in no particular order, vanilla, pencil shavings, leather, chocolate, and smoke may also appear at this stage.

This is not an exhaustive list of aromas because senses of taste and smell are very personal; where one taster may smell lemons, another may find limes. This doesn't mean that one is right or wrong, just that different noses have different sensitivities.

Do remember, however, that when we smell a wine, we are not looking to identify ingredients. None of these fruits or spices has been added to the wine! Because we do not have a specific vocabulary to describe the aromas of wines, we have developed descriptions of what the wines remind us of. We use our memory banks of aromas to help us remember what wines smell of, in the same way we use word games, like mnemonics, to remind us of important phrases or the colours of the rainbow.

Comparisons are often made to fruit and vegetables in order to describe the flavours and aromas of wine.

TASTING THE WINE

This is more serious than just drinking. To help you analyse the wine you have to incorporate some air into it. In other words, you slurp it! Noisy and attention-grabbing, I know, but there is valid reason for doing this.

Your tongue is a fairly simple tasting tool, recognising just five aspects of flavour. It used to be thought that these flavours were recognised on certain areas of the tongue but it is now known that sweetness, bitterness (normally caused by tannins in the wines), saltiness, acidity (which can last all through to the "finish" or end of the wine) and umami receptors are spread evenly over the tongue. Of these flavours umami is the most difficult to describe. First recognised in the Far East, it is best thought of as savouriness.

Think of soy sauce, parmesan cheese or Marmite and you might get the idea.

Now, if your tongue can only recognise these five flavours, where do we get the fruit and spicy flavours of wine from? To understand this we have to look at your anatomy. Within your nasal cavity is the olfactory bulb which is linked to your brain. It was originally part of your primeval fight-or-flee mechanism. This bulb can recognise over 5,000 different aromas. Nowadays we rarely need to smell danger but it is still an important part of our sense of taste. When we eat or drink something, the aromas are carried from the mouth to the nasal receptors along a passage and it is these receptors that allow us to identify tastes from our memory banks.

Drawing air through the wine and into your mouth releases the volatile vapours and sends them up to the receptors, which, if blocked, do not work efficiently. Which is why food is bland and unappealing when you have a cold.

So how do you slurp? To do this you need to imagine that you are drawing up the last bit of spaghetti into your mouth. Take a small amount of wine into your mouth, purse your lips (the spaghetti moment) and after tipping your head forward, draw some air through the wine and into your mouth.

Once you have slurped the wine, you will notice the way that more flavours are released, compared to simply sipping it. This exaggeration of flavours will help you examine the wine more easily. Look at the length of time that the flavours remain on the palate after you have either swallowed the wine or, as professionals do, spat it out. The longer they linger, the better the quality of the wine.

Think about the texture or "mouth-feel" of the wine: is it light or full-bodied? Does it feel rich and creamy? This could be a sign that the wine has been aged or matured in oak barrels or has gone through a malo-lactic fermentation.

Now you can come to your conclusions about the wine. Firstly, do you like the flavours? Is the wine balanced? In other words, are all the flavour components in harmony with each other or do one or more components dominate?

What is the level of quality? Is it a quaffing, everyday easy-drinking wine, or is it a fine example of the winemaker's craft? Is it mature enough? Does it need more time, or has it passed its peak? Are there any obvious faults? If you know the wine that is being tasted or other wines from the same region, do your conclusions match your understanding of that wine?

You may not want to slurp and spit your wine when presented with it in a restaurant, but remember—the wine waiter or sommelier is not really interested in whether you like the wine or not; you chose it, after all. However, he or she does want you to approve the wine before you are charged for it. Think of this as your last chance: use your senses of sight and smell and give the wine a discreet slurp to identify any faults before accepting it or asking for a replacement bottle.

CHAPTER 3

KNOW YOUR GRAPES

HOW VINES GROW

There are many species of grapevine in the world, but there is only one that is used for making wine. The Mediterranean vine, or *vitis vinifera*, to give it its botanical name, produces all the varieties of wine grapes that we have come to know and love.

It is generally agreed that wine production started over 8,000 years ago, in the Caucasus mountains in the country that we now know as Georgia. Mount Ararat is also in this area, and the Bible tells us that Noah planted the first vine there when the ark landed after the great flood. Since then, the vine has travelled, with the aid of traders, to Egypt, Greece, and, under the Roman Empire, to Spain, France, Germany and England.

Previous page: Merlot grapes in the Médoc. **Above:**
Young vines in the Napa Valley with a drip irrigation system.
Opposite: Chardonnay vines growing in Australia.

WHERE VINES GROW

The wine vine is a sensitive plant and only grows well enough to produce good quality, ripe fruit, in commercial quantities, between two distinct lines of latitude around the world. These are the lines 50–30° north and 30–50° south – the temperate zones in which the vines thrive. The vine will grow outside these zones, but the conditions are rarely suitable for large-scale production.

It is important to remember that the vine does not need heat to ripen the fruit; in fact, too much heat can 'cook' the grapes on the vine, with the result that the wine has, at best, the 'jammy' flavours of hot fruits or, at worst, burnt overtones. Instead, the vine ripens its fruit using sunlight and photosynthesis to convert starches in the grapes to sugars, and the most suitable climate is, therefore, a temperate one. The heat of the sun can be overcome by natural means, however: a mountain range may be the source of a cooling wind; and prevailing coastal winds or fogs can reduce the effect of the sun, as can planting vines at altitude.

The vines need copious quantities of water, as well as plenty of sunshine. Outside the European Union (EU) this can be supplied through irrigation – normally drip irrigation, where precise amounts of water can be fed directly onto the roots of the vines, as opposed to spraying or flooding entire vineyards. Inside the EU, however, the vine grower generally has to depend on the supply that nature provides. This can, and does, lead to variations in the quality of the wines from vintage to vintage, not only because rainfall is soaked up through the roots

and stored in the grapes, thereby diluting the flavours, but also because rainfall during harvest leaves a film of water on the grapes, which dilutes the juice when they are crushed.

In addition to the specific regional climate, each individual vineyard will also have its own 'micro' or site climate. This can be produced by the sheltering effect of a hill or forest, which gives

An example of a microclimate in action: these vineyards in British Columbia, in Canada, are protected from prevailing winds by the forest at the top of the slope, which also aids drainage and maximises exposure to the sun. The vineyards in the background are being irrigated with sprinklers.

protection from the prevailing climatic influence, or by planting vines on a slope in order to maximise exposure to the sun. In some cases, a cooling maritime breeze or fog will help create the ideal conditions. The effect of the microclimate on the developing vines explains some of the differences in quality between neighbouring vineyards.

Although different vine varieties need

different types of soil, there are two common factors regarding its quality: it needs to be well drained – vines cannot cope with wet roots – and it should be relatively poor or infertile. If the soil is too rich, vines tend to produce more foliage and fewer bunches of grapes. However, when a vine is stressed, it 'feels' the need to reproduce, and so, many grape bunches appear. It is for this reason that some of the best vineyards in the world consist of gravel, slate, clay, or even stony, soils. This combination of poor soil, microclimate, and, of course, grape variety, is referred to by the French as *terroir* – the environment that creates individual flavours and aromas in wines from different vineyards, villages, and regions; the 'magic' that makes all wines taste different and encourages us to explore and seek out new wines.

PETS AND DISEASES

Regardless of the characteristics that define each individual *terroir*, all vines are susceptible to a host of pests and diseases.

THE DEVASTATOR

Juicy, sweet, attractive grapes are obviously a luxury lunch for birds, and in some countries, nets, automatic scarecrows, and noisy motorbikes are used to keep them away. By far the biggest pest that attacks the vine, however, is not only extremely small, but is not interested in its sweet fruit either. *Phylloxera vastatrix* is an insect from the East Coast of the United States, which first arrived in Europe in the 1860s. At the time it lived on a species of vine unique to the continent – *vitis labrusca* – which had developed tough roots to prevent the larvae of the aphid from destroying the vine when biting into it, thereby allowing bacteria in and sap out.

Unfortunately, the Mediterranean vine had never been exposed to this little yellow bug, and, with its soft, sweet roots, it became an easy target. Within ten years or so more than six million acres of vines had been destroyed in France alone – hence the name *vastatrix* or 'devastator'. *Phylloxera* is now endemic in almost all the world's vineyards, having been transported on cuttings, in soil, in water, or simply by being blown for miles by the wind. The result is that, today, only one country is *phylloxera*-free, and that is Chile, which is protected by a desert to the north, the Andes to the east, and Antarctica and the Pacific Ocean to the south and west.

It was nearly twenty years before a method was found for controlling this pest. American viticulturlists realised that the insect was the same as the one found in the United States, and they began to develop a process of grafting the fruiting *vinifera* vine onto rootstocks from the resistant *labrusca* variety. This process continues to the present day, although some varieties of rootstock do not suit all soil types, while others seem to be less resistant than they once were. Another early attempt at finding a cure for this pest involved breeding entirely new strains of vine, by crossing *vinifera* vines with the American *labrusca* varieties. The results of these crossings were called 'hybrid', or 'direct producing', vines, and it was found that they had good

resistance to some fungal diseases and pests, including *phylloxera*.

However, the quality of the wines produced was not as good as that from the grafted vines, although they can still be found today in some French vineyards, but planting is discouraged. Outside Europe,

some of these vines are still used because they have a tolerance to intense cold.

In some areas of Canada and New York State, where the cold would freeze and split a normal vine, hybrid varieties, such as *vidal*, can be found producing some delicious wines.

Vines in the Mendocino Valley in the United States showing signs of an attack of the dreaded phylloxera that feeds on the sap in the roots.

OTHER PESTS

The roots of vines can also be attacked by microscopic worms called nematodes, which may also carry viruses and bacteria that can further harm the plant. While some rootstocks do show resistance to these pests, many vineyards will inject powerful insecticides into the soil to sterilise it before planting a new vineyard.

Two pests that do little harm to the plant on their own, but carry dangerous bacteria, are the glassy-winged sharpshooter and the leafhopper. These insects carry Pierce's disease, a bacterial infection that can destroy an entire vineyard in five years.

There is no cure for the disease and the insects are hard to control. However, natural predators, such as wasps, can be encouraged into the vineyard area to control the population.

Other pests include red and yellow spider mites, which infest the leaves and lessen the effects of them. These may be controlled by insecticide sprays, or, in organic vineyards, by the use of natural predators (see page 373).

FUNGAL DISEASES

The diseases that attack vines tend to be fungal in nature, because vine leaves act as a canopy, trapping dampness and creating the moist, warm atmosphere that encourages fungal growths.

• Oidium: this mildew shows as a white powder on the leaves and berries. If left untreated, it will cause the grapes to split.

Dormant Champagne vines in winter waiting for the arrival of spring. Really cold winters can freeze the sap in the stocks.

• Peronospera: this mildew shows as a furry fungus on leaves and reduces their ability to photosynthesise.

• Black rot: this fungus spreads in mild, wet weather, affecting both the leaves and the grapes. In some cases, up to 80 per cent of the crop can be ruined by this disease.

• Anthracnose: this mainly affects hybrid vines planted in damp soils, initially developing brown stains on the leaves, which then turn into holes if left untreated.

All of these diseases can be treated with a chemical mixture developed in 1885. 'Bordeaux mixture' is a blend of copper sulphate, lime, and water, and although it has been replaced nowadays by manufactured systemic fungicides, it is still recognised and its use permitted in organic vineyards.

• Eutypoise or dead arm: this fungal disease attacks the 'wood' of a vine, penetrating through old pruning cuts. Painting a new cut with a fungicide can control the disease, but it can be many years before the symptoms show in a vine, by which time, it is too late for treatment. The main effect of the disease is a dramatic reduction in the yield or number of grape bunches. This can have a devastating effect on the commercial value of the vineyard, although there is no real reduction in the quality of the grapes, just their number.

• *Botrytis cinerea* or grey rot: this fungal disease is not always an unwanted guest in the vineyard. Spread by damp, humid weather, if this disease attacks young, immature grapes it can soften and split the skins, allowing bacteria to get inside

the berries and ruin them. However, if it attacks ripe and healthy white grapes and the weather is hot enough to slow down the growth of the mould, then 'noble rot' results.

This rot removes moisture from the grapes, but retains acids and sugars. This results in very sweet grapes which, despite looking rotten and unattractive, can produce – especially in Sauternes – some of the world's sweetest and longest living white wines in the world.

The harvest consists of selecting and picking individual grapes that have reached the correct level of 'rot'. When they are pressed, a viscous, ambrosia-like nectar comes out that, after fermentation – which can be hard to start because there is so much sugar in the juice – produces wine with a high sugar content, and yet enough acidity to prevent it tasting like a cloying syrup.

CLIMATIC PROBLEMS

The vagaries of the weather can damage the vine during the growing season, affecting grape production.

Left: Sémillon grapes at the beginning of noble rot. Since the rot affects the grapes unevenly, they have to be picked individually.

Below: A hard year in the vineyard. These grapes show signs of mould and millerandage and many will need to be discarded at the winery.

FROST

Frost can be a great danger during spring, when the tender new shoots first appear from the buds. If these are 'burned', a vine's growth can be put back so far as to prevent the grapes from ripening before the end of the growing season. Planting vines on slopes with a river running through the valley will help prevent damage, as frost will simply roll down the hill and be carried away by the moving water.

Vine growers not fortunate enough to have a slope would traditionally light 'smudge pots' filled with oily rags, to generate smoke and fend off the frost. Modern methods of frost protection include the use of heaters and fans to circulate air through a vineyard or spraying the vines with water. The water freezes and expands to form a protective, insulating layer around the delicate shoots.

HAIL

A hailstorm during the summer, especially near the harvest, can devastate a vineyard, splitting grapes and smashing whole bunches. Many regions now employ planes to fly up and 'seed' clouds, forcing the contents to fall elsewhere.

COULURE AND MILLERENDAGE

Although the vine is a self-pollinating plant, it does need the correct conditions at pollination to ensure a good 'set'. If it rains or there is too strong a breeze, pollination can be poor. Coulure is the term used when the flowers fail to set properly and the small berries drop off

the bunch. Millerendage is caused by poor fertilisation of the flowers and results in small, hard, immature grapes forming on the bunches. These problems normally happen together; that is, the grapes that survive coulure will have a greater tendency toward millerendage later in the season. This leads to a poor harvest for the grower, with extra effort needed in removing the immature and bitter grapes, and hard work for the winemaker, trying to produce a wine with fewer grapes that are of a poorer quality than normal.

PRUNING VINES

Vines are pruned and trained for many reasons. A very practical reason is that the new fruiting shoots form on the previous year's growth; if the vines were not pruned, the fruit would soon be too high up to harvest easily. Pruning can also be used to restrict the yield of a vine by reducing the number of growing buds at the beginning of the growing year. The effect of this is to control the quality, as well as the quantity, of grapes produced because the vine can only produce so much flavour; if the vine were left to grow rampantly, there would be many grapes, but with little taste.

Pruning ensures that the grower can reach a balance between the number of grapes produced and the level of flavour in the juice. In many areas, legislation states both the maximum yield of a vine – normally expressed in hectolitres per hectare (Hl/Ha) – and the method of pruning to be employed in the vineyards.

Because Galicia can be quite overcast, the vines are trained so that the canopy exposes the leaves to the maximum amount of sunshine to ripen the fruit.

Once they have been pruned, the vines are then 'trained'. This will not only keep the vineyard neat and tidy, but will also allow the vine grower to control the number of leaves produced, so that a balance is created between leaves, offering shade and photosynthesis, and grape production. Nowadays, because of mechanisation in the vineyard, most vines are trained along wires to allow the easy passage of tractors when spraying or harvesting. The training method may be influenced by one of several factors in the vineyard: a vine may be trained high, to reduce the effect of heat radiation from the soil, or low, to increase the benefit of any reflected heat. Wind strength and the damage it can cause to the grapes may also be a factor.

Smudge pots in use in Chablis, France. When lit and combined with the slope, these pots offer frost protection to the tender vines.

SEND IN THE CLONES

We are all aware of the varieties of wine grapes that are available to growers. In some cases, the choice is set in local legislation: for instance, you cannot grow Chardonnay in Bordeaux and make an *A.P.* wine from it. However, growers also have the choice of 'subvarieties' or clones of the different vines. These are vines that have been developed over a number of years through selective propagation, in a bid to develop a desirable characteristic – earlier ripening, better fruit set, bigger yields, or resistance to disease, for example. These clones are given unromantic numbers to identify them from each other, and, again, legislation may prevent the use of certain clones because it is felt that the particular character harms the quality of the final wine. This is especially true of high-yielding clones, which tend to produce mediocre and dilute wines. So far, there have been few attempts to genetically modify vines in the laboratory, however, there are rumours of some developments to try to combat Pierce's disease (see page 45) in California.

As well as the cloning of vines, growers wanting to make better vines would cross different varieties of *vinifera* vines in order to produce new varieties with the best qualities of both parents. One of the best-known crossings was developed by the Swiss-born Dr Müller, when he was working at the German research station in Geisenheim. His aim was to develop a vine based on the quality fruit of the Riesling variety, but which would ripen earlier. Late-ripening fruit can be a problem in cool German vineyards, so he crossed it with an earlier ripening variety, either the Silvaner or Chasselas. Since he had been born in the canton of Thurgau, he modestly named this new variety Müller-Thurgau (see page 68). Unfortunately, although it does ripen early, it also produces rather dull wines. Nowadays, there are some interesting crossings coming from Germany, such as Ortega and Bacchus, producing attractively aromatic wines in cool areas of the world, especially England and Wales.

OLD VINES

It is generally accepted that older vines can make better wines—not that vine age is a prerequisite to a wine's quality, but it is a factor than can be taken into account.

It takes three or four years for a vine to begin to produce quality grapes in a commercial amount and after 20 to 25 years the yield of grapes from the vine begins to fall. However, as the yield drops the quality of the grapes' flavour, acid levels and sugar content grow. Age means that the vines tend to be drought-resistant and what has been described as "Darwinian" survival skills mean that the vines ripen earlier in the season. Ungrafted vines in *phylloxera*-free vineyards can continue like this for well over a hundred years, until the yields simply become economically unviable. Grafted vines in *phylloxera*-affected vineyards reach this state after about 80 years because grafting slows down the effects rather than curing.

For this reason you will often see the terms "Old Vines" or "Vieilles Vignes" written on a label to suggest a higher quality than another wine from the same producer. But what makes a vine old? At which birthday does the vine celebrate? Well, the answer is that there is no answer. There is no definition, so in a well established vineyard the old vines might be over 50 years old, whereas in a new vineyard or region the "old" vines might be young whippersnappers in their 20s. Still old, but only in relation to the surrounding vines.

To overcome any possible misleading use, the Australian company Yalumba sat down in 2007, looked at their vineyard records and came up with a charter to describe their vine stock, which they believed contained some of the oldest Shiraz vines in the world. This charter was soon the talk of the other Barossa Valley producers and in 2009 the charter (with a couple of amendments) was adopted across the region.

One reason for this was to identify the oldest vines in the region and preserve them (in the 1980s a "vine pull" scheme had managed to destroy many acres of old Barossa vines at the expense of younger ones).

The charter divides the old vines into four categories:

Barossa Old Vine: Vines that have documented evidence proving that they are 35 years old or over.

Barossa Survivor Vine: Vines that have survived the 1980s vine pull scheme and have documented evidence proving that they are 70 years old or over.

Barossa Centenarian Vine: As the name suggests these vines have documented evidence proving that they are 100 years old or over. They will have been planted before irrigation was fully developed and so site selection was paramount to ensure success. And finally:

Barossa Ancestor Vine: These vines can trace their roots back to the original Barossa pioneers—European settlers who saw the potential for wine in this region. These vines will have documented evidence proving that they are 125 years old or over.

It is at this point that young vine shoots are at their most vulnerable to early frosts and pests and diseases.

CHAPTER 4

MAIN GRAPE VARIETIES

PRINCIPAL WHITES

The following five grape varieties form the backbone for much of the white wine produced around the world.

Chardonnay

This seemingly ubiquitous grape variety comes originally from Burgundy in France, where it produces some of the finest white wines in the world. It is now planted in almost every wine-growing region in the world; in fact, it has almost supplanted its roots as a variety and become a 'brand' of fruity, dry, white wine in its own right. Chardonnay wines normally take well to oak fermentation and/or maturation, but the winemaker has to be careful not to allow the wood flavours to overpower the rounded buttery, pineapple, and tropical fruit flavours of the wine. The styles of wines produced vary from crisp, sparkling wines, through steely Chablis and the delicate Burgundies, such as Puligny

---

FOOD FOR THOUGHT

Chardonnay is such an extremely versatile wine that it can go with a wide range of food, but it is certainly happy with any poultry dish, especially a good roast chicken, as well as some white meats. Depending on the oak level, you can also try it with some of the oily, smoked seafood dishes or with any light, white fish recipe.

Montrachet, to the rich, buttery wines of California and the New World.

So what is it about Chardonnay that we, and winemakers, are attracted to? One thing is its malleability; Chardonnay is a very forgiving grape, and will produce an acceptable wine whatever the conditions. Drinkers like it because it is a reliable, lightly flavoured, dry wine. It has a touch of creamy vanilla, and is very soft on the palate. It is an unassuming, quaffing wine that sells in large quantities because it is exactly what it says on the label. And that is another reason for its success: the boom in production came at the same time as varietal labelling, when we could ask for a wine by the name of the grape it was made from. Furthermore, this was a pronounceable name – no more struggling with obscure French village or vineyard names.

Modern DNA fingerprinting techniques give us a clearer indication of the

---

BARE ESSENTIALS
Chardonnay

CHARACTER: Light, crisp dry wine with lots of tropical fruit flavours

CLIMATE: Tolerant of most climates, but does prefer limestone, chalk, and clay soils and the classic producers of this grape in France fulfil some or all of these requirements

BEST BUY: Domaine Leflaive Puligny-Montrachet, Premier cru "Les Pucelles" 2009

SNOB VALUE: Hugely popular at all levels of the wine-buying public, with Chablis and Champagne giving it real kudos

origins of this variety. It is now thought that Chardonnay's parentage lies in a marriage between the black Pinot Noir and the white Gounais Blanc, which used to be planted in France in the Middle Ages. So, one of the most popular white wine

Ripe Chardonnay grapes, the basis for some of the most popular wines in the world.

grapes in the world can trace its lineage all the way back to a classic red-wine grape and an obscure medieval vine.

Sauvignon Blanc

This distinctive white grape variety has its origins in Bordeaux, where it is thought to be one of the parents of the classic red grape, Cabernet Sauvignon. Its spiritual home is in the central vineyards of the Loire Valley, however, where it produces the crisply dry and aromatic Sancerre and Pouilly Fumé wines. Recently, it has discovered a new and important base in the cool climate of New Zealand. What makes Sauvignon Blanc stand out is its distinctive and pungent aroma. This has been described variously as being herbaceous, grassy, nettly, full of tart green fruits – such as gooseberries – or even musky like tomcats. One New Zealand producer aptly summed up the variety by calling his wine 'Cat's pee on a gooseberry bush'. Unlike Chardonnay, Sauvignon Blanc is very rarely oaked, and when it is, such as in the Napa Valley in California, it has to be carried out with care so that the flavours do not clash with each other.

As well as producing some wonderful varietal wines, Sauvignon Blanc is also an important blending component in some of the greatest white wines in the world. Sauternes and Barsac – sweet, dessert wines, made mainly from Sémillon that has been attacked by noble rot – would be too rich and cloying were it not for the addition of a small amount of the acidic Sauvignon Blanc to the final wine. On the other hand, the dry wines of the Pessac-Leognan and Entre Deux Mers in Bordeaux are softened out and given a more rounded 'mouthfeel' by the small addition of some Sémillon to the Sauvignon Blanc.

FOOD FOR THOUGHT

The acidity in Sauvignon Blanc wines means that it makes a great contrast to many foods which have quite forceful flavours. So you might like to try it as an accompaniment to any goat's cheese, or a seafood dish which has a rich sauce, or even the classic French dish of moules marinière with its lovely garlic-flavoured juices.

BARE ESSENTIALS
Sauvignon Blanc

CHARACTER: Light, tart dry wine with lots of 'green' flavours	
CLIMATE: Needs a cool climate and a limestone, flinty, or gravelly soil	
BEST BUY: Pierre Martin "Montes Damnés" Sancerre 2011	
SNOB VALUE: From poor to the pedigrees of Sancerre and Pouilly Fumé	

View over the vineyards towards the Château of Sancerre. The chalky soil reflects the sunlight to help ripen the fruit.

Sémillon

The Sémillon grape variety could be thought of as the vinous equivalent of a one-hit wonder when it comes to wine production. It is only really used as the backbone of serious wine in two main areas. In Bordeaux's Sauternes and Barsac, it produces some of the most intensely delicious dessert wines in the world, while in Australia's New South Wales, it produces a unique, dry, white wine and at least one delicious dessert wine. Australia has also found Sémillon a new blending partner in Chardonnay, where it pads out the wine without adding any extra flavours.

From a winemaking point of view, Sémillon's faults centre mainly on its lack of acidity, which means it tends to produce fatty, flabby wines that need to have a sharp grape, like the Sauvignon Blanc, blended in to add balance; it also has a thick skin, and it is this skin that makes the grape essential to the dessert winemaker. The thick skin is eaten away and 'thinned' when attacked by *botrytis cinerea*, or noble rot (see page 45). In this case the disease is restrained by warm autumn afternoons; it reduces the water content of the grape, while concentrating the sugar and acid contents. The result is a small harvest which produces relatively tiny amounts of ambrosia-like wine. Famously, Château d'Yquem produces just one glass of wine from each vine. Some vineyards of the Pessac-Leognan in Bordeaux, such as Château Haut-Brion, use the Sémillon to produce a dry wine but it will still have a fair proportion of Sauvignon Blanc wine blended in to add a little verve and some acidity.

Varietal Sémillons come into their own in the Hunter Valley in New South Wales, producing some of the most long-lived, white wines in the world. Here, the warmer climate results in riper fruit, with a higher acid content, and if the wine is to be oak aged, it will be left on the vine to ripen even further, so that it can stand up to the wood flavours.

The oaked wines really need to be drunk when young, while the unoaked wines from the Hunter Valley are at their best at five to ten years old, when they have a rich, nutty, honeyed note. In the

FOOD FOR THOUGHT

In its guise as a sweet dessert wine for which it is most famous, Sémillon is best served with any rich dessert, or the equally rich, but savory, foie gras pâté, or any blue cheese. In its dry form, however, it is best served with any shellfish or light white fish dishes, although some of the Sémillon wines produced in Hunter Valley go well with spicy foods.

Sémillon grapes growing in the Graves district of Bordeaux in France.

Riverina district of New South Wales, an Italian winemaker's son who had just come back from college noticed that the mouldy Sémillon grapes his father was throwing away seemed familiar. After persuading his father to let him experiment with some of them, he produced one of the best botrytised Sémillons outside Bordeaux. De Bortoli Noble One, as it is now known, is a classic example of this style of wine.

BARE ESSENTIALS
Chenin Blanc

CHARACTER: Crisp, dry wine with lots of acidity

CLIMATE: Prefers chalky soils, though will grow on clay, warm, dry conditions

BEST BUY: Didier Champalou Vouvray sec 2010

SNOB VALUE: Not great, as produces mostly middle-range wines

Chenin Blanc

This grape variety comes from the Loire Valley – not the Central Vineyards area so important to Sauvignon Blanc, but much nearer the coast in the Anjou, Saumur, and Touraine districts. This is also an important grape in South Africa, where it is known locally as the Steen. The Chenin is a versatile grape that can produce dry, medium, and dessert wines, as well as sparkling wines. This versatility comes from a combination of factors; the soil and climate are, of course, influences but, most importantly, the pruning and care of the vine greatly influence the final wine.

Chenin Blanc is a notoriously vigorous vine, which, if left alone, will produce huge quantities of uninteresting grapes and, subsequently, uninteresting wine. It is not unknown for the Chenin to produce over 100 Hl/Ha if left to its own devices – even on poor soils. To prevent this, the growers will sometimes revert to a 'green' harvest during the summer, picking perfectly healthy bunches of grapes from the vine during the growing season to reduce the yield and concentrate the flavours in the remaining bunches. It may seem a great waste, but it is the only way to produce quantities of quality Chenin Blanc wines. A further problem with Chenin is that it is a late-ripening variety, which is why sparkling wine production relies on the extra acidity from underripe grapes.

Yet there is one area of the Loire Valley in which the Chenin comes into its own: Coteaux du Layon and its

The Château at Saumur which dominates the town below and overlooks the Loire River.

subregions of Bonnezeaux and Quarts de Chaume, where, on a southern tributary of the Loire, between Saumur and Anjou, some wonderful dessert wines are produced almost every year from noble-rot grapes grown on a clay soil with a chalk subsoil and a foggy, autumn climate similar to that in Sauternes and Barsac. These are honeyed, acacia-flavoured wines with marmalade, toffee notes.

Saumur is the centre of sparkling wine production, with its chalk soils and caves, making wines full of the flavours of crisp, green apples. Touraine and its subdistrict of Vouvray produce sweet wines when they can. But they generally have dry or medium wines, which tend to be more rounded than the minerally dry white wines of Anjou. This is partly because of the Tufa chalk soil, which is the result of boiled chalk made during volcanic activity in the past, and which benefits from great drainage.

South Africa produces large quantities of dry, white wines from the Chenin, although they can be from overcropped vines and so have little flavour. When it is good, South African Chenin has some rich guava and pineapple, tropical-fruit flavours.

FOOD FOR THOUGHT

The lighter styles of wines made with Chenin Blanc make a good companion for a chicken salad on a summer's day, or any light, white fish dish. Depending on their richness, the sweeter styles of wine will go well with foie gras pâté, or any blue-veined cheese (soft or hard) and any desserts made with fresh fruit.

Riesling

Wine experts and journalists rave about Riesling, claiming it to be one of the finest white wine grapes around, and yet hardly anyone buys it – certainly not in the quantities that they buy Chardonnay or Shiraz. A hundred or so years ago, the Riesling wines of the Mosel and Rhine valleys were consistently more expensive than the finest red wines of Bordeaux. Now these wines are struggling to find a buyer at any price.

Why is this? One problem is that the Riesling has a taut, tight acidity of citrus fruits, and nowadays we prefer the softer, fruit-driven flavours of Chardonnay. This is a pity, because the high acidity levels give it flexibility; they help the wine to age, and are so high that it is unlikely for them to drop so low as to make the wine flabby. The high acidity levels also mean that the Riesling can produce intensely sweet wines and still have enough balancing acidity to stop the wine feeling cloying and heavy. Icewine was made for this grape variety (see page 207). Another problem is that the wine does not take well to oak, and so cannot be rounded out by smooth, rich, vanilla flavours.

From the grower's point of view, however, Riesling is a flexible, friendly variety. It grows well in the cool climate of Germany, its home, and in the much warmer climate of the Clare Valley in South Australia. It can produce lean, racy, dry wines, full of citrus notes, or delicious dessert wines, if allowed to hang longer on the vines – perhaps with an attack of noble rot. It also thrives on a variety of soils – from the slate of the Mosel to the red soil over limestone of Australia's Coonawarra. However, Riesling does not like hot climates, which is probably why it has not been a great success in the New World. This is unfortunate, because the New World winemaking methods would suit it very well; stainless steel, cool fermentation, with no new oak but, perhaps, some very large, old oak vats for maturation to allow some air interaction and add complexity. Its strong flavours and its German origins – where blending is frowned upon – mean that it is normally labelled as a varietal wine, with a few Australian exceptions, where some spicy Gewürztraminer is added (see page 72).

Riesling is considered an early-ripening grape (except in Germany, where the cool climate holds the process back) and has

BARE ESSENTIALS
Riesling

CHARACTER: Light, citrus-flavoured, dry wines and floral, sweet wines

CLIMATE: Can withstand a variety of soils, but prefers cool, dry conditions

BEST BUY: Dr Loosen Wehlener Sonnenuhr Riesling Auslese 2008

SNOB VALUE: Once great, now tarnished.

good resistance to the winter cold, so a small amount can be found in Canada. This also gives it some frost resistance. Overall, the key to great Riesling is a concentration of flavours – it is a high cropping vine, and yields of up to 100 Hl/Ha are not uncommon – but the best wines come either from old vines with low yields of around 30 Hl/Ha or from vines that have been pruned and trained to reduce the crop.

With such a variety of styles, there is a wide range of flavours in the wines – from crisp, young Riesling wines, with citrusy flavours to peachy, New World styles. As the wines age, a kerosene note can be detected.

Riesling grapes are very well served by the slatey soil of the Mosel Valley in Germany.

Unfortunately – and a further factor to Riesling's fall in popularity – there are large quantities of poor quality wine masquerading under the Riesling name. Some is the result of greedy winemaking, while much has come about through Germany's reluctance to protect the Riesling's name. Many non-German wines are made from grapes totally unrelated to the Rhine Riesling. Although some – Laski Riesling, Welschriesling (or Riesling Italico) – produce decent wines when care is taken, they are as unlike true Riesling as can be.

LESSER-KNOWN WHITES

There are several varieties of lesser-known whites – perhaps they are less popular outside their own regions, or they do not produce world-class wines, or they simply do not 'travel' well. Nevertheless, a few are worth a mention.

Aligoté

This is very much the second white grape of Burgundy, both in quality and in the area under vine. Most of the wine produced is labeled as the generic Bourgogne Aligoté, and is a thin, acidic wine, which does not like oak aging. Most locals will mix it with the local blackcurrant liqueur, cassis, to make the classic kir. There is one exception where a better quality Aligoté wine may be produced in good years, and that is around the village of Bouzeron, in the north of the Challonaise, which has its own *A.P.* Bourgogne Aligoté Bouzeron.

Grüner Veltliner

Austria's most popular grape variety is rarely seen outside its homeland, but over a third of Austria's vineyards are planted with this variety. What holds it back is the fact that it is very late ripening, so can't really be grown much further north. A lot of the production is, to be honest, everyday drinking white, but when it is grown in areas like the Wachau and Kamptal regions, with reduced yields and even late harvesting, it produces lightly aromatic white wines, with a peppery, spice note and a hint of honeyed citrus, which are capable of some aging.

Marsanne

This Rhône Valley grape produces white wine in conjunction with Rousanne (see below) – particularly in the northern Rhône Valley *Appellations* of St Joseph, Hermitage, and Crozes Hermitage – as well as the sparkling St Peray. However, much of the production is blended into the red wines in order to smooth them out. Like most white varieties, it tends to produce flabby wines if overcropped. There are small outposts of Marsanne production in California and Australia. Normally these are wines to be drunk young, but sometimes the Australian wines come into their own after ten or more years.

Rousanne

Rousanne has inconsistent yields and a low tolerance to powdery mildew. It is used in the white and red wines of Crozes Hermitage, Hermitage, and

Rousanne grapes growing in the stony soil of the southern Rhône Valley.

St Joseph, as well as in the white sparkling St Peray. Where it scores over Marsanne (see page 65) is that it is also permitted in the blend for red and white Châteauneuf-du-Pape in the southern Rhône Valley.

It is also grown as a varietal wine in the cool Central Coast area of California, where its herbal tea aromas are allowed to develop.

Verdelho

Both a grape variety and a style of wine in Madeira, Verdelho is used in the production of a fortified wine that comes between Sercial and Bual in richness. It is also found in Portugal's Douro Valley, hiding under the alias Gouveio, and is used to produce white port. It is in the hotter areas of Australia that Verdelho is producing some exciting table wines,

Silvaner grapes waiting to be harvested in the Franken region of Germany.

however. The Hunter Valley and McLaren Vale make crisp, dry wines with sharp lime and floral notes and a rich, oily texture.

Silvaner or Sylvaner

This variety comes from Germany. Although it is also found in Alsace, and some parts of eastern Europe, it is very rarely found in the New World. This is probably because the wines tend to be fairly neutral in flavour but with a crisp acidity. The best Silvaner wines (the 'y' is used in the French spelling) come from the Franken area of Germany. This tributary of the Rhine produces some concentrated flavours and racy acidity – enough flavour and acidity, in fact, to be one of the few areas to produce successful late-harvest Silvaner wines, especially around the town of Würzburg. The wines are recognisable because of the uniquely wide, round-shaped Bocksbeutel in which they are bottled.

Colombard

Originally from the Charente region, north of Bordeaux in France, this grape was used in the production of Cognac. Sales of the spirit have fallen and so more of the production is being used to make a table wine. It really comes into its own in the south-western region of Gascony, where its peachy, nectarine flavours form the backbone of the white IGP Côtes de Gascogne.

Palomino Fino

This variety has been adopted in southern Spain as that most suitable for the production of sherry. Its problems with downy mildew are overcome by the dry climate and chalky soil of the sherry region. As a table wine, it manages to produce a drink that is almost entirely devoid of flavour but, once it has been fortified and matured in the 'solera' system (see page 140), it develops amazingly complex aromas.

CROSS-BRED WHITES

These varieties have either been created by man or have naturally mutated in the vineyard.

Müller-Thurgau

This grape variety is a purely man-made entity. It is one of the first – and least successful – of man's attempts to improve on nature in the vineyard. It was developed by Dr Müller in 1882 at the Geisenheim Institute in the Rheingau region of Germany (see also page 211).

It was developed to produce a variety with all the positive elements of the great Riesling grape, but with the added benefit of ripening earlier in the cool German climate. The variety was originally thought to be a cross of the two *vinifera* varieties, Riesling and Silvaner. However, recent DNA research places the parentage firmly in the court of Riesling and a rather dull grape, the Chasselas de Courtillier.

The Müller-Thurgau grape has enjoyed some success: it does ripen earlier than Riesling, it is a prolific cropper, and it is not affected by soil type. Yet it produces some deeply forgettable wines, with cheap Liebfraumilch among them. There is some Müller-Thurgau planted in England, and more recent crosses are having greater success in producing attractive wines.

Bacchus

This cross of Silvaner, Riesling, and Müller-Thurgau was named after the Roman god of wine. It is far more successful than its mediocre parent and, when yields are kept low and the fruit is allowed to ripen fully, it can produce some full, aromatic notes. English producers are experimenting with, and getting interesting results from, oak aging.

Scheurebe

This variety is thought to be a Silvaner and Riesling crossing, but this is currently under review. Nevertheless, it is probably one of the most successful crossings to date. Named after a Dr Georg Scheu, this grape produces good acidity as well as sugar content. This means that it can produce good wines, even at the rich, sweet, Beerenauslese and Trockenbeerenauslese levels, if attacked by noble rot. In Austria, it is known by the less romantic name of Samling 88.

Ortega

This recent German crossing of Müller-Thurgau and Siegerrebe probably produces some of its best wines in England, where the cool climate restrains the tendency to produce lots of sugar, and therefore allows the grapefruit-like acidity to maintain some balance. Unfortunately, this variety is prone to disease.

Scheurebe grapes are generally left for much longer on the vine in order to reach higher levels of ripeness.

Pinot Blanc

The Pinot Blanc is a mutation of a mutation. It is thought to come from the Pinot Gris (see right), which is, itself, a pale version of the classic red grape, the Pinot Noir. It is grown in many parts of France, northern Italy (as Pinot Bianco) and Germany (as Weissburgunder), but in France, the only region that really supports it is Alsace, where it not only produces a varietal wine, but is also included in the sparkling Crémant d'Alsace.

Pinot Gris/Grigio

The Pinot Gris, a pale-coloured mutation of Pinot Noir, produces softly aromatic and perfumed wines, especially in Alsace. Although not as widely planted as Riesling or Gewürztraminer, the grape produces an exotic, musky note of fleshy nuts in a dry wine. You may find late harvest (*vendage tardive*) wines or some *botrytis*-affected *Sélection des Grains Nobles*. In Alsace the grape is most susceptible to noble rot and adds some deliciously-balancing, sweet notes in addition to the musky, spicy elements of the dry styles. This variety also has the ability to age.

AROMATIC WHITE VARIETIES

A group of grapevines that produce strongly perfumed grapes and wines.

Muscat

The Muscat is a rare grape variety, producing wine that actually smells of grapes! Wonderful, heady, grapey aromas emanate from most glasses of Muscat wine, as opposed to the leaner, mineral aromas of other varieties. It is thought by some that the Muscat is one of the original wine grape varieties. It has produced many mutations, all of which have developed into different varieties of Muscat. Today, you will find the Muscat à Petit Grains, Muscat of Alexandria,

Muscat grapes, seen here ripening on the vines, can either be used as table grapes or for producing sweet wines.

Muscat Ottonel, and Orange Muscat, among many others. But they all share the rare ability – probably owing to their distinctive flavours – to be both table and wine grapes.

Muscat is thought to have been brought to the south of France by the Romans, who themselves took it from the Greeks. It is also found in Spain, where it is called the Moscatel, and Italy, where it goes by the name of Moscato. It can produce light, frothy wines such as Asti Spumanti; heady, dry wines in Alsace; light, refreshing, sweet wines in the southern Rhône Valley; and rich, succulent, toffee-scented liqueur wines in Australia.

The Muscat is very much a Mediterranean vine, in that it does need more warmth than most grapes in order to ripen. In fact, it can only be grown in the sunniest spots of Alsace. On the other hand, it does not seem to need a specific soil type, and grows equally well on the clay soils of Beaumes de Venise, the sandy soil of Alsace, or the granite soil of northern Victoria in Australia. It is classed as a medium-cropping variety, but care still needs to be taken to prevent the vine overproducing.

The sweet wines are very rarely made from noble-rot grapes. Some may be made from dried or semidried grapes (*passito*), but it is much more common to find that the wine has been sweetened by the use of *mutage*. This involves the addition of brandy after pressing and before fermentation, which makes more than 6 per cent alcohol. The alcohol quickly raises the content of the wine to around 15 per cent alcohol by volume. This kills the yeast in the juice and creates a *Vin Doux Naturel*, a fresh, sweet wine that is delicious as an appetiser.

In the north of Victoria, around the towns of Rutherglen and Glenrowan, the Muscat is fortified and then aged, like a sherry, in a solera. However, the heat in the area virtually cooks the wine over the years and creates a wonderfully delicious, sticky-sweet concoction, which can be heavenly to drink.

Viognier

No one is quite sure where this vine came from, although it is assumed that the Romans brought it to its home in the northern Rhône Valley. Until a few years ago, Condrieu – the *appellation* most associated with this variety – was reduced to producing around 25 acres of virus-ridden vines and hardly any wine. And it is *some* wine: opulent and oily in texture, Voignier is exotically perfumed with floral, peachy, apricoty, and ginger-spice overtones.

The flavours in Viognier seem to develop late in the ripening process, which means that the grower needs to take care that the high levels of sugar in the grapes do not produce a lot of alcohol in the final wine. It seems to suit a cool climate best, and while the Condrieu vineyards are in a hot area of the northern Rhône Valley, they actually face in a direction that shades them from the intense heat of the afternoon sun.

An expansion of production in the past few years has been very quick, and as Viognier reaches New World producers in California and Australia, there is still much discussion as to the best soil. In

Condrieu, the soil is sandy with a granite subsoil and the only factor that growers seem to agree on is that the soil should be light and free-draining to maintain the freshness of the wine. The vine is a heavy cropper, with the intensity of the perfume dropping off as the yields increase.

There are several problems with this variety, one of them being that the base stock in Condrieu was virus-ridden, mainly with leaf roll, and producers are still trying to develop virus-free clones. Another problem is poor-setting fruit, even if the flowering has gone well. This millerendage can result in bunches of grapes with a mixture of healthy, ripe berries and green, immature ones. They have to be separated before pressing, which is an expensive and time-consuming process. Despite the intensity of its flavours, Viognier does welcome a small amount of oak aging, giving an extra creamy note to the final wine.

Viognier is used for blending in the Rhône Valley, but not with other white wines (although attractive Chardonnay/Viognier blends are beginning to appear from places like the South of France, Australia and South America). In the Rhône Valley, the Viognier is blended with the Syrah of Côte Rotie. About 20 per cent is permitted in the blend, although most producers use much less. The Viognier grapes are added to the vat of Syrah grapes before fermentation begins. The thinking behind this blend is that the perfumed and oily-textured Viognier adds softness to the final wine. Moreover, the phenolic compounds in the white grapes help to fix the red colour in the wine – a process known as copigmentation.

Gewürztraminer

Probably the most difficult grape variety to spell and pronounce, the Gewürztraminer is also one of the most easily recognisable varieties in a glass. The wine is full of exotic rose-petal, lychee, and violet floral aromas, with a sprinkling of black-pepper spice, and a rich, slightly oily texture.

Its wines tend to taste sweet, even if they are dry, which is the most common way of making the wine. When they are sweet, as in the late-harvest or *botrytis*-affected Alsace wines (see page 174), they can reach a further ethereal height of self-indulgence, although Gewürztraminer does not take *botrytis* well or easily.

The origins of this variety seem to be in the north of Italy, where the Traminer grape was recorded in the village of Tramin around a thousand years ago. How it got to its home in Alsace is less clear, but it is thought to have come via Germany, where pockets of production can still be found in regions such as the Nahe. The prefix of 'Gewürz,' meaning spicy, was added in the nineteenth century and describes the peppery, prickle of the wines on the palate.

The vine can be difficult to grow; it likes cool weather – otherwise it will lose acidity – but plenty of sunshine, and it finds this in abundance in Alsace, where the Vosges Mountains act as a giant wind-and-rain breaker. Soil, on the other hand, doesn't seem to be an issue, as long as it is well drained. Alsace's limestone-and-clay soil suits it well.

Problems with Gewürztraminer can begin in the vineyard. At the beginning

of the growing season the vine buds very early and so is susceptible to frost.

It is also a prolific cropper, if left to its own devices, and high yields dilute the perfume in the wine, as can be seen in the less successful producers of eastern Europe. It also suffers from uneven ripeness on bunches of grapes; it is not uncommon to find ripe and green berries on the same bunch.

Care needs to be taken in the winery as well. The fruit can contain so much sugar that the fermentation can be very rapid. This means that it could be finished before the flavours have had a chance

These pink-coloured Gewürztraminer grapes store up exotic aromas which are released in the wines of Alsace.

to develop in the wine. This can be controlled by cooling the vats to regulate the speed of fermentation and to stop the wine overheating, thereby spoiling its flavours.

The final problem for drinkers of Gewürztraminer wines is that all this flavour can be simply too much to handle; one glass is not enough but two is too many. This, along with a high price due to the relatively low yields, might explain why it is not hugely popular around the world.

PRINCIPAL REDS

The best wines in the world are produced from a small group of grapes, most of which owe their origins to three of the main regions of France: Bordeaux, Burgundy and the Rhône.

Cabernet Sauvignon

Commonly accepted as one of the greatest red-wine grapes in the world, Cabernet Sauvignon was first encountered in Bordeaux, France. Recent DNA research by the University of California, Davis, has discovered that the grape has its origins in Sauvignon Blanc and the Cabernet Franc of Bordeaux, which may go some way towards explaining the herbaceous, grassy, Sauvignon Blanc aromas sometimes found on the nose and palate of this great red grape. The mix is believed to be the result of an accident in the vineyard – where it was not uncommon to grow a mixture of varieties together – rather than from the actions of any wine grower.

What makes this a great grape variety? And why was it chosen as the predominant variety in Bordeaux? In some cases, it must be the simplicity of its aroma and flavour – Cabernet Sauvignon is blackcurrants, pure and simple, no matter where you grow it – and yet, this is by no means a simple grape.

One thing that sets Cabernet Sauvignon apart from the other great red varieties is a high proportion of phenols in the grapes' thick skins. Phenols are the compounds (including anthocyans and flavinoids such as resveratrol) that give red wine its colour and tannin, and are also seen as providing some of the health-giving properties of moderate wine drinking. By blending some Cabernet Sauvignon into a local wine, a winemaker can immediately give rich colour and flavour to his or her wine. In fact, the thick skin of Cabernet Sauvignon is one of the reasons for it being among the selected grapes in Bordeaux following the *phylloxera* blight of the 1860s: the high level of tannin in the final wines, resulting from the high ratio of skin to pulp as the grapes are split, acts as a preservative and gives the wines an ability to be laid down to age for a number of years. Furthermore, the thick skins slow down the penetration of fungal spores and allow fungicides to act before the grape skin is penetrated, thereby preventing spoilage.

Plump Cabernet Sauvignon grapes ready for harvesting in the Bordeaux region of the Medoc.

BARE ESSENTIALS
Cabernet Sauvignon

CHARACTER: Rich and fruity

CLIMATE: Tolerant of most climates, but likes a free-draining soil and warmth

BEST BUY: Château Mouton-Rothschild 2009

SNOB VALUE: High as it is associated with some of the premier wines in the world

FOOD FOR THOUGHT

As befits this most regal of grapes, Cabernet Sauvignon wines are best drunk with equally robust dishes: any grilled meats, but especially lamb, will provide an ample complement to its rich, fruity flavours. In addition, you could try it with a traditional steak-and-kidney pie, a classic beef casserole, or a hot-pot.

The Cabernet Sauvignon grape grows on most soils, especially if they are free draining and in a relatively warm climate. This means that the vine is easy to transport to most of the world's wine regions, and it is also grown in areas of France outside Bordeaux; expect to find it producing light-red and rosé wines in regions as diverse as Anjou-Saumur, in the Loire Valley, and Languedoc-Roussillon, in the south of France, where it may be presented as a varietal wine or blended with a local grape, such as the Tannat or the Negrette.

The blending potential of the Cabernet Sauvignon was first noticed in its home of Bordeaux, where it is blended in differing ratios, depending on where it is grown. The practice of blending Cabernet Sauvignon with Merlot, Cabernet Franc, and Petit Verdot (see pages 81 and 91), in order to form the classic Bordeaux blend (sometimes known as 'meritage' on Californian wine labels) was begun with care. In the temperate climate of Bordeaux, the Cabernet Sauvignon can find it hard to ripen by harvest time, so soft, plummy Merlot wine is added to soften out some of the harsher tannins of the unripe Cabernet grape. The Merlot

Harvesting Cabernet Sauvignon grapes in Bordeaux. The pickers transfer the grapes into small carts for collection before they are taken to the winery.

Harvesting Cabernet Sauvignon grapes in Bordeaux. The pickers transfer the grapes into small carts for collection before they are taken to the winery.

FOOD FOR THOUGHT

As befits this most regal of grapes, Cabernet Sauvignon wines are best drunk with equally robust dishes: any grilled meats, but especially lamb, will provide an ample complement to its rich, fruity flavours. In addition, you could try it with a traditional steak-and-kidney pie, a classic beef casserole, or a hot-pot.

The Cabernet Sauvignon grape grows on most soils, especially if they are free draining and in a relatively warm climate. This means that the vine is easy to transport to most of the world's wine regions, and it is also grown in areas of France outside Bordeaux; expect to find it producing light-red and rosé wines in regions as diverse as Anjou-Saumur, in the Loire Valley, and Languedoc-Roussillon, in the south of France, where it may be presented as a varietal wine or blended with a local grape, such as the Tannat or the Negrette.

The blending potential of the Cabernet Sauvignon was first noticed in its home of Bordeaux, where it is blended in differing ratios, depending on where it is grown. The practice of blending Cabernet Sauvignon with Merlot, Cabernet Franc, and Petit Verdot (see pages 81 and 91), in order to form the classic Bordeaux blend (sometimes known as 'meritage' on Californian wine labels) was begun with care. In the temperate climate of Bordeaux, the Cabernet Sauvignon can find it hard to ripen by harvest time, so soft, plummy Merlot wine is added to soften out some of the harsher tannins of the unripe Cabernet grape. The Merlot

also gives some welcome colour and 'backbone' to the final wine.

Growers of Cabernet Sauvignon know that some of the grapes will be affected by frosts in the spring and heavy rains at harvest time, and so will plant a number of varieties, which flower and are ready to harvest at different times. This ensures that there will always be enough of a harvest to make a wine every year, with the added bonus that, in a good year, all the fruit will be at its peak and the wines will be excellent.

Other reasons for this variety being chosen around the world are its distinctive style and its association with some of the greatest red wines in the world – the *Premier Crus* of Médoc in Bordeaux. These wines, identified as the best in the region in the classification of 1855, have set the international standards in red-wine production. Not all the wines made from Cabernet Sauvignon taste like the great Bordeaux red

Cabernet Sauvignon doesn't just grow in Bordeaux; these vineyards in the Southern French region of the Languedoc produce some very easy-drinking wines.

wines, but they do have a recognisable style: blackcurrant fruits, cedarwood, and pencil shavings permeate every Cabernet Sauvignon wine that has the ability – and is given the time – to age. In a blind tasting, in Paris in 1976, wine journalist Steven Spurrier championed Napa Valley Cabernet Sauvignons over

the great wines of Bordeaux – proof that, given the right conditions and with reduced yields, Cabernet Sauvignon produces quality wines no matter where it is grown.

It is rare to find a Cabernet wine that does not improve after contact with new oak. In some wines, prolonged contact (the top Médoc wines insist on twenty-four months) with new oak in barriques of 225 litres would overpower the fruit flavours of the wine. The blackcurrant flavours of Cabernet Sauvignon, however, seem to have a natural affinity with the vanilla and spice elements of newly made oak barrels, and this has probably influenced the selection of the barrique as the standard red-wine barrel around the world.

Cabernet Sauvignon is not just blended in the classic Bordeaux style; the Australians blend it with great success, in various proportions, with Shiraz. This blend may even have originated in Bordeaux, before the present *A.P.* legislation banned the production of Syrah in the region.

The Italians have also had success blending it with Sangiovese, in Tuscany (see page 228). For a long time, the restrictive *D.O.C.* legislation meant that these wines had to be classified as *Vino da Tavola*, or table wine, even though their popularity meant that they sold for far more than the approved wines of the region. These 'Super Tuscan' wines were a deliberate attempt to change the rules and make better wines, but winemakers have to be careful that the powerful Cabernet Sauvignon does not swamp the more delicate Sangiovese flavours.

Merlot

This Bordeaux grape variety is much more than an 'insurance policy' grape, grown to cover up for a bad Cabernet Sauvignon year. DNA research is still continuing as to the origins of this grape variety, but indications seem to be pointing towards one of the parents being Cabernet Franc, which would make it a close relation to Cabernet Sauvignon. Interestingly, the University of California, Davis, is also making the same claim for another old Bordeaux variety, Carmenère (see page 93).

The fact that Merlot buds and ripens at least a week before Cabernet Sauvignon means that it avoids the seasonal rains that can ruin a harvest in Bordeaux. This also means that the vine is more susceptible to frost damage, coulure, and millerendage, but it does like cool, damp soils, such as those found in the right-bank Bordeaux regions of St Emilion and Pomerol, where the water-retention properties allow the grapes to swell to full size. This, in turn, reduces the skin-to-pulp ratio and produces a softer, more approachable wine.

Its softness was one of the characteristics that led to the popularity of Merlot in the United States. The identification of the health benefits of red wine (see page 366) led to a huge increase in demand. Cabernet Sauvignon was too astringent for the new wine consumer, however. The wine industry soon recognised that the soft, plump, plummy, Merlot wines – with their relatively low

Merlot grapes ripening on the vine just outside the commune of St Emillion on the banks of the Dordogne.

tannin-induced bitterness and fruity cherry flavours – were perfect for the new red-wine drinker. This lower tannin level is due in part to the relative thinness of the grape skin and the lower density of the grape bunch. This does mean, however, that the grape is more prone to rot and downy mildew during the growing season, so spraying the loosely packed grape bunches is a frequent exercise.

Merlot is popular with growers because it will ripen in cooler climates than Cabernet Sauvignon and so there is a large amount of Merlot planted in the Alto Adige in northern Italy. Nevertheless, Merlot needs to be picked ripe – underripe and overcropped Merlot wines can have a noticeable 'green' streak of herbaceous flavours in them. One problem with Merlot is its tendency to yield too many grapes and so dilute its flavours. In such cases, the vine grower's skill lies in reducing the yield to create balance in the final wine. In the Bordeaux blend, Merlot is used to add fleshiness to the final wine. Lacking the tannin structure of Cabernet Sauvignon, Merlot tends not to be as long-lived on its own.

Merlot is France's third most-planted red-grape variety. This is, in some ways, because of its importance in a lot of the A.P. wines of south-west France, and its production of I.G.P. varietal wines from the southern regions of Languedoc-Roussillon and the Ardèche, as well as the cooler areas of the Loire Valley. Merlot is heavily planted in the United States – which produces both low-yielding, dense Merlot wines and the high-yielding, low-intensity, quaffing wines of the Californian Central Valley. The country could soon become the fourth largest producer of Merlot.

Chilean Merlot is more controversial. Recent research has shown that not all Merlot vines in Chile are, in fact, Merlot. Most 'Merlot' vineyards seem to

be a mixture of Merlot and its 'kissing cousin,' Carmenère. The two vines ripen at different times and there are definite bell pepper flavours and aromas resulting from the underripe Carmenère or overripe Merlot in the final wine.

Australia has recently seen a huge increase in the plantings of Merlot

Alto Adige in northern Italy produces varietal Merlot wines with the plummy characters associated with this grape.

vines, as it discovers cooler wine-producing regions.

In New Zealand, the South Island tends to be too cool, while northern areas of Hawkes Bay and Auckland are finding it much easier to ripen than Cabernet Sauvignon.

South Africa has recently joined the Merlot rush, but is still trying to find areas that are cool enough. If the climate is too warm, the grapes ripen before the fruit has developed all of its flavours and the grower is forced to leave the fruit on the vine to allow the flavours to develop, taking care to pick them before the acid levels drop off.

FOOD FOR THOUGHT

Not surprisingly, the variety of Merlot is matched by the wide range of food with which it goes: try it with some nice slices of cold ham, a generous helping of a coarse country pâté, or perhaps a roast game bird. A favourite of mine is a piece of ripe Camembert or Brie cheese, but you could also use it rather than Cabernet Sauvignon with a meaty casserole.

Pinot Noir

Pinot Noir is the grape of red Burgundy – the classic of all French red wines. Outside of Beaujolais, Pinot Noir is the only permitted red grape in this great region of France, and it produces wonderfully attractive, delicately flavoured wines with hints of cherries, violets, and somehow heady aromas.

The easiest way to describe Pinot Noir is that it is a 'capricious' variety, presenting growers with considerable hardship. Unlike Cabernet Sauvignon, it is a difficult grape to grow. It buds and flowers early in the season, so a location away from frost is vital. Linked with this is a propensity towards the related pollination problems of coulure and millerendage. The grape has a very thin skin, which is reflected in the relatively thin colour of the wines, but this also means that mildews and rots are a major problem in the vineyard during the growing season. Even in the winery, Pinot Noir can be, and is, an unforgiving grape. Mistakes do not always come to light straightaway; it may take a couple of years before an error shows itself in a wine, by which time it is almost impossible to correct

FOOD FOR THOUGHT

Given its variety, it is not surprising that the wine made from Pinot Noir can either be best drunk by itself, as in Champagne as an appetiser, or if used in a still wine it makes a good companion for anything from simple, grilled salmon (if the wine is light in style) to game casseroles, beefy stews, or even the ubiquitous coq au vin in a fuller-bodied wine style.

it. Despite, and possibly because of, the various difficulties, winemakers want to master the Pinot Noir, because the end result is well worth the challenge.

Pinot Noir vines have been cultivated for so long – there is some evidence of their cultivation in Burgundy as early as the fourth century – that they have mutated and produced a huge number of natural 'clones'. It is for this reason that

there is such a variety and intensity of flavours in wines from Burgundy. Some vineyards are planted with heavy-cropping clones, others with disease-resistant types, some lightly flavoured, others packed with dense flavours and colour, and others with lower-yielding vines.

The best Burgundian vineyards are situated right in the middle of the slopes, where there is optimum shelter from the

Small bunches of Pinor Noir grapes ripening on the slopes of the Côte d'Or in Burgundy, France.

elements and good drainage yet plenty of exposure to the sun. Pinot Noir prefers a lime-based soil, such as that found on the shallow clay slopes of the Côte d'Or, and the world's best producers of Pinot Noir look for limestone soils when planting this variety.

The cool climate of the Chilean valleys provides good growing conditions for the difficult Pinor Noir.

In the New World Pinot Noir is also producing some exciting wines. The cooler climates of Carneros and Oregon in the US, Bio Bio in Chile, the Yarra Valley in Australia, and Central Otago, New Zealand, are producing some great examples of light, floral-scented Pinot Noir wines.

Although best known for its fine, red wines, the Pinot Noir excels at producing some of the best sparkling wines: it is an essential component of most Champagne and traditional method wines, giving backbone and structure to the final wine. Blanc de Noirs is, in fact, made only from black Pinot grapes, and care must be taken when pressing to ensure that no colour gets from the skins into the grape must. The cool, chalky soils of Champagne produce the slightly underripe Pinot Noir fruit that is needed for wines about to go through a second fermentation.

BARE ESSENTIALS
Pinot Noir

CHARACTER: Light, with hugely variable fruit and floral flavours, depending on the type of wine produced

CLIMATE: Cool climate specific, but does prefer limestone, chalk and clay soils and the classic producers of this grape in France fulfill some or all of these requirements

BEST BUY: Louis Jadot Clos Vougeot grand Cru 2010

SNOB VALUE: High demand and low volumes push up the price of top Burgundy wines

Syrah/Shiraz

A vine with two names might be considered schizophrenic, and although there are differences in the flavours produced from this grape, whichever name it falls under, there is always the consistent spicy, note of freshly ground black pepper on the end of the palate.

Syrah wines from the northern Rhône Valley in France tend to be smoky, perfumed, and fruity, while Australian Shiraz is creamier, with a chocolaty sweetness and ripe, berry fruits. In other parts of the world, winemakers use the name that best indicates the style of wine they are trying to produce.

Syrah probably originated in the Rhône Valley, although there is a romantic notion that the name Shiraz – and so the vine – comes from the ancient capital of Persia, which once had the same name. Until recently this vine was largely confined to the Rhône Valley, with the only real exception being Australia, where a Scot, James Busby, planted some 400 different French cuttings in New South Wales in 1832, and found that Syrah was one of the best vines suited to the hotter climate of this new colony. The collection formed the basis for today's Australian wine industry.

Syrah is sensitive to heat (both too much and too little), so planting in the northern Rhône Valley has to be done with care in order to protect the vines from the worst excesses of the cold mistral wind that speeds down the valley, although the wind can help to dry the grapes after

a downfall of rain. Because the vine is late budding but early ripening, a hot climate will push the grapes into a state of overripeness very quickly.

Some rots will attack this vine, but generally it is disease resistant. In the Barossa Valley of southern Australia, the biggest problem is that of drought on the hot valley floor, and the best wines come from old vines, whose roots have dug down so deep, they are able to get more moisture out of the shallow water table. Irrigated vines can need up to five litres of water a day to keep going during the summer.

Syrah is a vigorous vine, so rocky, well-drained soils help to 'stress' the vine, thereby producing intensely-flavoured wines. The northern Rhône Valley has a variety of granite soils for achieving this, while Australian wine growers rely on the hot, dry climate to produce the same effect. Moreover, free-draining sandy soils, such as those of the Barossa, have resulted in southern Australia being *phylloxera* free. This means that there are still some eighty-, ninety- and even over a hundred-

Almost ready for picking, these northern Rhône Syrah grapes have survived the buffeting of the Mistral.

BARE ESSENTIALS
Syrah/Shiraz

CHARACTER: Fruity and slightly spicy, with either a smoky or creamy feel

CLIMATE: Neither too cold nor too hot, with a free-draining soil and lots of moisture

BEST BUYS: Penfold's Grange 2008; Côte-Rôtie La Turque 2009; E. Guigal

SNOB VALUE: Reputable in the Rhône and highly popular in Australia

THESE "SHIRAZ" VINES ARE THE "ORIGINAL" VINES PLANTED HERE IN 1860

Château Tahbilk has some of the oldest Shiraz vines in the world because it is phylloxera-free.

year-old, ungrafted vines growing here, giving some intensely flavoured wines.

Australian Shiraz has a great affinity for the American oak used in small barriques. Some wines are even poured into barrels before the fermentation is complete, because this increases the temperature slightly and helps the integration of the oak flavours, deepening the colour at the same time.

It wasn't until the 1970s that Syrah really started to move from these areas. California was an early exponent of Syrah, and a group of winemakers, known as the Rhône Rangers, soon showed that California could produce alternative wines to the usual Cabernet Sauvignon and Zinfandel. Since then, outposts of Syrah have appeared in Washington State, Chile, Argentina, and South Africa. Small amounts of Syrah are grown in Italy and in the warmer sites of Switzerland. You can also find it in the Lebanon wine, Château Musar, and some northern African wines, from Morocco and Tunisia.

One of Syrah's greatest assets is its ability to blend with other wines, giving them a welcome 'lift'. In the southern Rhône Valley, it has long been a partner in the blend of Châteauneuf-du-Pape, among others, and in the northern Rhône Valley it has been blended with white grapes such as Viognier, Marsanne, and Roussane to help soften the high tannins.

The typical Australian blend used to be with Cabernet Sauvignon, and some Tuscan producers blend it with Sangiovese, producing expensive table wines. There have even been rumours that unscrupulous Burgundy producers add a bit of 'improving' Syrah to boost a poor vintage.

FOOD FOR THOUGHT

Such a rich grape demands some equally rich dishes, and it is no surprise that meats such as venison and roast beef make good companions for the ripe fruit flavours of Shiraz. But you can also try it with other smoked or barbeque meats in the summer, and it is also possible to find some sparkling wines made using this grape that will go well with salads.

LESSER-KNOWN REDS

The following red grape varieties may not be as well known as the 'biggies' like Cabernet Sauvignon, but they make important contributions in their own small way.

Petit Verdot

Petit Verdot is an aptly named grape (a rough translation is 'little green one', which sums up the variety in its entirety). The small grapes have very thick skins and produce wines full of strong, vibrant colours. A small amount of Petit Verdot, added to a blend will give a welcome boost to otherwise pale-coloured wines. This variety has long been recognised for these benefits in Bordeaux, and especially in the Médoc, where as little as 1 per cent added to the final blend adds some tannin, colour, and an attractive violet flavour to the wine. Château Margaux, for example, has around 6 per cent of its vineyard planted with Petit Verdot and will add up to 8 or 9 per cent to the final blend (a considerable reduction from the 30 per cent that was common over a hundred years ago).

When the vine is taken to the warmer climes of Australia's McLaren Vale and California's Napa and Sonoma Valleys, not only do the grapes ripen earlier, but they can also produce varietal wines, and are used for blending in 'meritage'-type Bordeaux blend wines.

Cabernet Franc

Despite the popularity of Cabernet Sauvignon, which owes part of its heritage to Cabernet Franc, the latter is still regarded as an important constituent of a Cabernet Sauvignon-based wine blend. It tends to ripen earlier and more easily than its offspring, and so is less susceptible to harvest rains. This makes it a good 'insurance policy' in bad vintages, ensuring that the winemaker can still produce a wine.

Cabernet Franc also ripens in cooler areas of Bordeaux, where Cabernet Sauvignon would fail to mature – St Emilion, Pomerol, and especially Fronsac, where it is known as the Bouchet, which is reflected in the high

A collector's item, this bottle of 1953 Château Margaux has added interest because of its history.

proportions of Cabernet Franc in these blends of the wines.

Cabernet Franc is also grown in the cooler areas of the Loire Valley. It was selected by Cardinal Richelieu to be planted in the Abbaye de St-Nicolas-de-Bourgueil, owing to the reputation it had gained in Bordeaux. Here, the grape produces lighter-bodied, relatively soft, raspberry-flavoured varietal wines, when grown on the chalky, sandy soil.

The vineyards of Chile hid Carmenère for nearly 100 years.

For Cabernet Franc grown in California or Australia, the winemakers seem to revert to form. There are a few varietal wines coming from these areas, but the vast majority of the production does end up being used as a component in a 'meritage' Bordeaux blend.

Carmenère

Once the grape of choice in the finest vineyards of Bordeaux, this grapevine was abandoned when the Bordelaise were forced to replant their vineyards after the *phylloxera* blight of the 1860s; it was a difficult grape to grow, it was very susceptible to coulure, and this would result in uneven yields across the vineyard, while Cabernet Sauvignon promised much more stability and an easier life for the grower. In theory that was the end of Carmenère as a grapevine: no plantings survived the epidemic in France.

In the 1990s, however, the variety was discovered in Chile, possibly having been taken there in the early 1800s. At the time, Chile was becoming an affluent country and the nouveaux riches of the day looked toward owning vineyards as an outward sign of their wealth. The resulting demand for vines could not be met in Chile, so many vine cuttings were imported from France. It seems that a number of vines marked as Merlot were, in fact, Carmenère. (Anyone visiting a Chilean vineyard today will probably find that a high percentage of the Merlot vines are actually Carmenère, yet are still labelled Merlot.)

This may also account for some of the green-bell-pepper character found in Chilean Merlot wines (see page 270). Chilean winemakers now recognise the importance of the Carmenère variety as a 'signature' variety for Chile, and are working to understand the best way to grow and vinify this wine.

The results so far are encouraging: if the grape is left to ripen, the bell-pepper characters become subdued and are replaced by berry, plum and spicy flavours and aromas, with a definite savory, almost medicinal, cough syrup and soy-sauce note.

These vineyards in the Aconcagua Valley in Chile are a mixture of Merlot and Carmenère.

Gamay

The Gamay is the only permitted red variety in the region of Beaujolais. When looked after, it can produce delicious, refreshingly light, red wines. It is a variety that has hardly moved from its southern Burgundy roots, even if the name has: it has recently been discovered that Californian Gamay is, in fact, a much lesser French variety, called the Valdiguié, for example.

The Gamay Noir à Jus Blanc, to give it its proper name, produces wines that are easy to drink when young. The best examples are grown in the ten *Cru* Beaujolais villages, which are allowed to add their names to labels. Here, cherries, bananas, spice and pepper sit happily on this summery wine. It is this property that has allowed the vine to be planted in the Loire Valley – especially Touraine – and in

A visible sign of terroir, the granite sands of Mont Brouilly in Beaujolais are perfectly suited to the Gamay grape.

Switzerland, where it is normally blended with the Pinot Noir to make wine labelled as Dôle. This style probably owes its roots to the Passetoutgrains of Burgundy, a thirst-quenching, red wine, one part Pinot Noir to two parts Gamay, from the south of the region.

Grenache

Grenache, or Garnacha, is the most widely planted red grape in the world, the majority of it grown in Spain. The fact that the only top quality, French, red wine made from it is Châteauneuf-du-Pape, (even then, it is only the main variety in a list of thirteen), tends to support the argument that this is a Spanish variety, thought to have originated in Aragon, in north-east Spain. The fact that Roussillion, where a large amount of Grenache is planted, was actually Spanish until the French annexed the region in the 1600s, further compounds this argument.

The vine thrives on very poor soil –

These bush-trained Grenache vines are pruned low to take advantage of the stony soil of Châteauneuf-du-Pape.

you only have to look at the stone-covered soil of Châteauneuf-du-Pape to realise that it needs little moisture and lots of warmth (the stones over the soil radiate heat at night that has been stored during the day). This produces grapes that are full of sugars, ready for conversion to alcohol. Levels of 14 or 15 per cent alcohol by volume are not uncommon, and the wine is full of wonderful rich fruitcake and cinnamon-spice flavours.

This is a very versatile grape in Spain – producing anything from fruity *rosados* to deep, densely coloured red wines of the ancient vineyards of Priorat. The French and, to a certain extent, the rest of the world tend to see Grenache as a bit of a viticultural workhorse, producing vast seas of Côtes du Rhône wines, and using it as a blending grape to add some flavour and alcohol to the final wine. You can find Grenache in California and Chile, as well as North Africa. For quality Grenache, however, Australia has a few vineyards full of very old vines producing intensely flavoured wines, as well as some southern Rhône Valley-style wines with varieties such as Mourvèdre and Cinsault.

Sangiovese

Italy's premier grape variety has a literal translation – 'The Blood of Jove' – which supports the thought that this is one of the many grape varieties indigenous to the country. It is the main grape used in the production of Chianti and other wines of Tuscany, in western Italy. It is

The rolling hills of Piedmont provide many microclimates to create the conditions to ripen Nebbiolo grapes.

an ancient variety and, like the Pinot Noir, has mutated over the years, resulting in a large number of natural clones of varing quality.

Like most Italian grape varieties, despite producing some great wines, it has little reputation outside its homeland. There are a few outposts in California and Australia where immigrants created a demand for light, cherry-flavoured wines with good acidity and tannins. It is a late-flowering and ripening variety, which likes warm climates. It has a thin skin and so is very susceptible to rot in a cool, damp climate. Coulure can also be a problem. Despite this, when a good site is found and yields are controlled, Sangiovese can produce fantastic Brunello de Montalcino and Chianti wines, and is beginning to do just that in California and Australia.

Nebbiolo

Another Italian grape variety that makes some great wines in its homeland, but which winemakers have difficulty replicating elsewhere, the Nebbiolo is an old variety, with references made to a wine called Nibiol from Piedmont, as early as the thirteenth century. The name Nebbiolo probably comes from the Italian word *nebbia* meaning fog, a common occurrence during the October harvest. This is a very late-ripening variety and it is also early budding; wine growers have to be careful not to suffer from poor flowering and underripe fruit at either end of the same growing season.

With this variety, location is everything – even in its Piedmont home, it has to be planted on slopes with a southern exposure and not too high in order to keep it sheltered and warm. This contrary nature, demanding attention, is one reason why this variety hasn't moved far. Other areas seem to be too cool or too hot for this fickle variety. Soil can also cause problems: Nebbiolo will only produce its best on clay and limestone soils. Other soils produce pale imitations of the great wines like Barbaresco and Barolo, which are so full of alcohol and rich aromas of tar and roses.

The late harvesting of this variety has had a great influence on the style of the wines it produces. Traditionally, when the grapes were pressed there was very little natural warmth in the winery, which meant that the fermentation was slow to start and lasted for a long time. One of the results of this was a high level of tannin extraction, and the only way to soften the wine was to give it a long, barrel age. Even today, legislation states that Barolos have to be aged for three years – of which two are in the barrel – before it can be sold.

In moving to nearby regions, Nebbiolo has become known by different names: in parts of Piedmont, it is called Spanna, and in Lombardy it is known as Chiavennasca, where some long-lived Valtellina wines demonstrate the quality of this grape variety.

Left: The morning mists in Piedmont can cause problems for the growers who need to delay the harvest of late-ripening Nebbiolo. **Right:** Softer Barbera grapes are becoming more popular in the Piedmont region.

Barbera

Unfairly known as Piedmont's second grape after Nebbiolo, Barbera is now more planted in Piedmont than its famous rival, and has also travelled throughout the world, carried on a wave of Italian emigration to California, Argentina, and Australia. Its ability to grow on most soils, combined with high acidity and low tannins, and a full body, make it popular with winemakers and far less problematic than the Nebbiolo.

Its versatility is also reflected in the styles of wine produced from this grape. Barbera wines can be light and cherry flavoured, or intense, with a bitter-cherry tang on the palate. New winemaking techniques, including barrique-aging rather than using the traditional large barrels, can introduce a softer, more plummy note to the wine as well. If Nebbiolo is a wine to mature and nurture for a long time, then Barbera is one to enjoy on a daily basis.

Zinfandel/Primitivo

Californian winemakers like to promote Zinfandel as 'California's grape variety'. They probably have a case, even though the vine is European in origin. Research, begun in the 1960s, has proved that Zinfandel is the same variety as the Primitivo from Puglia in southern Italy. Furthermore, DNA fingerprinting by the University of California, Davis, has now shown that its origins also belong somewhere in Croatia, with the Crljenak variety. The variety is thought to have arrived in California soon after the 1849 Gold Rush, when a demand for vines led to a shipment arriving from the East Coast with a number of 'Zenfendel' vines, which had been imported from the Austrian imperial nursery.

No matter where the variety comes from, the Californians can certainly claim to have secured its place as a quality wine grape. And this, despite large-scale uprooting of Zinfandel vines in the modern rush to plant Cabernet Sauvignon and Chardonnay. White, or blush, Zinfandel – a medium-sweet, rosé-style wine – first became popular in the 1970s and 1980s and the subsequent demand brought an end to the uprooting of vines and encouraged growers to look at this variety again.

The vine displays its southern Italian roots in its love of a hot, sunny climate. It is a late-ripening variety, but ripens unevenly, so that green, unripe grapes and overripe raisinlike fruit can be found on the same bunch. Grapes therefore have to be left on the vine for as long as possible, which leads to very high alcohol contents. Fourteen per cent is not uncommon and 17 per cent alcohol is not impossible, although such high levels can overpower the flavours and make the wine taste Port-like.

Zinfandel suits poor, well-drained, mineral-rich soils, and the concentration of flavours this gives to the grapes and wine is shown in the date, ripe berry, and raisin notes with spicy hints on the palate. Nowadays, the wine is matured in oak barriques, although large Californian Redwood vats are used for fermentation in some of the older wineries.

Recently, and much to the annoyance of Californian Zinfandel producers, European law was changed to allow Italian Primitivo wines to be labelled as Zinfandel. In some ways, this is simply a backhanded compliment to the effort made by those Zinfandel pioneers who opened the world's eyes to the possibilities of this vine.

Tempranillo

Along with Garnacha, Tempranillo is the main grape in Spain's Rioja region, where it produces a variety of styles of red wines from light, young wines, through to deep wines that have the ability to age for twenty to thirty years. It also features in Ribera del Duero, Penedés, Toro, and Valdepeñas under a variety of names such as Tinto Fino, Ull de Llebre, Tinto de Toro, and Cencibel, and it even travels across the border to Portugal, where it appears as Tinta Roriz, one of the permitted grapes in Port. There are also some small plantings in southern Australia.

Temprano is Spanish for early, and this reflects the early-ripening aspects of the variety. It ripens some two weeks before Garnacha, even though it buds at about the same time. This suits the cool Riojan climate, which is influenced by the Atlantic Ocean, and the grapes' thick skins ensure a rich colour, while

The vineyards of Rioja are protected by the High Sierras that moderate the influence of the Atlantic Ocean.

rot is not a problem. It takes well to oak aging, especially in barriques that were introduced to Rioja by Bordeaux merchants looking for replacement wines when their own were decimated by *phylloxera*. The rich vanilla flavours enhance the wine's fruitiness. Instead of the new barrels used for a quick burst of flavour, winemakers prefer long-term aging in old barrels to allow more controlled oxygen contact. Spanish *Gran Reserva* wines spend at least two years in these barrels and a period in bottle before they are sold at five years old.

Chalky, clay soils suit this variety best, but it does grow well on limestone as well. In Spain, the clay helps the soil to retain moisture in the hot summers and reduces the need for irrigation (permitted in Spain but not the rest of Europe).

CHAPTER 5

WINE STYLES

Here you will find the classic wine styles which winemakers all over the world attempt to imitate.

It is probably fair to say that there is nothing new in the wine world. Wines might come from new regions or countries, but whatever wine is made can probably be pigeonholed into a small group of wine styles. These wine styles are identified by, and based upon, the standard-setting wines of the European – and by that I mean mainly French – wine regions, the Blue Riband wines, which new and ambitious wine producers strive to emulate.

But what is it about these wines that makes them so good? Why do they become a sort of 'Holy Grail' for winemakers? Is it the grape varieties they use, the techniques employed in the vineyards and the wineries, the skills of the winemakers, or some magical combination of all of the above?

This section attempts to identify those categories and explain what it is about these styles, and the resulting wines produced, that has made them so popular with a growing number of winemakers and wine consumers around the world today.

Red Bordeaux

Red Bordeaux wines, and in particular those of Pauillac, set the standards that all other red wines, especially those based on Cabernet Sauvignon, try to reach. Why is it so popular? What is it about this mixture of grapes, winemaking style, and *terroir* that appeals to us? First, we have to consider the flavours – dense, dark, blackcurrant fruits, spicy cedarwood, cigar-box and oak notes, with leathery notes appearing as the wine ages. There are not many wines that have a combination of such top quality varieties in the blend (or *cépage*, as the French call it) as Bordeaux. Cabernet Sauvignon, Cabernet Franc, Merlot, and Petit Verdot are all used in varying amounts depending on where in Bordeaux the vineyards are. The thick skins of the Cabernet Sauvignon and Petit Verdot give the wines their tannins, which act as preservatives and give the wines their ability to age.

Historically, the beginning of international interest in Bordeaux wines can be linked to 1152, and the marriage of Eleanor of Aquitaine to the future Henry II of England. As part of her dowry, Eleanor brought the land that we now know as Bordeaux. For the next 300 years, until John Talbot, Earl of Shrewsbury, lost the battle of Castillon, this area was administered from London, and the wines, naturally enough, received a tax 'break', which made them less expensive than other imported wines. It was about this time that the English gave this wine style a nickname, which helped carry it around the world. Claret was a corruption of the French term *clairet*, which was used to describe wines that had had a short period of skin contact and were probably similar to today's rosé wines. Demand for the wines was so high that when England went to war with France (a frequent occurrence in those days), the wines had to be smuggled in from friendly (to the French) countries, such as Scotland and Ireland.

After the Dutch drained the land that is now known as Médoc, in the seventeenth century, new vineyards began to appear on this well-drained gravel soil, producing the premium wines that we recognise today. Even the famous diarist Samuel Pepys had bottles of Château Haut-Brion in his cellar. This launch of the 'New French Clarets' led to the Classification of 1855, which was devised at the request of Napoleon III for his grand Exposition Universelle in Paris. It divided the châteaux of the *Médoc* into five *Cru*, or growths. The wines were grouped according to the prices they had reached at auction over the previous years. This classification still holds well today, with the best wines demanding the best prices. There has only been one alteration to this list in all that time. In 1973, Château Mouton-Rothschild, after many years of lobbying, and as the result of a presidential decree, was raised from a second to a first growth, joining

FIVE TOP TASTES

1.	**Château Latour**, 2009
2.	**Bealieu Vin. de Latour. Cab. Sauv.**, 2005
3.	**Errazuriz Vinedo Chadwick**, 2007
4.	**Cullen Diana Madeline**, 2006
5.	**D'Arenberg Coppermine Cab. Sauv.**, 2005

Châteaux Latour, Lafite-Rothschild, Margaux, and Haut-Brion from next-door Graves.

In fact, the wines that we recognise as Claret today did not really appear until the late 1800s, when the vineyards of Bordeaux were replanted after the devastation of *phylloxera*. The growers took this opportunity to replant their

Majestic Château Margaux sits among the vineyards that have taken its name around the world as part of the select group of premium Médoc producers in Bordeaux.

Château Latour still grows roses at the end of each row of vines as an early indicator of pest and mildew attacks.

vineyards with varieties that they had realised were easier to grow. They also looked at the location in which the vines were being planted, to optimise their ripening potential. So, out went Carmenère, long considered a difficult grape, and Petit Verdot plantings were heavily reduced, as were those of Malbec. In came the Cabernet Sauvignon, which, with its thick skin produced deeply coloured wines with lots of tannin, giving the wine a great aging potential. Around the same time there came the arrival of the small, wooden barrel, or *barrique*, in which the wine now spends the first two years of its life.

Nowadays, the wine is made with care. The best houses still harvest by hand, because this allows a field selection of the best grapes, and pickers can remove diseased or underripe grapes as they collect the bunches. This sorting, or *tirage*, continues in the winery where each bunch is reinspected to remove excess leaves and rotten berries. The grapes are then destemmed in a *fouloir-égrappoir*, or destemmer-crusher, to separate the tannic stalks from the grapes and ensure that the seeds do not release their bitter oils by being split.

The individual grape varieties are fermented separately, either in oak vats, or, as is more common nowadays, in stainless steel, before they are blended by the cellar master to ensure that the final wine has the attributes it requires to make it what he or she wants. At this point, it will be placed in the standard

Bordeaux barrel or *barrique* of 225 litres for two years. During this time, it is 'racked', or separated from its sediment, or 'lees', by moving it to a different barrel to keep the wine clear and allow oxygen to 'soften' the tannins and remove any excess sulphur that has been absorbed by the wine. This racking may take place four times in the first year and another two times in the second.

After two years, the wine is bottled and sold, although it may not be ready to drink for a number of years, depending on the quality of the vintage.

It was the international recognition of the quality of these wines which drew winemakers from the New World towards Bordeaux and encouraged their attempts to emulate the techniques and style as a way to gain recognition for their wines on the world's market. As Robert Mondavi said, 'I wanted to make wines like these, wines that have grace and style, harmony and balance.' They quickly realised that the easily recognisable, blackcurrant-and-mint Cabernet Sauvignon flavours were a means to prove to everyone that they could make serious wines. The Californian homage to Bordeaux is the 'meritage' blend, which takes the same grapes as Bordeaux and matures them in similar, French oak *barriques*.

Californian Cabernet Sauvignon exploded onto the international wine scene after a blind tasting organised by the wine writer Steven Spurrier in Paris in May 1976. This tasting placed the best of the Napa Valley against the best of Bordeaux. The judges' result? After tasting the wines blind – that is without knowing which wine was which – and adding up the scores, these top-notch French wine judges found that the winner was Warren Winiarski's Stags Leap Wine Cellars' 1973 SLV Cabernet Sauvignon, beating several first-growth châteaux from Bordeaux. The wine was grown on well-drained, volcanic soils, on the slopes above Oakville.

This was described at the time as a 'shot heard around the world', and proved to the wine world for the first time that great wines did not have to come from France. At about the same time, Robert Mondavi and Baron Philippe de Rothschild of Château Mouton-Rothschild were agreeing to work on a joint venture to produce a wine in the Napa Valley, using Mouton's winemaking techniques. It was the birth of Opus One.

When the Opus One vineyard was planted, the site selected was on the richer valley floor. To overcome this, the vines were planted much closer together than was the norm in the valley. This density of planting did a number of things. First, it made the vineyard twice as expensive to plant and maintain, but it also put increased pressure on the vines. The large number of vines had to fight for the nutrients in the soil. This pressure on the artificially stressed vines resulted in fewer bunches of better-quality grapes, a quality which, along with the traditional winemaking techniques used in the state-of-the-art winery, carries through into the bottle.

The ground-breaking winery of Opus One is the result of the collaboration between Robert Mondavi and Baron Philippe de Rothschild.

Red Burgundy

It would be hard to find a red wine in France that was so unlike red Bordeaux as red Burgundy. First, and probably most importantly, this wine is a single varietal wine. Pinot Noir is the difference that causes most of the variation in wine style between these two regions. Its thin skin means that the wine very rarely reaches the tannic intensity of Bordeaux, and never has the depth of colour. Second, because there are no set rules regarding its production, there can be great differences in the styles of wines. Some are quite full-bodied, while others can be delicate and floral.

All this, of course, means that it is difficult to explain the qualities that make a great red Burgundy wine. The common factor is one of concentration: the better wines all have more flavour and colour than those produced from lesser locations on the region's slopes.

The aromas vary according to the age of the wine: young wines display red fruit characters, such as raspberries, cherries, and plums, which, as the wine ages, turn to more vegetal aromas of brassicas and truffles. Some say that there is also 'something of the farmyard' about these aged wines.

One of the wine consumers' problems with Burgundy wines is the plethora of producers compared with Bordeaux. In Bordeaux, the great estates are still owned by a family or a company (Chinese entrepreneurs seem to be the only people with enough money to buy a great estate nowadays), whereas in Burgundy, the combination of the Revolution and Napoleonic law has resulted in each of the vineyards having a number of separate owners.

When the Revolution swept by on its way north to Paris, the monasteries were stripped of their lands, which were divided up among the peasants. As each generation has married and passed on, the law, which insisted that property was divided equally among the offspring, has resulted in great vineyards, such as Clos de Vougeot, which is only some 50 Ha, being divided between more than 80 separate owners, each looking after their own vines. Because this situation is repeated over almost every vineyard, it means that, for once, simply knowing the name of a great vineyard is not enough. Families may own small parcels of more than one vineyard, and they will make small amounts of wine from each holding. So there will be a number of different wines, each entitled to use the vineyard names, and all of a sudden it becomes as important to know who has made the wine as it is to know where it has come from.

This has led to the growth of the *négociant*, or merchant, who buys wines from a number of growers, and blends them together to produce a larger amount of wine from that vineyard. Some of these merchants, who may own parcels

FIVE TOP TASTES	
1.	**Clos Vougeot GC, Louis Jadot**, 2000
2.	**La Tâche, Dom. Romané Conti**, 1990
3.	**Pinot Noir, Coldstream Hills**, 1997
4.	**Pinot Noir, Dom. Drouhin**, 1999
5.	**Anderson, Marl. P. Noir, NZ**, 2001

of vineyards themselves, buy grapes and make their own wine, while others may buy already made wines. The result of this complex web is that one producer's Vosne Romanée will taste different to another's.

The climate in Burgundy also has a great influence on the wines. Because it is so far north, the grapes sometimes have difficulty ripening, and in bad years the wines, even the best, can taste thin and tart. But it is this cool climate that

A traditional wine press at Clos de Vougeot dating back to the time when the monastery owned the entire vineyard.

brings out the best in the Pinot Noir, and this is reflected in the New World areas that are working best with this variety. Tasmania, New Zealand, and Oregon and Washington State in the Pacific Northwest are all developing a similar, powerful style of Pinot Noir as that found in Burgundy.

White Burgundy

Once again, this is a varietal wine made entirely from Chardonnay, but, depending on where it comes from, it will have a variety of tastes. As with red Burgundy, the consumer has to take into account the fact that the reputation of the wine's producer is as important as the reputation of the vineyard when it comes to the quality of the wine. One Montrachet could taste completely unlike another, depending on the quality of the fruit purchased from the growers and the winemaking techniques employed.

There is no set rule about white Burgundy production – it all depends on the district that the wine comes from. The main differences in the methods used for the production of white Burgundy are the use of oak barrels for fermentation and/or maturation and the use of malolactic fermentation. This is not fermentation in the manner of the yeast fermentation, which puts the alcohol into wine, and it normally occurs during the maturation period. It is a 'secondary' fermentation, which converts the harsh appley, malic acids present in the wine to a softer, creamier, buttery-flavoured lactic acid. This conversion sometimes happens naturally in the winery because of a build-up of the lactic bacteria necessary for this fermentation to occur. Nowadays, winemakers may deliberately add a cultured strain of lactic bacteria to the new wine, to ensure that a controlled malolactic conversion takes place.

One of the results of this secondary fermentation is that some white Burgundies, such as those from the Côtes de Beaune, take on a buttery flavour and

texture, and because the overall acidity is reduced, have a gentler finish to the wine, reducing the dominance of mineral acidity on the palate.

Chablis wines, produced to the north of the main part of Burgundy, are almost never treated with new oak barrels in the fermentation and maturation period, giving the wines their streak of acidity and mineral notes on the palate. However,

some producers use older barrels with no dominating influence on the wine's flavour, but may add a little complexity, for the short storage period before bottling. Most Chablis producers now rely on inert stainless-steel vats, to allow the flavour of the *terroir* to come through on the wine. As a rule of thumb, wines that are not *Premier* or *Grand Cru* will rarely see any oak.

The light, clay soils of Montrachet, combined with the slope of Côte d'Or, show Chardonnay-based wines at their best.

The wines of the Côte d'Or, mainly the *Grand* and *Premier Cru* of the Côte de Beaune, on the other hand, normally have oak-barrel fermentation and maturation, spending anywhere between one and two years in wood, depending on the quality of the wine. During this time, the wine will be racked, or transferred, to a fresh barrel to separate it from the main deposit of sediment caused by the fermentation. Once this large deposit has been removed, the wines receive an occasional 'stirring', or *batonnage*, to mix up the small amount of lees which settles in the barrel. This encourages the malolactic fermentation and reduces some of the influence of the wooden barrel on the wine.

It is this Côte d'Or-style of wine which the New World producers have tried to emulate, with ripe Chardonnay flavours and oak influences which, depending on the price of the wine, can be created either by using new oak barrels or the less expensive oak chips. Traditionally, casks have been used to transport wines for thousands of years.

Their shape makes it easy to transport the wine by rolling it, and the bulge in the side can collect any sediment 'thrown' by the wine as it matures, so that the wine can be easily drawn off and separated from it.

Casks can also add flavours to the wine as it ferments and matures (the amount of flavour added will depend upon the size and age of the cask). Smaller and newer casks will add more flavour than older or larger ones.

The flinty flavours in Sancerre wines is not surprising when you look at the terroir of the area.

The demand for oak casks has risen, and this has an obvious influence on the price of a standard *barrique* of 225 litres. A one-year-old *barrique* can cost over $350, while a second hand barrel will cost £165 in the Napa Valley. This has an immediate inflationary effect on the price of a bottle of wine.

A cheaper alternative is to add oak chips to the fermenting vat. These chips can vary in size, from pencil shavings to a small nut. Adding as little as seven grams per litre of fermenting wine allows them to give similar vanilla and coconut flavours to the wine at a twentieth of the cost of a new barrel.

Unfortunately, the use of these chips, while giving the flavours of a barrel, cannot replicate the other influences of barrel aging. There is none of the slow oxygenation that helps stabilise the wines and give some prebottling maturation. They may also give a big up-front boost of flavour to the wine, but it can fade after a while, leaving bitter notes in the wine and meaning that the wine is unsuitable for aging.

A good guide as to the type of oak influence used in making a wine is the price. Less expensive wines, designed to be drunk straightaway, will seldom have seen a barrel, or if an older barrel has been used, they will have been given a chip 'boost'. In this respect, it is the Sonoma Valley and cooler parts of Australia that have beaten the path which almost every other wine-producing country has followed.

FIVE TOP TASTES

1.	**Clonale by Kooyong Chardonnay**, 2012	
2.	**Clos Grand Cru Chab.**, 2011, **W. Fevre**	
3.	**Chambertin-Cl. de Bèze, D Chanson**, 2010	
4.	**Marimar Est, D. Mig "Acero" Char.**,2009	
5.	**Leeuwin Est., Art Series Char.**, 2010	

Sancerre and Pouilly Fumé

This style of wine produces the single, varietal, dry Sauvignon Blanc wines, which originally come from the Central Vineyards of the Loire Valley, in France, and it is centred on the two adjacent towns of Sancerre and Pouilly-sur-Loire. At this point the River Loire almost runs south–north as opposed to the east–west path which is its normal course. These two towns lie almost opposite each other on the banks of the river, and their well-drained chalk slopes face south and east to maximise their exposure to the sun.

The Fumé in Pouilly Fumé is meant to demonstrate the gunflint note on the wine from the soil, which separates it from the green, spicy characters of the wines of Sancerre. Both wines share the green, grassy notes of what is, at best, described as gooseberry fruit, hay and nettles, but can sometimes be recognised as cat's pee, and a lean streak of mineral elements that shoots across the tongue. But Fumé also helps to identify the wine as different from the easily guzzled Pouilly-sur-Loire wine from the same area, which is made from the lesser Chasselas grape.

This area has been well and truly shaken up by the arrival of New Zealand Sauvignon Blanc wines, especially those from the cool, sheltered Marlborough region of the South Island. These crisply dry wines fully allow the aromatic elements of the grape to develop. One sniff of them fills the nostrils with pure scents of limes, gooseberries, grass, nettles, tropical fruits, and asparagus, in varying quantities. The palate finishes with a rich tang of refreshing acidity.

New Zealand vineyards, such as these in Blenheim, are now proving the quality of their Sauvignon Blanc wines .

Both these wines share a common element of little or no oak aging or maturation, leaving the grape to display its qualities 'unplugged'. This cannot be said of the Californian style of Sauvignon Blanc developed by Robert Mondavi. His Fumé Blanc Sauvignon Blanc wines are aged for a year in French oak barrels. This rounds out the astringent acidity and makes the wines more approachable to drinkers who find Sauvignon Blanc too zippy.

Sauvignon Blanc wines can also be found in the cooler areas of South Africa and Australia. The styles in these countries tend to fall between those of the Loire and California, having riper stone fruits on the palate and lacking the mineral notes of the Loire. Chilean Sauvignon Blanc is a bit more complex – a lot of what was believed to be Sauvignon Blanc vines have turned out to be a lesser variety called the Sauvignonasse, although these vines have now been replaced. More importantly, new, cooler areas have been planted and the best Sauvignon Blanc wines now come from the Casablanca, Limari and Leyda valleys.

FIVE TOP TASTES

1.	**Forrest Est Marlboro Sauv. Blanc**, 2012
2.	**Sancerre André Dezat**, 2011
3.	**Blanc Fouilly Fumé D. Dagueneau**, 2010
4.	**Suckfizzle. Sauv. B./Semillon**, 2008
5.	**Ch. Carbonnieux. Pessac Léognan**, 2010

Riesling

Riesling wines vary a lot in style. Germany, where the grape has its origins, will traditionally make a wine that is full of tight, zippy acidity, yet has some residual sugar with low alcohol. Probably because this balance is so hard to achieve, New World producers tend to remove the residual sugar by turning it into alcohol, while keeping the trademark zippy acidity and floral notes of the variety.

German Rieslings vary from region to region. The floral wines of the Mosel are lighter and more delicate than the more honeyed wines of the warmer, south-facing slopes of the Rheingau. Yields are as important in Riesling production as they are with other varieties. It is essential to concentrate the flavours to produce top quality wines, but at first glance, the yields in German vineyards can appear huge: 100 Hl/Ha is not an uncommon figure, though this can be explained in part by the fact that German vineyards tend to be very healthy in comparison with others. This is due to the diligence of growers, who tend to plant disease and virus-free plants and uproot unhealthy vines at an early stage. These healthier, fitter vines then produce more bunches with little impact on the flavour.

Concentration also occurs as the grapes move from a ripe state to one of overripeness. German wine law reflects this in the quality classification of the wines. As the grapes get riper on the vine, the sugar content increases, and this indicates the quality level that the final wine can achieve. *Spätlese* wines are late harvested, normally a couple of weeks after the main harvest. *Auslese* wines are made from selected bunches of late-harvested grapes, *Beerenauslese* wines are made from selected berries of late-harvested grapes and, finally, *Trockenbeerenauslese* wines are made

from selected berries that have been attacked by *botrytis cinerea*. Each level concentrates the flavours by reducing the yields from the vines.

Of course, with all this excess sugar, acidity is vital in order to stop the wines

You either have to be a mountain goat or extremely nimble in order to work in the vineyards above Piesport in the Mosel Valley in Germany.

becoming cloying, and the type of acid is important to the flavour of the wine. As the grapes ripen, the malic acid in the grape changes to tartaric and the flavours move from those of harsh, cooking apples to sweeter, citrus lemon and lime flavours. The acid content of the Riesling is so high that wines with 50 grams or more of sugar per litre of wine can, in fact, taste medium rather than sweet.

In France, the Riesling can only be planted in Alsace, which was under German control for a long time, but the style is completely different to its German neighbours. This is due in part to the soil and the fact that the region is much further south than the main German regions and so warmer. The main difference is the alcohol content: 12 per cent is not uncommon here (whereas 8 per cent is not uncommon in Mosel) so the wines are drier in style because more of the sugar content has been converted to alcohol. *Vendange tardive* (late harvest) wines, which can be dry or semi-sweet, and *Sélection de Grains Nobles*, which is always sweet, can be found here too, especially the latter, which tend to be rare.

In Germany's other neighbour, Austria, you again find dry Riesling is the norm, with a relatively high alcohol content of 13 per cent. The best sites are found in the Wachau district, and sometimes need a few years aging in the bottle to reach their peak. In addition, a small amount is made from *botrytis*-affected grapes in the Neusiedlersee area.

The only New World countries to make a success of Riesling-style wines have tended to use the Alsace model rather than the German. Silesian Germans introduced the Riesling to Australia when they emigrated to the Barossa Valley in South Australia. However, they soon found that the area was too warm. The vines ripened too early, making flat wines, which needed to have acidity added, first proof that even top quality vines cannot just be planted anywhere and produce top quality wines. On the other hand, the nearby Clare Valley, and its subdistrict of Polish Hill Valley to the north, has proved to be a significant producer of quality Riesling wines, which have searing lemon and lime acidity and tropical-fruit and floral notes which age well, giving a gasoline-like complexity to the wine.

New Zealand is a relative newcomer to the Riesling world, with the first vines only being planted in the 1970s. But its cool climate is beginning to produce some exciting, dry, Riesling wines in the Marlborough region in the South Island, where the combination of a sheltering mountain range and poor, well-drained soil bring out the best in the vine. They also produce a small amount of sweet, late-harvest Riesling wines.

The incline of the vineyards of Winninger Uhlen in the middle Mosel maximises the exposure of the slate soil to the sun.

Champagne

The secret of quality sparkling wine lies partly in the vineyard – in the selection of good quality but underripe fruit to give those crisp, appley flavours – and partly in the method which is used to put the sparkle into the wine and give the creamy mousse that smooths out the acidic edge of the wine. At its very simplest, the winemaker can take a still wine and inject it with carbon dioxide (CO_2) to make it fizz. This is only used for the least-expensive fizzy wines. No, to make a wine sparkle, it has to be fermented for a second time in a sealed container, and it is the size of that container which influences the quality of the wine.

Sparkling wine can be made in large tanks and filtered under pressure into the bottle; it can be made in a bottle and once more transferred or filtered under pressure into the bottle; or it can be fermented in the bottles that you purchase, after the sediment caused by the fermentation has been removed. This final method ensures that the small quantity of wine is in contact with a relatively large amount of sediment giving a definite yeasty, toasty note to the wine.

It is this method, rather than the 'Tank' or 'Transfer' methods, that is used in the production of Champagne and the best sparkling wines around the world. In fact, the base wine for quality Champagne and sparkling wines needs to be very underripe to allow it to survive this second fermentation. For this reason, the best

The cool, chalk cellars of the Champagne region are perfect for maturing the wine after its second fermentation. Some of the caves have even been decorated.

sparkling wines come from really cool climates, in France, Australia, New Zealand, and so on. Fully ripened fruit just does not make good sparkling wine; it becomes too fat and rounded in taste, instead of offering the lean and crisp flavours that are so refreshing and exciting.

Champagne history was recently turned on its head.

For many years, the accepted story was that a Benedictine monk, Dom Pérignon, was the 'inventor' of Champagne. Dom Pérignon was the cellar master at the Abbey of Hautvillers, north of Epernay, in what is now the Champagne region, from 1668 until his death in 1715. Recent research by wine writer Tom Stevenson, however, has found that a paper lodged with the Royal Society in London, some twenty years earlier by Englishman, Christopher Merret, describes in detail the process for putting the sparkle into wine. He also goes on to record the fact that sparkling wines were already enjoying a following in London at that time. The Champagne wines of that time used to sparkle because the cold cellars had actually stopped the fermentation prematurely, only for the yeasts to reawaken in the warmth of spring, or an attractive ale house, to complete the process and give a fizz to the wine.

In fact, it is now thought that a lot of Dom Pérignon's research was to *prevent* this secondary fermentation in his wines, not encourage it. However, Dom Pérignon did have an influence on Champagne, the wine, which has propelled it to the top of the world's sparkling wine tree.

I say sparkling wine because, as the Champenoise say, 'Champagne is a

Above: Pinot Noir grapes growing in the Montagne de Reims. **Right:** A view of the Abbey of Hautvilliers where Dom Pérignon reigned.

sparkling wine but not all sparkling wine is Champagne.' They continue to be very protective of the name 'Champagne', and will use the power of the courts to ensure that the name is not abused.

But, back to the Dom: his influence was to reduce yields on the fruit that was given to the Abbey as 'rent', so increasing the flavour. Even today the *A.P.* rules insist that only 2,500 litres of juice can be extracted from 4,000 kilograms of grapes. This means that it takes nearly 2 kilograms of grapes to make one bottle of Champagne. The juice left in the grapes after the legal amount has been extracted is normally sent for distillation.

He also developed the idea of 'regional blending' in the wines that he made. This is achieved by separately vinifying the three permitted varieties of Chardonnay, Pinot Noir and Pinot Meunier, from different vineyards around the region, and then blending the resulting wines to form the 'base' wine, before it is fermented for the second time.

This process is the rationale which ensures that each Champagne house, or brand, tastes unique. In the spring, the modern cellar master may have up to 300 different wines to taste and blend to form the wine that will be transformed, by the second fermentation, into Champagne.

For non vintage wines, the cellar master also has the option to add some reserve or older wine into the blend to give some consistency. A vintage Champagne is made from the wines of a single year, that is, there are no reserve wines added. Any year can be a vintage year, but the larger houses only produce vintage Champagnes in the best. It can be said that non-vintage Champagne reflects the style of a house, whereas vintage Champagne reflects the style of a year.

Once the base wine has been blended, the cellar master (working to a formula first devised by a local pharmacist of the early nineteeth century, André Françoise) adds sugar and yeast before the wine is bottled

and sealed. This formula overcomes an early problem with the production of sparkling wine, that of bottles exploding due to the pressure created by the second fermentation. Early Champagne cellars were not safe places to work.

Bottled wine is placed in the cellars for a minimum of fifteen months for non vintage and three years for vintage wines. During this period, the magic of Champagne occurs. The yeasts eat the sugar in the wine and convert it to alcohol and carbon dioxide. At this point, another of the great coincidences of life occurs. Carbon dioxide is the most soluble gas known, and normally, during a fermentation, this gas floats off into the atmosphere (don't stick your head over a vat of wine in mid-fermentation), but when it is trapped in a vessel, the gas gets absorbed by the wine. This gives the wine its sparkle, but

also builds up the pressure, meaning that the wine has to be placed in heavier, thicker bottles than those used for table wines. At its maximum pressure, the bottle has to withstand up to seven or eight atmospheres, or around 90 pounds per square inch.

As the wine slowly ferments in the cool cellars of the Champagne region, the yeasts consume all the sugars in the wine and slowly die, falling to the side of the horizontally stored bottle. At this point the cells break down and a process known as autolysis begins. This has a greater effect in a small bottle than in a large tank, because of

Above: The home of James Bond's favourite Champagne – 'The name's Bollinger, Champagne Bollinger'.
Right: Monument to the master: the statue of Dom Pérignon outside the headquarters of the company which now uses his name for their prestige cuvée.

the smaller volume in contact with the yeast cells. Autolysis inhibits oxidation, helps prevent a refermentation later on, and adds amino acids, which give the wine its acacia, floral aromas and some biscuity notes. This process can last for over five years.

The next problem facing the Champagne maker is to remove the yeast

FIVE TOP TASTES
1. **Krug Grand Cuvée NV**
2. **C. Heidseick Bl. des Millénaires Br.**, 1995
3. **Mailly Grand Cru, Bl de Noires Br.**, NV
4. **Billecart-Salmon Brut Rosé NV**,
5. **Nyetimber Class. Cuv. Eng. Spark.**, 2008

The formidable Veuve Clicquot-Ponsardin, founder of the world-famous Champagne house that bears her name.

sediment, without allowing the gas to escape. Dom Pérignon overcame this problem by storing his wines neck down in a bed of sand, so that the sediment would naturally settle next to the cork. The huge amounts of Champagne produced nowadays would probably need a sand bed the size of France to do the same, so bottles have to be stored in large stacks. It took a young widow, whose husband had left her a Champagne house, to devise a method of moving the sediment gently from the side of the bottle to the neck. Rapid movement would disturb the sediment and leave a fine haze of suspended matter in the wine – not very attractive to the consumer.

The process that the Veuve (widow) Clicquot-Ponsardin developed is still used today. The story goes that she ordered a kitchen table to be placed against a wall with slots cut into it. Bottles of Champagne, still stored on the horizontal, are placed in these slots in a 'pupitre'. Over a period of three weeks, these bottles are gently shaken, turned, and raised until they reach near vertical and the sediment has spiraled down the bottle to rest against the cork. This 'riddling', or *rémuage*, process is still carried out by hand on the best wines in the region, but costs have forced the producers to look at mechanical methods to replicate this process, for all but the prestige marques of each house.

When the sediment has been moved to the neck, the bottles have to be stored *sur point*, or upside down, between straps on the floor and the wall. At this point a further use for the 'punt', or depression in the base of the bottle, is found. In addition to preventing the bottom of the bottle flying out under the pressure, another bottle can be placed in the punt to add a second or third level to the bottles being stored in this way.

Once the wine is ready to be sold, the producer must remove the sediment, without allowing the gas to escape. This was done by hand, a dangerous technique that involved the operator, wearing protective leather clothing, opening inverted bottles and quickly tilting them up so that the sediment, but not too much Champagne, fell out. Timing is everything. A Belgian engineer, named Walfart, who recognised the ability of saltwater to remain liquid below freezing point, solved this problem in the 1880s.

Dipping the neck of Champagne bottles into brine at -16°C (3°F) causes the neck and its contents to freeze. At this point, the bottle can be turned the right way up and the wine will fall away from the frozen sediment in the neck. Then, when the bottle is opened, the sediment will be forced out by the pressure of the

gas behind it, leaving a space needing to be filled by wine. As the 'dosage' or top-off Champagne is introduced, some sugar is added as well. This is designed to set the final style for the Champagne – remember that the yeasts will have eaten all the sugar in the wine, so a little sugar, perhaps as little as three or four grams per bottle, is added to round off the acidity. Sweeter, *doux* Champagnes have much more sugar added, perhaps as much as 40 grams, than the drier *brut*, or 'English' style, preferred in the UK.

Once the wine has been resealed with a fresh cork and clamped down with a 'cage' of wire, it simply needs to be labelled and decorated prior to sale.

Champagne is the benchmark sparkling wine against which all other sparkling wines are measured. This is reflected in the fact that where most 'flying winemakers' come from Australia to Europe, 'sparkling winemakers' will fly from Champagne to all points in the New World, to act as consultants and pass on their techniques. As a consequence, Champagne houses have made a massive investment in the New World, to make more sparkling wines, in their attempts to satisfy demands that cannot be met in Champagne. Moët & Chandon, for example, have now got outposts making quality wines, using the same traditional method used in Champagne, in the cooler areas of Australia, California and Argentina.

Right: Smaller producers still freeze the bottles' necks by hand in order to remove the sediment from the Champagne.
Left: Towards the end of the remuage process the yeast sediment sits next to the cork ready for disgorging.

Crémant

This is a term used to describe sparkling wines from France that are made using the same method as in Champagne, but outside the Champagne region. It is a strange quirk that, as a result of the legal lobbying of Champagne producers, the only winemakers permitted to use the term *Méthode Champenoise*, the

Still family-owned, Château d'Yquem sits patiently waiting for the mists that bring noble rot.

Champagne producers themselves, don't use it. The result has been to find a term for these other sparkling wines.

Crémant wines are produced using local grape varieties, in regions as diverse as the Loire Valley, using the Chenin Blanc; Alsace, where the Pinots Blanc, Noir, and Gris are used; Burgundy, with its Chardonnay and Aligoté, and Limoux in the south of France, where the Mauzac forms part of the blend.

Crémant was originally a term used to describe a style of Champagne that had a much lower gas pressure inside the bottle, so making a less fizzy wine.

FIVE TOP TASTES

1.	**Cr. Chevalerie Blanc NV, C. de Saumur**
2.	**Cuvée Flamme Brut NV, Grat. & Meyer**
3.	**Cr. de Bourgogne Brut NV, C. de Lugny**
4.	**Cr. de Alsace Brut NV, Wolfberger**
5.	**Dom. de Brize, Saumur, Brut Rose NV**

Sauternes

One of the great dessert wines of the world, which although the techniques are copied wherever possible, has few contenders growing up in its shadows. This wine helps to demonstrate how influential and varied are the wine styles of Bordeaux. No one is sure when the idea of making a sweet wine from grapes that had been attacked by rot was formed. But the wines of Sauternes and its five communes, including Barsac, were classified in a similar manner to the wines of the Médoc in 1855, when the wine of Château d'Yquem was, quite rightly, put head and shoulders above the rest in a *Premier Cru Supérieur* category on its own.

But, of course, the grapes have to be attacked by the correct type of rot. *Botrytis cinerea*, or noble rot, when it forms on the Sémillon grapes, reduces the water content and concentrates the sugars and acids in the juice, as well as changing the chemical structure of the juice to produce glycerol. This means that the yields in the vineyard will be less than a quarter of the expected amount in

Mists cover the vineyards of botrytis-affected grapes in the Mosel Valley in Germany.

FIVE TOP TASTES
1. **Ch. d'Yquem Sauternes**, 2010
2. **Ch. de la Tour Blanche Bommes**, 2009
3. **Noble 1 Botrytis Sém. De Bortoli**, 2009
4. **Roy. Tokaji Essencia. Tokaji, Hung.**, 2000
5. **Opitz 1, Weingut W. Opitz, Aut.**, 2006

the Médoc, and this results in the rich, unctuous liquid that comes out of the press. Because *botrytis* does not attack every bunch uniformly, the grapes have to be harvested in a series of selective pickings. These pickings are all fermented separately and blended before bottling.

Botrytis is not a given occurrence every year, its arrival can be patchy or even nonexistent. When this happens, Sauternes can lack the spicy, honeyed intensity for which it is known. If there is no *botrytis*, the wines have to be made with overripe grapes because the law forbids Sauternes to be a dry, white wine. Otherwise, Sauternes producers have two choices: either to make a sweet Sauternes or a dry Bordeaux Blanc, with the huge reduction in price that that *appellation* brings. New World *botrytis* wine producers are permitted to inoculate their vineyards with *botrytis cinerea* spores to ensure that this does not happen.

A controversial process, which can be used in Sauternes production – although the high cost is proving prohibitive – is cryoextraction, which can help overcome the problems of a wet harvest. This, as you can imagine, is the worst thing that can happen to a Sauternes producer. You spend all your time encouraging a growth

of mould to reduce the water content of your grapes, and then the rain comes, soaks them, and puts it back!

Cryoextraction involves placing the damp grapes in a huge refrigerator for around twenty hours, which freezes the water on the surface of the grapes, so that when they are pressed, only the concentrated juice runs out. It does not replace noble rot, but can save the crop, and the quality, of a wet harvest. But it does make a wine that is already expensive even more so.

Once the juice arrives at the winery, the fermentation will slowly begin. Believe it or not, there is just too much sugar in the juice for the yeast to work efficiently – like a child locked in a sweet shop who starts wolfing the chocolate then slows down, and eventually stops, so does the yeast. When the wines reach somewhere in the region of 14 per cent alcohol by volume, the yeasts just give up and go home, leaving lots of residual, or unfermented, sugar in the wine. This gives the honeyed, apricot-and-marzipan flavours of the wines, which get a splash of new oak barrel aging to add vanilla notes to the final wine. All this means that the sweetness of the wine is not the sweetness that comes from refined sugar. It is more like the natural sweetness of honeycomb, which can have a twist of acidic Sauvignon Blanc wine added, if necessary, to stop the wine being too rich and cloying on the palate.

The high sugar content can act as a preservative, so that while young Sauternes can be far too easy to drink, if it can be resisted and left to age, the flavours will improve over the years.

This technique of making wine is found wherever the climatic conditions encourage the growth of noble rot. Other parts of France that produce *botrytis*-affected wines include the area around the River Layon in the Loire Valley. The *appellations* of Coteaux du Layon, Bonnezeaux, and Quarts de Chaumes produce a lighter style of wine than Sauternes, from the Chenin Blanc grape, and the Alsace *Sélection de Grains Noble* are also *botrytis*-affected wines, but are only produced in exceptional years.

In Germany, *Trockenbeerenauslese* wines are made from *botrytis-* or *edelfaule*-affected grapes, normally Riesling, producing rich and honeyed wines, with great concentration and aging potential. In this case, the word 'Trocken' refers to the 'dried' state of the grapes rather than the flavour of the wine.

It is more common to find *botrytis*-affected wines in neighbouring Austria, where the huge Lake Neusiedlersee produces the correct growing conditions for noble rot much more frequently. Hungary's famous Tokaji wines are made from a percentage of *botrytis*-affected grapes. The bigger the percentage, expressed in the number of *puttonyos* on the label, the sweeter the wine.

In Australia, the NSW Riverland area has also found that the climatic conditions encourage *botrytis*. It is now the centre of production of a *botrytis*-affected Sémillon wine and is bringing out world-class dessert wines that are starting to rival Sauternes.

Sherry

The development and production of Sherry has, like that of Port, and, to a certain extent, red Bordeaux, been heavily influenced by its main export market, Britain. This can be seen in the names of some of the large merchants in the area: John Harvey & Sons, Croft, Sandeman, and others owe their origins to the British and Irish interest.

This fortified wine is made in a unique way that is copied in other regions and countries, but has very few rivals. A number of influences set the style of this wine. First, the soil – the Jerez region in southern Spain, near the port of Cadiz has a chalk soil, which absorbs water when it rains, and then seals it in when the top layer is baked by the sun. This ensures that the vine has access to supplies of water during the growing season.

Second, there is the effect of 'flor', a yeast infection, on the wine as it matures. Normally, once an alcohol fermentation is over, the yeast dies. However, the yeasts in Jerez somehow change, and in some barrels will continue to live and form a fatty or creamy film over the surface of the wine. Living off the alcohol in the wine, they change the wine giving it a strong apple and nuts aroma and flavour, and the film also acts as a barrier protecting the wine from oxygen and so keeping it fresh. But not every barrel of maturing Palomino wine will have this film forming in it. Those that do receive a lower fortification, or amount of alcohol (a local brandy), to raise the content to around 15 per cent, and are known as Fino sherries, unless they come from the seaside town of Sanlucar de Barrameda when they are called Manzanilla sherries.

If the barrel is not affected by flor, the wine is fortified to a higher lever, raising it to 17 per cent alcohol, and is classified as an Oloroso.

The wines are then matured in *bodegas*, or cellars – a bit of a misnomer because these are actually large, cathedral-like buildings that stay cool because the air never really moves or heats up no matter how sunny it is outside. Within these *bodegas* the wines are matured in 'soleras'.

The solera system is a method used in the production of a few fortified wines only. Its main aim is to keep the flor alive by adding fresh wine every few months, and so is essential in the production of Fino and Amontillado sherries. An Amontillado sherry is actually an aged Fino sherry that has been allowed to come into contact with oxygen. This oxidisation gives a rich element of dried fruit to the nutty flavours of the dry wine.

The solera allows a 'fractional' blending to take place over a number of years. Imagine a stack of barrels, each layer containing wines of different ages, the youngest at the top and the oldest at the bottom or base. As you remove some wine to bottle and sell from the bottom

FIVE TOP TASTES
1. **Bod. Barbadillo Manzanilla, Extra Dry**
2. **Lustau Fino del Puerto En Rama**
3. **Apostoles 30yo Palo Cortado Gonz. By.**
4. **Nöe 30yo Pedro Ximénez Gonz. Byass**
5. **Lustau "Los Arcos" dry Amontillado**

barrels, being careful never to empty them, you replace it with wines from the layer above. This continues until you reach the top layer, when you place fresh, new wine into it.

It can take the wine at least seven or eight years to travel through the entire solera, ensuring that any variation in vintage quality is blended out of the wines. Any Sherry bottle that has a date on it will be the date that the 'base' of the solera was laid down, and, since the solera has never been emptied, the theory is it will have some elements of the original wine in its makeup.

Oloroso wines are also matured in a solera, but after the wines are removed they can be treated in a number of ways, depending on the desired style of the

Chalk vineyards of Palomino grapes sit in the sun in the vineyards of Jerez.

final wine. Because they have not had the protective covering of the film of flor, these wines will have a more pronounced oxidised note on the nose and palate. This gives a darker colour and a toasty, fruitcake flavour to the wine. They are sometimes sweetened by the addition of a rich sherry made from sundried Pédro Ximénez grapes. This intensely sweet Sherry can be found on its own, but is commonly used as a blending wine to take some of the austerity away from a dry Oloroso. Commercial Oloroso wines are sometimes labelled as Cream Sherries and Pale Cream Sherries are simply sweetened, uncoloured Fino wines.

Port

One of the great fortified wines of the world, Port is made in many styles, but is rarely copied to the same level of quality as, say, red Bordeaux. To a certain extent, this wine came about by accident. The Methuen Treaty of 1703 was a trade treaty signed between the British and Portuguese governments, and it included sending wines to England. It was common practice to add some brandy to wines that were being transported a fair distance in those days to stabilise and preserve the wine. Soon, the brandy was being added during fermentation to kill the yeasts and leave some residual sweetness, so beginning the development of the Port wines that we enjoy today.

The important factor in making Port is the rapid extraction of colour from the grapes. The early fortification results in residual or unfermented sugar being left in the wine, and, because the wine is then placed in barrels, it has to be separated from the skins.

So maximum and efficient extraction of the colour from the skins is essential. This is one of the reasons for the large number of grapes permitted in the production of Port. Some have thick skins and one or two are members of that small group of grapes that have a coloured juice.

Traditionally, treading the grapes by foot helped this process. The foot is an almost perfect pressing implement. It is hard enough to split the grapes and gently squeeze the skins to extract the colour and tannin required, without splitting the seeds and releasing their

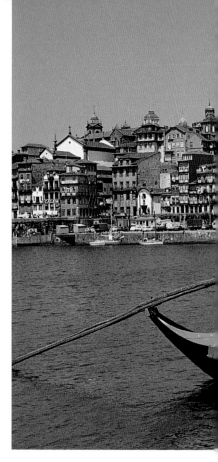

bitter oils into the wine. After a hard day in the vineyard, the pickers would jump into the shallow troughs or lagars (with clean feet, one hopes!), have a party and tread the grapes. Nowadays, costs mean that this practice is only used on the top quality vintage Ports of some producers.

Over the years, other methods have been developed to extract the colour. The most commonly used method is the

Barcos rabelos like this moored across the river from Porto used to transport wines down river from the quintas.

'autovinifier'. This is a sealed vat, which uses the pressure of the carbon dioxide produced during the fermentation process to pump the fermenting juice over the 'cap' of skins that floats on the surface of the juice.

Recent research, however, has led to the development of a mechanical process, which replicates the human treading process, the aim of which is to make a wine with the intensity of colour and structure, aroma and elegance, and concentration of phenolics, that you find in vintage Ports, without the costs involved in treading by foot. To date, the producers have, by comparative experimentation, developed a piston process, the Port Toes, that is used to produce all styles of Port with

the exception of vintage Port. It has been found that, while the machine cannot equal humans yet, it is a great improvement on the autovinifier.

In the spring, once the wine has settled down after the shock of fortification, it is transported down the Douro Valley. After a journey of about 125 miles to the coastal town of Vila Nova de Gaia, which sits opposite the town of Oporto that gives the wine its name, the wine is matured in the producers' Port Lodges or warehouses.

The method of maturation used and the time of bottling will vary according to the style of wine that is being produced.

Above: From the youngest Port on the left to an aged Colheita on the right, the colour difference of mature tawny Ports can be clearly seen.

Vintage Port

This is the product of a single, exceptional year. Port vintages have to be declared and so this wine is only made two or three times a decade. The best wines from a number of vineyards are blended and matured for about eighteen months, in large vats, before bottling when they are still fiery and tough. They need at least fifteen years' slow maturation in the bottle before they soften out and the brandy becomes integrated with the sweet, yet spicy, damson, plum, and blackcurrant flavours.

Single Quinta Ports

These Ports come from a single vineyard and are produced in the years when a vintage is not declared. Once again, they

FIVE TOP TASTES
1. **Dow's Vintage Port**, 2011
2. **Graham's 20-year-old Tawny Port**
3. **Taylor's Single Quinta Vintage Pt.**, 2001
4. **Graham's Colheita Port**, 1969
5. **Fonseca Lt. Bott. Vint. Unfiltered.**, 2007

Right: Still under single ownership, Taylor's Ports are some of the most sought after by aficionados.

Ille terrarum mihi

TAYLOR'S®

praeter omnis angulus ridet, ubi virus
floret vinifera Hiberica, Ibi natum, et
quercus ligneis vasis in iuventate mea
conditum, per multos viginti annos quiesco.
Merum rubrum simplex ingredior : evenio

YEAR OLD TAWNY PORT

Aged for 40 years in wood

vinum involutissimum flavum. Nunc est bibendum
nunc vino pellite curras.

ESTABLISHED IN 1692 • PRODUCT OF PORTUGAL

BOTTLED IN OPORTO BY
TAYLOR FLADGATE & YEATMAN
VINHOS S.A., VILA NOVA DE GAIA

20% VOL   75 CL

are the product of a single year and are produced in the same way as vintage Port. They normally come from the best estates, and in vintage years, would probably end up in the vintage blend. They are matured in bottles in the Port lodges and are not released until they are around nine years old, as opposed to vintage Ports, which will be released a lot earlier to be matured elsewhere. They share the same flavours as vintage Ports, but have less intensity.

Late Bottled Vintage Ports (LBV)

Again, these are wines from a single year, and like, vintage Port, are blended from wines from a number of estates. They differ from vintage Port in a couple of ways however. The wines are not of the same quality as vintage Port, but share some of the characteristics and they spend a longer period of time – anything between four and six years – in large vats. When they are filtered and bottled, they are ready to drink. The filtering process means that the wines will not 'throw' a sediment in the bottle, and so do not need to be decanted.

Ruby Ports

These are blended Ports, which are also matured in large vats. They are inexpensive wines that have an appealing, fiery note, because the brandy has not yet had the time to integrate into the wine.

Tawny Ports

Instead of the large vats used for 'dated' and Ruby Ports, Tawny wines are matured by being placed in 600-litre pipes. Most Tawny Ports have an age marked on them – ten, twenty, thirty, or forty years being the average amount of time that they have spent in the barrel. The lengthy aging gives the wine softer, oak-influenced, raisiny flavours and allows it to change colour from a ruby-purple colour to an orange-brick, or tawny, color. Once again, they do not need decanting, because the sediment has formed in the barrel rather than in the bottle. They should be served chilled and, like LBV Ports, can be drunk straightaway.

Colheita Ports

A variation on Tawny Port, instead of being a blended wine of different years, Colheita Port is the wine of a single vintage, which is placed in 600-litre pipes and bottled anything up to sixty years later, when it is ready to drink.

Many traditions have developed about the way Port should be consumed. The idea of 'passing' the Port came from the Royal Navy. As a fortified wine, Port kept for longer, and so was popular with the officers. However, long sea voyages meant that care had to be taken to get the maximum pleasure out of limited supplies.

Many bottles were knocked off the table as the ship rolled. To prevent this, the Port was passed from right to left, round the table, and could not be placed on the table until it had completed a circuit and everyone had a glass.

CHAPTER 6

WINE AROUND THE WORLD

FRANCE

If the area of the Caucasus mountains, now in Georgia and Armenia, can lay claim to the origins of vine cultivation, then France can claim to be the modern home of the vine.

How else do you explain the worldwide influence of its wine styles? From Bordeaux (including Sauternes), Champagne, Burgundy, and many other regions, wines have been exported around the world, and winemakers have tried to copy them.

The wines of France are not simply a reflection of the *terroir*, climate, and

skills of the winemaker, they are also intertwined with the history and culture of the country. Would the British still have their love affair with the red wines of Bordeaux, if it had not been for the marriage of Henry II and Eleanor of Aquitaine? Would the wines of the Southern Rhône have found favour, if it were not for the ambitious aims of

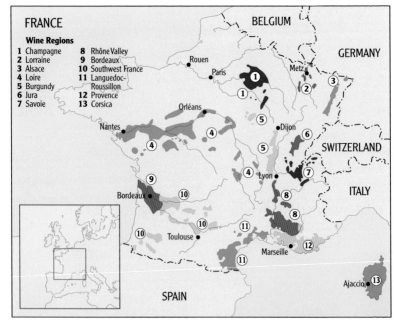

FRANCE

Wine Regions

1 Champagne	8 Rhône Valley
2 Lorraine	9 Bordeaux
3 Alsace	10 Southwest France
4 Loire	11 Languedoc-Roussillon
5 Burgundy	12 Provence
6 Jura	13 Corsica
7 Savoie	

1990

CHATEAU
LANGOA BARTON

SAINT-JULIEN

APPELLATION SAINT-JULIEN CONTRÔLÉE

S.A. DES CHATEAUX LANGOA ET LÉOVILLE-BARTON
A St-JULIEN-BEYCHEVELLE - GIRONDE - FRANCE

FIDE ET FORTITUDINE

Previous page: An Appellation Contrôlée marque on a bottle of St Julien. **Below:** The citizens of Avignon relax and enjoy the wine made famous by the rival papacy set up in their town by Clement V.

Clement V and his rival papacy in Avignon? What would the wines of Burgundy taste like if the land had not been given to the citizens during the Revolution, and the vineyards then further subdivided by each generation?

A France without wine? Unimaginable!

FRENCH WINE LAWS

It is not just in the styles of wines that France has been the trendsetter. The wine laws of France are also the blueprints from which most other countries pick and choose their own. French wine laws are based around the concept of *terroir*. This is an ambiguous term, with no real translation into English, which covers the interaction between not only the geology of the soil in which the vines grow, but also the macro and microclimates of the district, formed by the topography of the surrounding landscape. The theory is that, as each district will have its own *terroir*, so each wine will display different characteristics, some more subtle than others. The influence of *terroir* affects the choice of grape variety, the method of training the vine, and the individuality of the district.

There are positive as well as negative aspects to this. It is clear that this system has maintained the great variety in the types and styles of wines produced in France, by removing the ability of the winemaker to follow fashionable trends, for example, replanting their vineyards with nothing but Cabernet Sauvignon and Chardonnay, chasing the quick sale. On the other hand, it has stifled experimentation, with stories abounding of the 'Vin Gendarmes' turning up at vineyards and digging up unapproved vines in the dead of night, even if they are full of nearly ripe grapes! And some claim that the regulations have also stifled innovation in the winery, where there is no incentive to improve the quality of wine because of the belief that it all comes from the *terroir*, with little or no intervention from the winemaker.

Even with these strictures, it is important to point out that, in common with almost every set of wine laws in the world, the French wine laws are not a guarantee of quality. The term *Appellation d'Origine Protégée*, or

Appellation Protégée, or *A.P.*, simply states that the wine or food (the system does not just classify wine) comes from a certain area and has been made following certain rules.

The *A.P.* regulations control:
• The delimited area that can be planted.
• The grape varieties and clones that can be planted.
• The maximum yield that can be extracted from the vines normally expressed as a number of hectolitres per hectare.
• The minimum alcohol content of the wine.
• The viticultural methods, such as method of pruning, density of planting, and so on.
• The vinification methods used, including how the wine should be matured, size of cask, length of time, and so on.

These regulations are enforced by a local committee, which organises the blind tasting that all the wines have to pass. But, again, the criteria that the wines have to pass are ones of typicality rather than quality.

Appellations vary in size from the large, generic, regional ones, such as *A.P.* Bordeaux, through the districts, such as Médoc, down to villages like Margaux and even the Burgundian *Grand Cru* vineyards like La Tâche. So, despite the level of the classification on a wine's label, the name of the producer is still the best guide to the quality of the wine.

Appellation Protégée wines form the peak of the classification system in France. The other levels are:
• *Vin Délimité de Qualité Supérieure*: this category is slowly being phased out

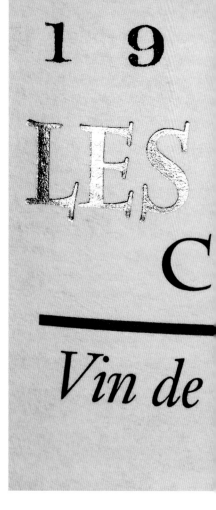

as the wines are promoted to *A.P.* status.
• *Indication Géographique Protégée*: this category was introduced in the late 1960s to identify the mainly southern, country, or regional, wines that had a definite character. The regulations are a bit more flexible than the older *A.P.* regulations but still cover such things as permitted

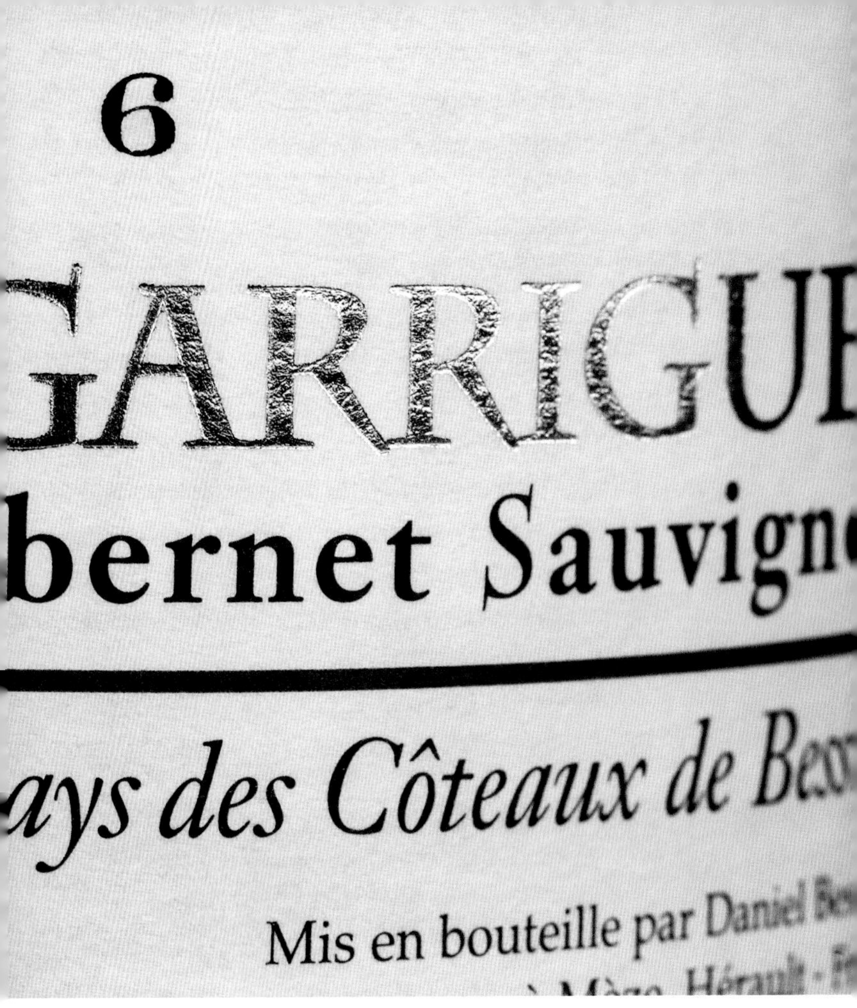

6

GARRIGUE

bernet Sauvigne

ays des Côteaux de Be

Mis en bouteille par Daniel Be

varieties, minimum alcohol content, and the area of production. This has allowed the more enterprising winemakers in the south to make whatever wines they want outside the restrictions of the *A.P.*

• *Vin de France:* this is the basic wine of France. Almost 40 per cent of the wines produced in France fall into this

Vin de Pays, now I.G.P., regulations allow producers to show the vine variety used and experiment with different styles.

category. There are no restrictions on the grape varieties used, or the yields and the labels can show the variety and vintage but no area of production, simply stating 'Produce of France'.

Bordeaux

Bordeaux wines, especially the red wines of the Médoc and Graves, have long been recognised as iconic wines of France, if not the world. The region is unique when it comes to wine production in France. Not only is it the largest and most productive French wine region, it also produces a wide variety of wine styles. Apart from the eponymous red, you can find rosé, dry white wines and luscious dessert wines here, some of them long recognised as being among the best in the world.

How did this region, situated on the coast of the Bay of Biscay in south-west France, achieve this status? Firstly, as with many European wine regions, we have to thank the Romans who first planted vines in the area, so answering the long-debated question "What have the Romans ever done for us?"

However, the land of the Médoc as seen by that forward-thinking Roman centurion would have looked very different to the land we know today. Then the view would have been of a flat land with a few hillocks standing proud of a wet marshland. Further investigation would have shown that these hillocks were in fact banks of gravel with a thin layer of topsoil. Now, I can't say what

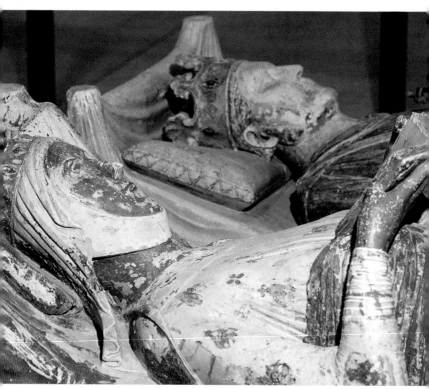

his thoughts were, but in my mind's eye either he was shrugging his shoulders and thinking, "Well, this is a cold, wet flatland—let's plant something and see what happens" or, as I prefer to believe, "Hmm… gravel—good drainage that. Poor quality soil and a marginal climate? Great—let the vine struggle for better quality. THIS is the land I've been looking for. Let's plant, lads!"

Why? Well, if you look at the location of the great first growths of Médoc , they all sit on top of these gravel ridges or "croupes".

Bordeaux's international reputation, however, really began with the marriage of Eleanor of Aquitaine and the future Henry II of England in 1152, which opened up the English market to the wines of this region, a market that is still important today.

Of course the wines were not the same as we find today, The main region was the Graves to the south of the city and the wine style was a deep rosé wine known as Clairette, a term the English translated to "Claret" which is used to describe all the red wines from Bordeaux today.

But this still does explain the world-class status that Bordeaux wines have achieved today. For that we need to look at a few other influences.

Firstly, there is England's on-off relationship with France. From the fourteenth to the nineteenth century there has been a succession of wars between the countries. One of the results of this was a shortage of French wine on the English market and high taxation on the wines that were available. Officially, England bought more wine from Portugal to make up the

The tomb of Eleanor of Aquitaine whose marriage introduced the English to the delights of claret.

difference or auctioned French wine seized from vessels along the French coast. But there is some speculation that a lot of the "seizing" was in fact pre-arranged between English and Bordeaux wine merchants, with some of the money raised from the sale making its way back to Bordeaux. There was also a lot of trade through Scotland and Ireland.

In the seventeenth century the other great trading nation of Europe arrived in Bordeaux. The Dutch not only opened up new markets for Bordeaux wines but in order to meet new demand planted new vineyards. And because they needed more land, they used their engineering skills to drain the land of the Médoc and created the terrain, criss-crossed with drainage channels, that we recognise today.

However, this did not solve the problem of poor wine sales in England where the tax regime made French wines much more expensive even when the two countries were not at war. Recognising this challenge the producers of Bordeaux, led by Baron Arnaud de Pontac, the owner of Château Haut Brion, began to develop the idea of the luxury brand. Firstly they insisted that the wine was exported under the Château name, not just the region name. They also began to develop the process that we recognise today as producing quality wines, reducing yields and rejecting poor-quality grapes.

It is this style of wine that Samuel Pepys noted drinking in his diary in 1663, although his French let him down when he described it as "Ho Bryan".

The revolution was kinder to Bordeaux than Burgundy. Rather than break up the estates (see page 187) and give the land

Above: Most French wine villages are rightly proud of their products. **Right:** Not all châteaux are as impressive as Pichon Lalande in the Médoc.

other varieties such as Cabernet Franc, Malbec and Petit Verdot and abandoning "difficult" varieties (which would only ripen in exceptional years) such as Carmenère and Syrah.

Along with the variety of grape, the type of soil is one of the dominant factors in deciding the blend, or cépage, of the wine. The warm gravel soil of the Médoc and Graves areas, on the left bank of the river, suits the later-ripening Cabernet Sauvignon grape whereas the heavier clay soils of St Emilion are better suited to the early-ripening Merlot variety. So a typical cépage in the Médoc might be

Cabernet Sauvignon	55%
Merlot	20%
Cabernet Franc	20%
Petit Verdot/Malbec	5%

Whereas a St Emilion cépage is more likely to be:

Merlot	60%
Cabernet Franc	30%
Malbec	10%

to the workers, the state needed money when it came to look at the seized estates of Bordeaux. Because of this, the estates were auctioned off in their entirety. The purchasers were either rich bankers such as the Rothschild family or merchants like the Irishman Thomas Barton who kept the estates under single ownership.

The Bordeaux merchants were also the first to grade their wines with the 1855 classification (see page 161), something that we take for granted in other regions today.

The next major impact on Bordeaux wines occurred around 1870 when the *phylloxera* scourge arrived, devastating the vineyards and causing them to be completely replanted with grafted vines by the late 1890s. This led to the dominance of Cabernet Sauvignon and Merlot as growers, desperate to earn some money, took the opportunity to plant varieties that were easier and more reliable, downgrading

The land of Bordeaux is well drained, having three rivers running through it. The Gironde is supplied by its two tributaries: the Dordogne to the north and Garonne to the south. These rivers not only drain the soils, but have also aided transportation as the Bordeaux merchants developed international trading routes with the world. Mind you, the merchants were also quite smart in that they placed a higher shipping fee on wines from outside the region—thus making them more expensive on the open market.

The climate also has a major influence on the wines of Bordeaux. The Gulf Stream runs down the coast and, when combined with the expanse of the Gironde estuary, helps to keep early-season frosts at bay. The vineyards are protected from the prevailing Atlantic winds and rain by the Landes forest (the largest in France) and the large sand dunes which line the sandy beaches. Combined, they form a windbreak and rain shadow and create a warm and relatively dry microclimate around the vineyards of the Médoc.

The basis of wine production in Bordeaux is the château system. The château, not necessarily a grand castle or even a country house, is an estate under single ownership that makes its own wine. The size of these estates is not regulated, so over the years estates have varied in size as they have sold or acquired land. The château name is really no more than a brand.

Médoc

The Médoc is, in the eyes of the world, one of the premium red wine producing districts in the world; in fact, any white wines grown here can only be classified as lowly *A.P.* Bordeaux Blanc. This reputation is based on the production of a handful of châteaux and a classification system devised for the grand Exposition Universelle in Paris, organised by Napoleon III in 1855, which listed the wines of the Médoc in five growths, or *Cru*. The wines were divided according to the price they had raised at auction in the previous years. Four *Premier Cru*, or First Growth wines, were declared (this included one famous wine from neighbouring Graves, Château Haut-Brion, or as Samuel Pepys recorded it, 'Ho Bryan').

This league table of wines has not changed since then, apart from one revision in 1973. After forty years of lobbying, and the issue of a presidential decree, Baron Philippe de Rothschild finally saw his beloved Château Mouton Rothschild promoted from second to first growth. But, as he recorded on that year's label, 'Once I was second, Now I am first. Mouton has not changed'.

The district is divided into two sections: Médoc and Haut Médoc, Médoc being to the north, with a more clay-dominated soil. The Haut Médoc is the centre of quality red wine production, and is further subdivided into a number of villages or communes, each with their own *A.P.* Those with the best reputation

The late Baron Philippe de Rothschild.

lie nearer the river, on beds of gravel that were deposited thousands of years ago. From north to south they are:

Saint Estèphe

These full-bodied, tannic red wines are slow maturing, and, because of the higher percentage of clay in the soil, now tend to have more Merlot in the blend to soften the wines. Look for the Châteaux of Cos d'Estournel, Calon-Ségur, and Montrose among others.

Pauillac

The home of the great wines of the Médoc and, by association, of Cabernet Sauvignon, Pauillac produces full-bodied wines with cigar-box and blackcurrant aromas as evidenced by the fact that some of the top wines will have up to 85 per cent Cabernet Sauvignon in their *cépage*. Pauillac is the home of three of the classification's first-growth wines:

The neoclassical elegance of Château Beychevelle is home to one of the great red wines of Bordeaux.

Château Lynch Bages shows the Irish influence in this area. John Lynch, the original owner, was Mayor of Bordeaux.

Château Lafite-Rothschild, Château Latour, and the promoted Château Mouton-Rothschild. If you can't afford these wines, there are a number of other classified Châteaux, such as Pichon Longueville Comtesse de Lalande, Lynch-Bages, and d'Armailhac.

St Julien

Situated next door to Pauillac, these two communes are separated only by the Juillac stream. The wines are similar to Pauillac's, if slightly less intense and well known. Look out for the Châteaux of Léoville-Barton, Beychevelle, and Léoville-Lascases.

Margaux

The wines of Margaux are more silky and soft than those of Pauillac and St Julien, mainly due to a higher proportion of Merlot in the *cépage* – up to 20 per cent rather than Pauillac's 5 per cent. There is one *Premier Cru* wine in this commune, the elegant, violet-scented, Château Margaux. Try and find wines from Châteaux Palmer, Rauzan-Ségla, and

d'Angludet to discover the qualities of this area.

Graves

Named after the soil that is an extension of the left bank's gravel, so important in the Haut Médoc, this area has slowly shrunk over the years, under the twin attacks of creeping suburbia – Château Haut-Brion, the *Premier Cru* vineyard, is now surrounded by the urban sprawl of the city of Bordeaux – and delimiting legislation. In 1987, the area to the north of the district, which includes most of the best vineyards, was split off to form a new *appellation* of Pessac-Léognan.

Graves wines were classified in 1959 and consist of two lists, one of fourteen red wines and one of ten white, with six châteaux appearing on both lists. In an egalitarian manner, the lists are in alphabetical order and are not subdivided into classes.

There are two *appellations* in this area. The *A.C.* Graves is for dry, white wines made from Sémillon and Sauvignon Blanc grapes, and a red wine made mainly from Cabernet Sauvignon and Merlot grapes.

The red wines are similar in style, if a bit lighter than those produced by their neighbours to the north. Reflecting the change in wine consumption, the production of this region has moved, in the last few years, from a majority of white wine to somewhere in the region of two bottles of red wine for every bottle of dry white. This is despite the

Nowadays lying within the town of Bordeaux, Château Haut-Brion still produces top-quality Bordeaux wines.

improvement in the quality of these dry white wines.

The second *appellation* is the somewhat inappropriately named *A.C.* Graves Supérieur for not very exciting, sweet white wines that have not been attacked by noble rot.

Pessac-Léognan

Formed in 1987, from the better, northern section of the Graves, this *appellation* is based upon the two communes of Pessac and Léognan, which gave it its name. The soil here has a higher proportion of gravel in it than the remaining district of Graves to the south. The free-draining soil is well suited to the Sémillon and Sauvignon Blanc grapes, which produce the medium-bodied, dry, white wines, and the Cabernet Sauvignon and Merlot grapes, which dominate the *cépage* of the tobacco and blackcurrant red wines. It is in this *appellation* that Château Haut-Brion now lives, reflecting the fact that the red wine is much more similar in style to the reds of the Haut Médoc than the wines of the Graves.

As the city of Bordeaux has expanded, houses have surrounded the vineyard of Haut-Brion, which makes one wonder what the owners grow in their gardens! This has happened because growers in the area chose not to replant their vineyards after the *phylloxera* attack, and over the years have sold the land for redevelopment.

Apart from Château Haut-Brion, look out for Châteaux such as Smith-Haut-Lafite, La Mission-Haut-Brion, Bouscaut, and Carbonnieux.

PARIS

Sauternes and Barsac

In the south of the Bordeaux region, a couple of small communes lie on the banks of the Garonne, surrounded by the Graves region. Here, the topography of the region, combined with the location of the rivers, produces the perfect conditions to make sublime sweet wines. In the autumn, early morning mists form on the rivers and are trapped in the vineyards. When the sun breaks through, the warm, moist atmosphere encourages a mould to grow on the grapes and begin to rot them. A problem for the grower? Hardly, in fact, they can't wait for it to arrive.

Of course, this is not any old rot but *botrytis cinerea* – the noble rot that

Part of the Exposition Universelle of 1855 for which the wines of Médoc and Sauternes were divided into the classification that still holds strong today.

dehydrates the Sémillon and Sauvignon Blanc grapes, turning them into slimy raisins, and concentrates the sugar and acids, and subtly changes some of the chemical make-up of the juice to produce the honey-like texture and flavours of the wine. Because the rot does not attack bunches evenly, the grapes have to be picked by hand. Actually, in most cases, it is individual grapes that are picked, by experienced people who can sort through the bunches and select only those grapes at the proper stage of rot, leaving the rest

to hang on the vine for a bit longer, until they too are ready. This means that the harvest in Sauternes and Barsac takes a lot longer, as the pickers may have to go through the vineyards three or four times before the harvest is over.

Botrytis does not arrive every year, and if it does not, then the wines will be made with late-harvested grapes, those which have been left on the vine longer to shrivel and concentrate the sugars. The wine will be sweet, but will lack the concentration and complexity of a *botrytised* wine. If the grapes cannot be left on the vine because of the weather (for example, rain would bring the wrong sort of rot), then the winemaker has simply to swallow his or her pride and make a dry wine. If they do this, then they have to classify the wine as a simple Bordeaux Blanc, as the Sauternes and Barsac *appellations* are for sweet wines only.

The wines of Sauternes and Barsac were classified in 1855 for the same Paris Exposition as the wines of the Haut Médoc. Even at that time, it was clear that one wine stood head and shoulders above the rest. For this reason, there is a special category of First Great Growth, or *Premier Cru Supérieur*, for the wines of Château d'Yquem in Sauternes. The other classified wines were divided into two classes, *Premier* and *Deuxièmes Crus*. Among the first growths, Château la Tour-Blanche, in the commune of Bommes, is actually the wine label of the local agricultural college. The vineyard was left to the French government in the early 1900s, with a stipulation that it was to be used for this purpose. Once, it had a

Château Figeac, one of the top producers of soft, Merlot-dominated St Emilion wines.

reputation for not being all that good, and this was put down to letting the students loose on the wines. Nowadays, the wines are much improved and have regained a reputation for their quality. Other first growths to look out for are the Châteaux of Rieussec, Suduiraut, and Coutet.

St Emilion

Lying on the right bank of the river Dordogne, St Emilion is probably the second best known area of Bordeaux, after the Haut Médoc, for red wines. But because it is located farther from the coast, and has a cool, clay-dominated soil, the Cabernet Sauvignon is hardly found and this affects the style of wine produced in the area.

The wines of St Emilion are dominated by the Merlot grape and supported by the Cabernet Franc, resulting in softer, plummier flavours, and because of the thinner skins and lower tannin content of the grapes, they mature earlier than the Cabernet Sauvignon-dominated wines of Médoc.

This large production area is subdivided into three areas: the Côtes, the Graves, and the Sables. The Côtes, or slopes, provide the best wines from their limestone and clay soil. The Graves is a flat plain, with surprisingly little gravel deposits in it, despite its name, with only a couple of great vineyards – the Châteaux Figeac and Cheval Blanc (it means 'white horse', and is not to be confused with a white wine of Château

Cheval). As for the Sables, this sandy-soiled area, down near the river, is used to produce quantities of not very interesting *A.P.* St Emilion.

Classification Clash

Since I wrote the first edition of this book the wine-producing region of St Emilion in Bordeaux has been in turmoil. Since 1955 the producers of St Emilion have worked with a classification system to grade their wines. I am sure that the date, exactly 100 years after the famous classification of the wines of the Médoc, is no coincidence. One differing aspect of their classification system, however, was a built-in review of every wine's position in the classification every decade or so. This meant that, depending on a wine's performance defined by certain criteria and a blind tasting, a property could find itself promoted or demoted within the categories of Premiers Grands Crus Classés and Grands Crus Classés.

This system seemed to be accepted and carried on with little upset until the re-classification of 2006. When the results of this classification were published, four producers who had been demoted complained to the courts. Subsequent investigations seemed to substantiate their claims that the 'blind' tastings weren't as blind as they should have been and that judges with an axe to grind may have come to biased conclusions regarding the quality of the wine.

The result was that after much expensive wrangling the 2006 classification was scrapped and the

1996 classification reinstated, with the addition of a number of properties that had been promoted in their new categories.

A new classification system was announced in 2012. This time the inspections – based on dossiers submitted by the producers – and tastings were outsourced to wine experts from Burgundy, Champagne, the Rhone valley and the Loire, who made up a seven-person commission. But even this attempt at impartiality has proved controversial. The commission promoted two producers to the prestigious Premiers Grands Crus Classés "A" category, adding Châteaux Angélus and Pavie to Châteaux Cheval Blanc and Ausone. They also promoted a number of producers to Premiers Grands Crus Classés "B" and demoted a few others. The result is that there are now 18

These modest-looking buildings surrounded by vines are in fact the winery of the famous Château Pétrus.

Premiers Grands Crus Classés and 64 Grands Crus Classés wines. Peace at last, you might think… but this is the world of wine. In January 2013 three producers filed a complaint with the courts, claiming that there were procedural errors with the selection process. One of the original 2006 complainants found that it still had not been reinstated whilst the other two had either been demoted or not promoted to a level that they thought they deserved. So, "plus ça change", as the French might say.

Pomerol

This small, flat, and uninteresting-looking commune to the north of St Emilion produces some of the most powerful and expensive Merlot-based wines in the world. And all this without having to classify the wines. There is simply an A.P. Pomerol for the red wines produced in this area.

The expense is easy to calculate, because most of the producers here are small, producing only a few hundred cases of wine every year. Huge interest and demand drives the prices for these wines through the roof. How else do you explain a price of £1,500 a bottle, which was paid for some 1982 Le Pin in 1997? Really, who can afford £250 for a glass of wine? Again, the sandy, clay soil is hardly suited to the Cabernet Sauvignon grape, so the wines are full of the plummy Merlot flavours.

Some of the wines from this area get extra oak, not only by being fermented in new oak *barriques*, but also by being racked into new oak after a few months to boost the vanilla content. This makes for powerfully flavoured wines, especially if the growers are extremely strict with the quality of the selection, or *tirage*, of the grapes at harvest. By throwing away the grapes that don't come up to the mark, the winemaker can produce opulent wines, full of concentrated flavours.

This area can also produce wines with more finesse and elegance. Château Pétrus has for a long time been recognised as a wine with superstar status, because of its full-bodied yet supple style, with soft tannins on the fruity palate.

Entre-Deux-Mers

Literally, if slightly exaggerated, between two seas. This area, lying between the Garonne and Dordogne rivers, produces dry white wines from Sémillon and Sauvignon Blanc grapes for the A.P. of the same name. Red wines are labelled as basic Bordeaux Rouge, or, if they have a higher level of alcohol, they fall into the Bordeaux Supérieur category.

Cérons

This small *appellation* lies next to Sauternes and Barsac, and in good years produces 'sauternes-like' wines, when *botrytis* pays a visit. In the other years, the growers hedge their bets by being allowed to label their dry, white wines as A.P. Graves.

Cadillac – Côtes de Bordeaux

This thin strip of land runs up the north bank of the Garonne, in the south of the region, producing, on the whole, rustic, red wines. But in parts of the commune opposite Sauternes and Barsac, sweet, white wines are produced in the *appellations* of Cadillac, Loupiac, and Ste-Croix-du-Mont which resemble their neighbours across the river.

Blaye – Côtes de Bordeaux

This *appellation* to the north of the region, on the right bank of the Gironde, produce rustic, red wines with black fruits and cigar notes, for early drinking.

Fronsac and Canon Fronsac

Lying on a tributary of the Dordogne, the River Dronne, just to the north of Pomerol, these small *appellations* produce powerfully scented wines that are very much dominated by the Merlot and Cabernet Franc grapes.

Champagne

This *appellation* lies in the north of France, about an hour's drive to the east of Paris, which has proved helpful in the past, when Parisian household rubbish was shredded and spread on the chalk soil as fertiliser. Although maybe it was a little disconcerting to realise that the blue bits in the soil weren't minerals, but the remnants of rubbish bags!

The name Champagne comes from the Latin *campania*, meaning rolling countryside, and it describes the undulating chalk hills perfectly. Based around the three towns of Reims, Epernay, and Château Thierry, the region is divided into four sections: the Montagne de Riems, Côte des Blancs, Vallée de la Marne, and the Aube.

Being so far north, it is cold rather than cool in the vineyards, and ripening the grapes can be difficult, but that is not a real problem, since you need extra acidity in wines that have to undergo a second fermentation, otherwise the final wine might be too lush.

The *A.P.* regulations for Champagne go against the grain with regard to *terroir* in other *appellations*, where the source of the grapes is paramount. In Champagne, it is sufficient that the grapes come from the region. One of the reasons for this is that regional blending helps to eliminate vintage variation. If the grapes have not ripened well in one part of the region, Champagne producers can use grapes from other parts of the region to compensate.

Reims' medieval cathedral was badly damaged during the First World War when Champagne was on the front line.

This was one of the ideas of the man the French believe discovered Champagne. Dom Pérignon was a Benedictine monk and cellar master of the Abbey at Hautvillers, an important job, since the abbey used the sale of the wine it made from the grapes it purchased as income. Dom Pérignon realised that the cool climate meant that the wine occasionally did not finish its fermentation cycle and that the dormant yeasts sometimes restarted the fermentation in the warmth of spring. However, by the time he had worked out how to remove the bubbles, the Parisian market was beginning to ask for sparkling wines.

The legacy of Dom Pérignon in the Champagne houses of today is reflected in the fact that most of them own very few of the vineyards from which their grapes are sourced, meaning, of course, that there are two powerful lobbies in Champagne production – the producing houses and the growers. This can, and does, lead to tensions, because the growers want the best price and the houses want to pay as little as possible in order to stabilise the wine's price.

Dom Pérignon's legacy is also reflected in the *cépage* of permitted grapes in Champagne. Of the three permitted varieties, two, Pinot Noir and Pinot Meunier, are red, because Dom Pérignon found that these grapes usually made wines which tended not to referment in the spring. The third variety is the classic white grape, Chardonnay. Champagnes can be made from the red grapes only, in which case they are labelled Blanc de Noirs, that is, a white wine from red grapes. While Blanc de Blancs on a label means that the Champagne was made entirely from Chardonnay grapes. Rosé Champagnes are made in one of two ways: either the skins of the red grapes are left in contact with the juice for a short period, to colour the wine, or a small amount of still red wine is added to the base blend.

Once purchased, the grapes from each vineyard are kept separate and fermented in relatively small batches. In the spring, the cellar master of the house will sit down with up to 300 samples from the wines made at the end of the harvest. He can then blend the wines to create the 'house' style of the final Champagne.

Nonvintage Champagne

This is the mainstay, the prop, of any Champagne house, on which its reputation is built. The aim of the cellar master is to produce a uniform style of wine that reflects the house. The cellar master can create a single wine using wines from a number of different vintages. This not only evens out any differences in quality and in the vintage, but also the older, or reserve, wines add some of the mature, nutty elements to the final wine.

Vintage Champagne

In exceptional years, the cellar master may find that the quality of the wines is such that a wine can be created without the use of any reserve wines. In this case, the house can declare a vintage. Not every house has to declare a vintage in the same year; depending on where the houses source their fruit, they may not feel that the quality is good enough.

De-Luxe Cuvées

I suppose that these wines are the equivalent of the great châteaux of Bordeaux and the vineyards of Burgundy. They are produced in small, expensive, amounts by some houses, using only the best grapes available to them. Names to look for are Moët & Chandon's Dom Pérignon, Louis Roederer's Cristal, and Veuve Clicquot's La Grand Dame.

The secret of Champagne lies in the miles of cellars that run beneath the towns of Champagne. These create a stable, cool environment, perfect for storing wine during the second fermentation and the maturation period (see page 127). During this time, sediment, or 'lees', will have formed from the dead yeast in the bottle, and as the yeast cells absorb wine

some will explode and give a biscuity note to the wine.

Once the wine is ready for sale, the sediment needs to be disgorged (see page 134). This process is still carried out by hand for the de-luxe *cuvées* and magnums. The standard bottles and non-vintage wines in most houses use a mechanised process.

When all the sediment and the minimum wine had been expelled, the bottle is topped up with its *liqueur d'expedition*, a mixture of Champagne and sugar that sets the final style of the wine. The more sugar that is added to the liqueur, the sweeter the wine.

Some growers grow and produce their own wines, and only sell it at the cellar door. I remember a surreal experience

Champagne is only produced in bottle or magnum size; the larger bottles are the result of decanting under pressure.

with some friends when, one Sunday afternoon, we sat in the living room of a small house in Champagne, tasting the family's wines, while they sat next door having their dinner. These small growers are known as *récoltants-manipulants* as opposed to the major houses who are known as *négociants-manipulants*, but there are also a number of cooperatives producing large amounts of wines.

Champagne also produces a still table wine, but it cannot be labelled as *A.P. Champagne*, as this is reserved for the sparkling wines. Coteaux Champenoise is the still, red or dry, white wine from the region.

Alsace

When is a German wine not a German wine? When it comes from Alsace, in France, of course. Alsatian wines are heavily influenced by their German neighbours, lying, as the region does, right on the eastern border of France. Like most border areas, it has been fought over for centuries, with 'ownership' changing hands on a regular basis, and this is reflected in the number of fairytale castles that dot the landscape.

How is this reflected in the wines? Well, the grape varieties which grow in the region are those that you would expect to find in Germany – Riesling, Sylvaner, and

Gewürztraminer, for example, plus other permitted varieties including Pinot Gris, Muscat, and Pinot Noir.

The Alsace *A.P.* is the only French *A.P.* that permits the naming of the variety on the label, another influence from the folks next door. The regulations also insist that the wine is sold in a German-style 'flute'-shaped bottle, rather than the more usual 'pot' shape which is common in France.

The result of this mélange is probably best described as a German wine with a very French twist. The wines are drier and have more alcohol (no bad thing) than if they were made across the border.

The geography of the area is partly responsible: Alsace lies in a huge rain shadow formed by the Vosges Mountains, making it one of the driest places in France, which reduces the yields of the vines and concentrates the flavours.

There is a second *appellation* for the wines of Alsace, the *A.P.* Alsace Grand Cru, which covers just over fifty vineyards. These vineyards are allowed to put their name on the label of the wine, and there is a further restriction on the types of grapes that can be used to make *Grand Cru* wines – they can only be made from Riesling, Muscat, Pinot Gris, and Gewürztraminer.

Vineyards on the slopes of Alsace overlooking the picturesque town of Riquewihr.

There are, however, a couple of exceptions to the dry wines made in Alsace. *Vendange tardive* wines can be sweet, being made from late-harvested grapes that have been left on the vines to dry out in the warm autumn air and *Sélection de Grains Nobles* wines are few and far between, since they are sweet wines only made when noble rot arrives in the vineyard. The other exception is Crémant d'Alsace, a sparkling wine made in the traditional method, which very rarely leaves the region.

Loire Valley

The Loire is the longest river in France, rising in the Massif Central and winding its way north, and then west, before running into the ocean at Nantes. It was the medieval equivalent of the motorway, transporting goods and wine over a long distance.

The length of the river gives the region a number of soil types, as well as different climates: warm and maritime near the sea with cool winters, yet hot and continental with cold winters in the Central Vineyards area. This variety is reflected in the number of wine styles produced in the region. In fact, you can get every style of wine from the Loire. The region is normally divided into four separate districts: the Nantaise, Anjou & Saumur, Touraine, and the Central Vineyards

Nantaise

Around the town of Nantes, at the mouth of the Loire, lies the *A.P.* Muscadet and the *A.P.* Muscadet de Sèvre-et-Maine, providing wines that are both neutral in flavour and dry, with a twist of acidity, which make them perfect accompaniments for the local seafood dishes. Of the two, the latter is the best.

The grape variety for these wines, known locally as the Muscadet, but better known as the Melon de Bourgogne, is only found in this area, but actually comes from Burgundy. The *appellation* is unique in that it sets a maximum alcohol content rather than a minimum, the relatively low alcohol content being seen as a quality factor in this wine. Look out for the term *sur lie* on the label, as it means that the wine has been stored 'on the lees' in the

barrel, which keeps the wine fresher and gives it extra flavours.

Anjou-Saumur

This large area produces some very ordinary wine, but also some delicious wines. It is probably best known for the *appellation* Anjou Rosé which, to be perfectly honest, can be awful. Better rosé wines appear under the *appellations* Cabernet d'Anjou and Rosé de Loire, which are based upon better quality Cabernet Franc grapes. The *appellation* of Anjou Rouge can produce deliciously light red wines, full of the grassy, black-fruits flavours that the Cabernet Franc and Cabernet Sauvignon can deliver. There is also an Anjou-Villages *appellation* for the better vineyards here. Chenin Blanc is the permitted grape for the white wines in the area. The basic *appellation* is Anjou Blanc, but the smaller *appellations* of Savennières and Savennières Coulée-de-Serrant produce some excellent, honeyed Chenin Blanc wines.

South of the Loire, on the River Layon, is a tributary providing a microclimate, which, in some years, can encourage the growth of noble rot. The *A.P.s* of Coteaux du Layon, Bonneazeaux, and Quarts de Chaume produce intensely sweet dessert wines, with great aging potential, from the Chenin Blanc grape.

Further along the Loire is the town of Saumur. Best known for its sparkling wine, *A.P.* Saumur is made using the traditional method, using mostly Chenin Blanc grapes but often with small

The delightful château at Angers, the capital of the Anjou-Saumur region.

amounts of Chardonnay, Sauvignon Blanc and even Cabernet Franc, in the blend of the base wine. Still wines from the area are classified as *A.P.* Saumur Blanc or Saumur Rouge, although the best reds are classified as Saumur-Champigny.

Touraine

Further east lies the *A.P.* of Touraine, which produce everything from dry whites, from the Sauvignon Blanc grapes, to rosé and medium red wines, from the Cabernet Franc or Gamay grapes. It is also the centre of production of Crémant de la Loire, a sparkling wine based on the Chenin Blanc grape.

In the west of the area are the small *appellations* of Bourgueil, St-Nicolas-de-Bourgueil, and Chinon, which produce light red wines from the Cabernet Franc grape. These wines are full of strawberry and blackcurrant fruits and can have great aging potential. Some of the vineyards of Chinon lie up against a nuclear power station, but don't seem to come to any harm, or glow in the dark!

The *appellation* of Vouvray, lying on a plateau of tufa chalk, or chalk that has been boiled in volcanic action, is for Chenin Blanc white wines only. Vouvray Demi Sec is for medium-sweet white wines, and Vouvray Moëlleux, which

is reserved for sweet wines, produces intensely flavoured, peachy wines. There is also an amount of sparkling Vouvray produced in the region's caves.

Sleeping Beauty's castle: the Château of Amboise lies in the area of Touraine in the Loire Valley.

Sancerre and Pouilly-Fumé

These two villages lie opposite each other as the Loire turns west. They form the main part of the Central Vineyards area and lie about sixty miles to the east of Touraine. Here, the Sauvignon Blanc takes over from the Chenin Blanc, and wines gain a green, gooseberry-fruit streak. This style of wine has been copied around the world, with the best results coming from New Zealand. Sancerre also has an *appellation* for red and rosé wines produced from Pinot Noir grapes, which can be light, cherry-flavoured wines good for early drinking. Smaller *appellations* in this area are Quincy, Reuilly, and Manetou-Salon, which, while as pungent as the aromatic wines of Sancerre and Pouilly-Fumé, tend to be lighter in style. There is a lesser *A.P.* in Pouilly: Pouilly-sur-Loire is for what can be best described as a general drinking wine produced from the lowly Chasselas grape.

The Rhône Valley

This region, in the south of France, runs north to south and follows the Rhône Valley. It was here that the Romans first planted the vine in France. The styles of wines vary from the steep-sided northern district, to the flatter, wider, and hotter southern area.

The main difference in the styles of wines can be seen in the *cépage* of the two areas. In the north, the wines are either varietals or may have small percentages of a couple of other grapes blended in. The south, on the other hand, can have over a dozen permitted varieties in an *A.P.*, even though only eight or nine might be used. This is due to the heat, since the elements that go towards making up a great wine cannot be found in a lesser number of grapes. Best known for full-bodied, dense wines, the Rhône also produces wonderfully fragrant whites and delicious sweet wines. The generic *appellation* is Côtes-du-Rhône and most of the production for this wine comes from the southern district.

Côte Rotie

Literally, the 'roasted slopes', this *appellation* produces fragrant Syrah red wines, sometimes with a small amount of the white grape Viognier blended in to soften them. There are two subdistricts: the Côte Blonde, with limestone soil, and the Côte Brune, whose soil has a notable iron content. The wines of the Côte Blonde tend to be lighter and earlier drinking than those

The chapel of Hermitage surrounded by some of the best Syrah vineyards in the northern Rhône Valley.

of the Côte Brune, although, for this reason, most Côte Rotie wines are a blend of the two.

Condrieu and Château-Grillet

Just to the south of Côte Rotie, these areas produce some of the best aromatic, white wines made from the Viognier grape. Château-Grillet, at just under ten acres, is the smallest *A.P.* in France and, since the Viognier can be so difficult to grow and deliver incredibly small yields, I wonder how they make any money from it.

Condrieu and Côte Rotie are planted on such steep-sided slopes that the vineyards are terraced and have to be tended by hand. The main climatic effect on this area is a kalabatic wind, the Mistral, which runs from the Alps down to the Mediterranean. It is so strong that the vines cannot be trained in the normal manner. Instead, they are braced between three poles in a wigwam shape. However, the wind does dry the grapes slightly, and this helps to raise the alcohol content of the wine. It is also a blessing if there is a rainstorm before the harvest, as it dries off the excess moisture and means that the grapes are not soaked or the wines diluted.

St Joseph

This *appellation* is another Syrah red wine, but it is softer than the neighbouring wines, being full of dark sweet fruits with spicy notes.

Crozes Hermitage

The largest *A.P.* in the northern district, Crozes-Hermitage produces red and white wines from the Syrah, Marsanne, and Roussanne grapes.

Hermitage

This is probably THE *appellation* of the northern Rhône. Situated on the hill of Hermitage, with full-bodied, bold flavours, the wines from these vineyards were once as popular and as sought after as red Bordeaux and white Burgundies. It is only recently that they have attracted attention again. The white Hermitage wines are made from Marsanne and Rousanne grapes, and are full of stone-fruit and pear aromas and flavours. Some are oak

The appellation of Cornas on the southern edge of the northern Rhône Valley.

aged with good aging potential, but some producers are eschewing this to create wines that are ready to drink after only a couple of years.

But it is the red, Syrah-dominated, wines which make this *appellation*. They are intense, full-bodied wines, with plenty of smoky, spicy, tar aromas and black fruits that need years to soften out. A wine with an Australian lifeguard's shoulders and, when matured, slim hips.

Cornas

Lying to the south of Hermitage, this *appellation* is growing in confidence in the quality of its wines. Again, the red wines produced here are dominated by the Syrah grape.

St Peray

This *appellation* seems to have arrived here by mistake! A sparkling wine? In the home of big reds? Surely not. To be perfectly honest, it is not the best sparkling wine in France. The climate is too warm to produce the tart flavours that we expect from Champagne.

Southern Rhône

Here, the valley opens out and becomes flatter and easier to work. The Mistral still influences the wines, but the vines can now be staked or trained along wires, although some growers still plant the vines at an angle so that the wind can blow the vines upright over the years. The heat means that the wines all have a large number of permitted vines in the *cépage* because overripe grapes become jammy and lose intensity of flavour. This is overcome by using the large range of grapes, to create the complexity of flavours normally found in a cool-climate grape.

The generic red, white, and rosé wines come under the Côtes du Rhône *appellation*. Côtes du Rhône Villages wines come from a restricted number of sixteen communes in the south. They are allowed to add the name of the village to the label if all the wine comes from that village. Look out for Cairanne, Rasteau, and Valreas. Two communes of Rasteau and Beaumes-de-Venise make sweet wines, called *vins doux naturels*. These are fortified wines, which, in a similar manner to Port, have the fortifying alcohol added soon after pressing, to make a fresh dessert wine, using Grenache for the Rasteau red and Muscat for the Beaumes-de-Venise white.

Châteauneuf-du-Pape

This *appellation* takes its name from the château built for Pope John XXII, and used by Clement V when he decided to

It is easy to recognize the 'soil' of Châteauneuf-du-Pape with its distinctive poudin stones.

set up a rival papacy in Avignon. It is also within this *appellation* that, in the 1920s, a producer called Baron Le Roy de Boiseaumarié devised the rules which form the modern *A.P.* system. These rules, describing permitted varieties, limiting yields and delimiting areas, were adopted by the Institut Nationale des Appellations d'Origine in 1935. The wine, like most Southern Rhône wines, is made from a mélange of thirteen varieties, but is dominated by Grenache.

The soil is fairly unique, in that it consists of rounded stones, called *poudins*, which store up the heat of the day and so protect the roots of the vines.

Then, like a storage heater, they radiate it out at night, to help slowly ripen the grapes and dry them out a little, to increase the alcohol content of the wine. The spicy, raspberry wines are ready to drink at a young age, but the best will improve with a little keeping. The bottles of the Châteauneuf-du-Pape are still decorated with the papal keys as a sign of the wine's heritage. There is also a small amount of white wine produced here.

Gigondas

A small *appellation*, in the east of the area, which was once one of the listed Côtes du Rhône Villages, Gigondas has wine styles that are similar to Châteauneuf-du-Pape, as is the *cépage*, but they are not quite as fine.

Vacqueyras

This is a small *appellation*, which lies to the east as well. Although the wines can be described as rural and rustic in style, they can contain attractive notes of dusty, spicy red fruits.

Lirac and Tavel

These *appellations* are in the south of the district and produce rosé wines, as well as a deep red from Lirac. The rosé wines are quite high in alcohol and have some deep cherry flavours and an 'onion-skin', browny-pink colour. The white wines from this area need to be drunk young.

Clairette de Die

This sparkling wine is made on a tributary of the Rhône, from the Clairette and Muscat grapes. It is an attractive, apple-flavoured wine.

Burgundy

Extending as far north as Champagne, these lands were once the property of the Duchy of Burgundy. The vineyards in Burgundy were developed by the monasteries, which were funded by the sale of the wines that they made. The scientific brethren plotted and surveyed the land, which runs from Chablis in the north to the outskirts of Lyon in the south, and made small batch fermentations to prove the theory of site significance, or the importance of *terroir*, in making wines with different flavours. The maps that they produced form the basis of the vineyard sites of today.

All this changed in 1789. The Revolution dispossessed the monasteries and divided the vineyards among the populace. Each generation has subdivided them even further, so that one vineyard can have as many as eighty owners. For some reason, this division has not resulted in cooperatives working together. Instead, it seems to have encouraged a process whereby each owner produces small amounts of wines from a number of vineyards under their control. In most cases, it is not economically viable to bottle such a small production, so the wines are sold to a merchant, who blends them to make bottling viable. Therefore, in Burgundy, it is as important to know the merchant as it is the vineyard, because not every owner makes wines of the same quality and each merchant does not buy wines of the same quality.

Dijon, in northern Burgundy, marks the beginning of the Côte d'Or, but is more famous for its mustard than its wine.

The *appellation* system in Burgundy is just as confusing. The basic *appellations* are the generic *A.P.s* of Bourgogne Blanc and Rouge, as well as the white Bourgogne Aligoté, made from the grape of the same name and Passe-Tout-Grains, a red wine made from blends of Pinot Noir and Gamay. The next stage up are the regional *appellations*, which cover wine from more specific areas, such as Chablis and Côtes de Nuits, and which do not have a village *appellation* of their own.

Village *appellations* cover the best villages on the slopes of the Côtes d'Or, with the next level up being the *Premier Crus*, or second-best vineyards, within those villages. The best vineyards have their own *appellation* of *Grand Cru*. These vineyards are so famous that they do not bother to put the village name on the label, the vineyard is enough. Don't be confused with village *appellations* that include the name of a *Grand Cru* title in the name. Wily French mayors have long affixed the name of the vineyard onto the village name to prove its status. Hence Aloxe-Corton, which was once simply Aloxe, with the *Grand Cru* vineyard of Corton within its boundaries.

Chablis

This white wine producing area is probably one of the best known regions in the world. The small northern *appellation* is very prone to frosts, so the best vineyards are situated on slopes, and all growers employ a number of methods to protect the vines – from placing lit smudge pots between the vines to warm the air, to spraying the vines with water to insulate the tender buds from the frost.

Ripening the Chardonnay vines can be difficult, and the classification of the vineyards all depends upon their ability to do so. In some cases, the difference is due to the slope of the land and the amount of limestone in the soil, as the white limestone reflects the sunlight and helps to ripen the fruit.

The Petit Chablis *A.P.* is not used much nowadays, but produces a lighter style of dry, white wine, normally from younger vines. In fact, the wines of Chablis are all dry and are seldom oaked, thus allowing the mineral steeliness of the wines to shine through.

Chablis is the generic *appellation* and accounts for approximately half of the production from the area. *Premier Cru* wines come from a range of sites that have been upgraded because they have a better aspect or *terroir*.

The top vineyards in Chablis are the *Grand Crus*. These seven vineyards – Les Blanchots, Bougros, Les Clos, Les Grenouilles, Les Preuses, Valmur, and Vaudesir – lie side by side, to the north of the town of Chablis, facing south on the banks of the river Yonne. They all gain help from the River in carrying away frosts and reflecting sunlight into the vines.

Côte d'Or

These golden slopes form the heart of Burgundy. Consisting of two districts, the Côtes de Nuits and Beaune, the slopes face east overlooking the River Saone. The name 'golden slopes' echoes the colour of the vines and their leaves in the autumn sunshine, or could it just be that, at the current prices for a hectare of prime vineyard, 'there's gold in them thar hills'?

Côtes de Nuits

This district, to the north of the area, is centered around the town of Nuits-St-Georges, and runs from Dijon in the north to the town of Nuits-St-Georges in the south. It is the red wine production area of the Côte d'Or.

Marsannay

This is the first village in the north, producing an attractive rosé wine, as well as a red from Pinot Noir grapes.

Fixin

The vineyards here are responsible for small amounts of red wines that show their rustic origins.

Gevrey-Chambertin

The quality of Côte de Nuits really shines through here.

The *Grand Crus* of Chambertin, Chambertin Clos de Bézé, and Latricières-Chambertin are among the best Pinot Noir wines in the world, with plummy, gamey, and chocolaty flavours, but the quality of the village wines from this area can, unfortunately, come very far behind them.

The Château at Clos de Vougeot lies among some of the most expensive real estate in France.

Morey-St-Denis

This *appellation* produces some relatively good value, if unexciting, Pinot Noir wines.

Chambolle Musigny

Chambolle-Musigny also generates some wonderfully fragrant wines, if you find the right merchant.

Vougeot

This *appellation* is more famous for the *Grand Cru* vineyards within its boundaries than for its own wines. Clos de Vougeot is the world-famous walled vineyard of about 50 hectares producing wonderfully concentrated wines, full of soft summer fruits. But with so many owners, the quality from some can be suspect.

Flagey-Echézeaux

There are two *Grand Cru* vineyards here: Echézeaux and Grand Echézeaux. Both produce fragrant Pinot Noir wines with raspberry flavours, but, like most Burgundy vineyards, demand pushes up the price.

Vosne-Romanée

Here is another famous, and therefore expensive, *appellation*, containing four *Grand Cru* vineyards including the sublime Romanée-Conti. The others are La Tâche, Romanée-St-Vivant, and Richebourg. They all produce concentrated, plummy wines, with attractive savoury and gamey notes.

Nuits-St-Georges

Although it has no *Grand Cru* vineyards, Nuits-St-Georges does have a number of *Premier Cru* vineyards. I have to admit to having a soft spot for the prune-like, chocolaty, smoky, red-fruit-flavoured wines of this *appellation*, as one of these was the first wine that I can remember drinking and enjoying.

Côte de Beaune

The soil changes as we enter this area. Much more limestone breaks through the clay soil, and where it does, great white Chardonnay wines abound. The

Pinot Noir grapes growing in the vineyards of Aloxe Corton on the Côte de Beaune.

town of Beaune that gives its name to the area is full of medieval buildings, which reflect the artistic aims of the Duchy of Burgundy. The most important building in the old town is the Hôtel Dieu, or the Hospices de Beaune, with its attractively coloured tiles on the roof. From the very beginning the Hospice has been funded by the sale of wines from its vineyards. Over the centuries, more sites have been bequeathed to it and every year there is a grand auction – and party – on the third Sunday in November as the Hospice's wines are sold. The prices at this auction not only fund the operation of the modern Hospice, but also set a guide price for the other wines from the vineyards for that vintage. For some reason, the prices very rarely fall.

Corton

The district starts with the impressive hill of Corton. There are three villages on the hill: Ladoix wines are almost never bottled under the village name, since most of the production consists of the red and white wines of its *Grand Cru* vineyard, Ladoix-Serrigny; Pernand-Verglelesses comprises hardly more than the *Grand Cru* vineyard that gives the village its name, although part of the Aloxe-Corton *Grand Cru* vineyards of Corton Charlemange, for white wines, and Corton, for red, spill over into its boundaries, meaning that it can produce all three labels. The majority of the Corton Hill and, of course, its vineyards lie within the village boundary of Aloxe-

Corton. Find the right producer and the whites have intense buttery, melon, and pineapple notes, while the red will be fragrant with a gamey or vegetal note.

Savigny-les-Beaune
This *appellation* produces relatively inexpensive, light red wines which make a good 'starter' wine for the Burgundy novice.

Chorey-les-Beaune
A neighbor of Savigny-les-Beaune, here too, you will find good, light reds, created from grapes grown on generally flat land.

Beaune
In addition to being the main town of the area, Beaune, much like Nuits-St-Georges, has no *Grand Cru* vineyards, but a number of *Premier Cru* wines are produced in the area, making soft, red-

fruit flavoured Pinot Noir wines for easy drinking.

Pommard
The second largest wine-producing area in the Côte de Beaune, Pommard has a reputation for strongly flavoured, savoury wines with aging potential.

Volnay
On the other hand, the commune of Volnay makes soft, delicately fragrant, red wines, and the *Premier Cru* vineyards make better versions of the same.

Monthélie
A recent newcomer to the village-wine level, in the past, most of the production from Monthélie was bottled as Côte de Beaune Villages, but the *Premier Cru* vineyards are producing some interesting Pinot Noir wines.

Market day in the centre of the town of Beaune, home to some of the best négociants in the region of Burgundy.

Auxey-Duresses

Sharing a similar history to Monthélie, a lot of the wines from Auxey-Duresses are being labelled as Meursault.

We now come to the white wines that all Chardonnay growers try to emulate. The limestone soils of the south of the Côtes de Beaune produce some of the best white wines in the world, with nutty notes from the use of oak barrels, and buttery elements from malolactic fermentation.

Meursault

Meursault does produce a small amount of red wine, but it is washed away on a sea of top quality white wine. Having said that, it is the next villages which contain the best of the best.

Puligny-Montrachet

This is the village that sets the world standard for white wines, with its *Grand Cru* vineyards of Montrachet, Bâtard-Montrachet, Bienvenues-Bâtard-Montrachet, and Chevalier-Montrachet. The wines from this area are dry, but full of the richness developed by proper use of oak and malolactic fermentation, and when combined with riper fruits and a mineral steeliness similar to that found in Chablis, you have the qualities to which other white wines aspire.

Chassagne-Montrachet

Although it contains a bit of the *Grand Cru* vineyards of Puligny-Montrachet within its borders, Chassagne-Montrachet also produces red wines and white under its own name.

St Aubin

Easily missed, this rather hidden away *appellation* produces good quality *Premier Cru* red and white wines, which are a good value for the money.

St Romain, Santenay, and Maranges

These three small *appellations* produce some good, if workmanlike, red and white wines.

Hautes Côtes de Nuits and Beaunes

Two lesser *appellations*, which run across the top of the slopes, these two reasonably small areas produce red and white wines that are light and easy drinking.

Côtes Chalonnaise

Lying to the south of the Côtes de Beaune, the wines from Côtes Chalonnaise are very different. This is partly due to the aspect of the vineyards, which have a more southern exposure, and partly to the variety of soils that abound in the area. It produces red wines from the Pinot Noir and Chablis-style whites from the Chardonnay. The district is also the centre of production of Bourgogne Aligoté and Crémant de Bourgogne.

Bourgogne Aligoté de Bouzeron

This *appellation* is purely used for Aligoté wines from the village of the same name.

Rully

The centre of Crémant production in Burgundy with its traditionally fermented white or rosé wine, the *A.P.* for Rully itself is for red and white wines which are lighter in style than its illustrious neighbours to the north.

Mercurey

Actually the main wine-producing *appellation* of the area, its name was once used for the whole area, which was then known as the Region de Mercurey. The *appellation* is for red and white wines, but the majority of the production is light, red-fruit flavoured red wine.

Givry

Not to be confused with Gevrey in the Côtes de Nuits, Givry is another red wine dominated *appellation*, which produces sweet, easy-drinking, cherry-flavoured, Pinot Noir wines.

Montagny

While Montagny only bottles white wines under its *appellation* name (the reds are bottled as Bourgogne Rouge), there are some *Premier Cru* vineyards in this area, as there are in Mercurey and Rully, but they are nowhere near the standard of the *Premier Cru* vineyards of the Côte d'Or.

Mâconnaise

The rock outcrop of Solutré, which overlooks the villages of Pouilly-Fuissé, Vinzelles, and Loché, dominates this region, which is centred on the town of Mâcon. There are a number of *appellations* within this area.

Mâcon

The *A.P.* Mâcon is for white wines made from Chardonnay and reds from the Gamay grape.

Mâcon Superieur

Virtually the same as Mâcon, these wines need to produce an extra degree of alcohol.

Mâcon-Villages

The white wines of the better villages (over forty at the last count) of the Mâcon area can use this *appellation*. If the fruit for the wine is sourced from a single village, then the name of that village, such as Lugny or Viré, can add their name to the label.

St Véran

The wines in this *appellation* come from eight villages lying next to Pouilly-Fuissé.

The town of Mâcon lies on the edge of the vineyards and is also home to an annual wine fair.

They are crisp, dry, white wines, which, from decent producers, can be good value for the money.

Pouilly-Vinzelles and Pouilly-Loché

Cleverly, these two villages next to Pouilly-Fuissé have managed to add its name to theirs, unlike the St Véran producers. The wines, though, are lighter than their neighbours' and, because demand is less, are less expensive.

Pouilly-Fuissé

A dry Chardonnay wine grown in the shadow of the Solutré outcrop, Pouilly-

Fuissé is not to be confused with the Pouilly-Fumé, Sauvignon Blanc wines from the Loire. The limestone soil produces rich, mineral notes, which combine with ripe, melon Chardonnay notes, to produce stunning wines when they are made correctly. Demand has driven the price up, but find a good producer and the price will seem worth it.

Beaujolais

As you drive south from the village of Pouilly, you come to a crossroads, and all of a sudden, the French idea of *terroir* makes sense. On one side of the road, the white limestone soil belongs

One of the many small villages producing Beaujolais, Jarnioux lies on the western edge of the region.

normally with a couple of years' age and still possessing some cherry-bubble-gum notes, with elements of dried bananas and herbs?

The common factor of these wines is the carbonic maceration method of production. In this, whole bunches are placed in sealed vats (some producers refer to this as whole-bunch or cluster fermentation). The weight of the berries crushes the lower bunches, which begin a normal fermentation, while the whole berries above are blanketed in carbon dioxide (CO_2), which softens the skins, allowing the yeasts to enter the grapes without splitting them. So the fermentation takes place inside the grape, permitting colour to be extracted rather than tannins. When the fermentation is finished, the grapes are then pressed to release the wine.

Beaujolais or Beaujolais Superieur

These are the basic *appellations* – the word *Supérieur* is added if the wine has an extra degree of alcohol – and most of them are produced in the south of the region.

Beaujolais-Villages

Produced in thirty-nine villages on the better soils to the north of the region, the best villages in the *appellation* are recognised on their own merits. The ten *cru* are Brouilly, Côte de Brouilly, Regnié, Morgon, Chiroubles, Fleurie, Moulin-à-Vent, Chénas, Juliénas, and St-Amour. These wines are the epitome of a wine style that drops all pretense and cries drink me.

to Chardonnay's Pouilly-Fuissé, while on the other is the red, granitic, sand soil of Beaujolais with its juicy, Gamay red wines. There is a small amount of dry white wine made from Chardonnay, but as far as the world is concerned, Beaujolais is red. But what red?

Is it the young, cherry-dominated Beaujolais Nouveau, which we tend to ignore nowadays, but in good years can be just the wine to cheer up those cold, damp, November nights? Or is it the more serious red wines from the top villages,

Southern France

Stretching from the southwestern Pyrenees, all the way across to Provence, the *appellations* throughout this area include Irouléguy, Jurançon, and Bearn, which make some full-bodied reds, peachy-dry and sweet wines, as well as some very ordinary red, white, and rosé wines. Madiran wines can be red or white and are made from a melange of grapes. The reds are dominated by the Tannat, and the whites by Petit Manseng. Gaillac wines are also red or white, but some more classical grape varieties, including Syrah and Cabernet Sauvignon, are permitted in the blend.

As you move north towards Bordeaux, the influence of that region becomes more apparent. Cahors, for example, is based upon the Malbec grape, which has fallen into misuse in Bordeaux and the Buzet *appellation* is a Bordeaux-like wine which, on a good day, can be better than a basic Bordeaux rouge wine. This continues as you come to the *appellations* of Côtes du Marmandais, Côtes du Duras, and Bergerac. On the other hand, the Monbazillac *appellation* is better known for its Sauternes-style of dessert wines, produced from *botrytis*-affected grapes. They are lighter, though, and less expensive, but can be attractive in good years.

Languedoc-Roussillon wines mark the beginning of hot, Mediterranean-influenced wines, which reach their pinnacle in the southern Rhône Valley. Some of the best-known *appellations* are Fitou, Minervois, and Corbières, which are all made from a number of permitted varieties, such as Mourvèdre, Carignan, and Syrah, to produce full-bodied reds.

Some whites are also made, but the climate is much better suited to red wine production.

The Coteaux de Languedoc produces some decent red and white wines, but is also the base for *A.P.* Blanquette de Limoux, a sparkling wine made from the local Mauzac grape. Some producers claim that Dom Pérignon took the idea of sparkling wine from here to Champagne, but that might just be jealousy.

Moving eastwards, the region of Provence produces some wonderfully attractive rosé wines, as well as full-bodied, perfumed reds from the smaller *appellations* of Cassis, Bellet, Bandol, and

Full-bodied, herbal-scented wines come from vineyards like these in Provence.

Palette. Finally, from the foothills of the Alps come the wines of Savoie and Jura. Most of these never leave the area, but a small number of *vin jaune* wines are produced. This is a white wine, which has been deliberately allowed to oxidise to give it some sherrylike characters, and it is very much a local specialty.

Indication Géographique Protégée/Vin de Pays

Consisting of regional wines, with some distinguishing character that elevates them above the sea of *Vin de France*, *I.G.P.* wines have to conform to local standards and pass a blind-tasting panel. This allows the good producers a degree of experimentation in order to create high quality wines, which, in some cases, can command prices as high as those of some classed wines. One example of this is the wine Mas de Daumas Gassac, a red, which is based on the Bordeaux blend of Cabernet Sauvignon, Cabernet Franc, and Merlot, which has a degree of aging in new oak. The white wine from the same area is also unusual in that it is a blend based on Viognier and Chardonnay.

There are a number of different levels of *I.G.P.'s*, depending on the size of area they cover. The largest of these is the regional *I.G.P.'s*, which are then subdivided, firstly, into departments and then, secondly, into zones. The driving influence in the southern areas, such as the *I.G.P.* Pays d'Oc, has been the arrival of flying winemakers, mainly from Australia.

GERMANY

Here is a country producing quality wines that the world seems to have forgotten about.

Germany contains the most northerly vineyards in Europe. For this reason they have to use every trick in the book in order to make quality wine. And they do make quality wines here. For many, the general impression of German wines is one of mass-produced, semi-sweet, sugary wines. This is based

The village of Assmannhausen produces light, red wines from the Späteburgunder or Pinot Noir grape.

upon the large amounts of inexpensive Liebfraumilch and Niersteiner Gutes Domtal wines, which seemed to fill the supermarket shelves 20 or so years ago. These were bulk wines made from vines that were squeezed until every possible drop of juice was extracted from them, and they bear little or no resemblance to the country's quality wines.

Why were they made? Well, it is really difficult, expensive, and time consuming

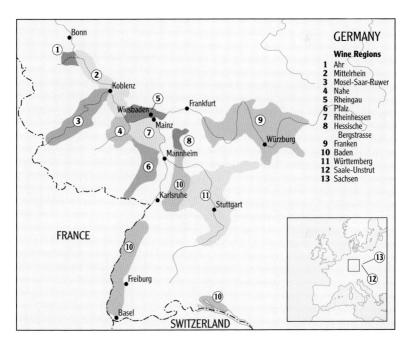

GERMANY

Wine Regions
1 Ahr
2 Mittelrhein
3 Mosel-Saar-Ruwer
4 Nahe
5 Rheingau
6 Pfalz
7 Rheinhessen
8 Hessische Bergstrasse
9 Franken
10 Baden
11 Württemberg
12 Saale-Unstrut
13 Sachsen

Stahleck Castle overlooks the Mittelrhein region and the Lorelei rock that lured many a sailor to his doom.

to make good wine this far north. Bulk wines need much less care and attention when they are being grown and made, compared with quality wines – unless, that is, you are trying to make the best possible wines from the fruit that is available. If you have a market that wants cheap wine and is not too concerned about quality, human nature being what it is, you take the easy option. The problem with that is, what do you do when your market changes, becomes more educated, starts to look for better tasting wines, and wants to progress up the quality ladder? If you can supply the demand, no problem. If you can't, it can take years to change your methods, you may even have to change the vines in the vineyards. Changing the vineyards is essential. The quality grape in Germany is the Riesling, a comparatively low-yielding and late-ripening grape, which cannot produce the volumes of juice required to make huge quantities of inexpensive wine.

Over the years, the Germans have tried to overcome this by crossing the Riesling with a number of other varieties, in order to improve the yields and ripen the fruit earlier, without dropping the quality of the fruit. The results have been a great number of grapes that don't taste of Riesling but do produce a huge volume of grape juice. Varieties such as Ortega, Bacchus, Scheurebe, and Wurtzer now abound in Germany and Austria, a few have even made it to the UK, and, when carefully cultivated, these grapes can produce some interesting, drinkable wines.

This is the situation that Germany found itself in. By being seen as a producer of these cheap, and perhaps not so cheerful, wines, Germany is not perceived as a quality wine producer. The country's quality producers are aware of this fact, and are continually trying new marketing campaigns to introduce new and returning wine drinkers to their products. They are also working to change the styles of wines produced.

Traditionally, German wines are made with sweetness and a low-alcohol content. The German quality system is based upon the sugar content of the

grapes at harvest time. The more sugar in the grapes, the higher up the quality ladder the wine can progress. This is easy to measure and is a sign of technically well-grown grapes. The coolness of German vineyards means that the better locations and growers will produce the riper berries. The Germans prefer sweeter wines, so, traditionally, the winemakers have not allowed the yeasts to convert all the sugars into alcohol by stopping the fermentation early, usually with a dose of sulphur, which leaves some residual sugar in the wine.

Younger winemakers have begun to question this style of winemaking, and groups, such as the Charta organisation of the Rheingau, have dedicated themselves to producing dry or off-dry Riesling wines to the higher standards that the legislation demands. The aim in the Rheingau is to produce high quality wines that are easy drinking, go well with food, and are capable of aging. In addition, there is a limit to the amount of sugar that can be in the wine. This is controlled by ensuring that the level of residual sugar cannot exceed the acidity by any more than a tiny amount. This ideal is also being copied in areas such as the Pfalz and the Nahe.

The Romans introduced the vine to Germany, and that is one reason why the wine regions are centred on the river

A grape harvest in Germany: vines are trained high to allow frost to roll down the hill without damaging them.

complex of the country. Apparently, the natives didn't take too kindly to the invaders, and used to hide in the forests and throw things such as rocks down onto the passing Roman boats. To counter this, the Romans cut down the trees and planted vines. They were harder for the Germans to hide behind, and provided a useful cash crop as well.

The other reasons were based upon trade: the Rhine runs through the whole of Germany and most of Europe, before reaching the North Sea, so ships could load up in Germany and take wines as far as the UK without stopping.

The river also helps ripen the fruit. It can act as a mirror to reflect sunlight into the vineyard. To take advantage of this, most German vineyards are planted so that the rows run vertically down the slopes, rather than horizontally, following the contours of the hill. This allows the reflected light to run up the slopes and affect the maximum number of vines. The moving water, combined with the angle of the vineyards, also helps to carry away banks of frost as they settle and roll down the slopes. Again, the growers have addressed the effects of this frost by pruning the vines in such a way as to encourage them to grow higher, which means that the frost will settle and flow below the tender shoots and flowers.

In the Mosel Valley, the slate soil absorbs heat during the day and radiates it out at night to help the ripening process as well. To maximise the exposure to the sun, the vines are only planted on the south-facing slopes. So, as you drive along the banks of the river, you will see the vineyard plantings stop and start, and even jump across the river, just to find the maximum sunlight. Now you can understand what I mean about the amount of tricks that the growers have to employ.

GERMAN WINE LAW

These laws were first implemented in 1971, and originally laid out eleven delimited regions that could produce quality wines. When East and West Germany were reunited, a further two areas were recognised, making the number thirteen.

The German term for these regions is *Anbaugebiete*, and they are subdivided into groups of villages, or *Bereiche*, which are then further divided into groups of vineyards, or *Grosslagen*, before the final identification of individual vineyards, or *Einzellagen*.

In theory, as with the French classification system, the smaller the area of production that is identified, the more the quality of the wine improves. The only problem is that it can be difficult to tell the difference between an *Einzellage* wine and a *Grosslage* wine from the label. This is because both these wines must show the community, or *Gimeinde*, name on their label, meaning that the buyer has to be aware that Piesporter Michelsberg is a *Grosslage* within the area of the town of Piesport, whereas Piesporter Goldtropfchen is an *Einzellage* in the same town.

Just to make things more confusing, the individual vineyards, much as in Burgundy, can have a number of different owners, because the monasteries that were once the major owners were stripped of their property when Germany was invaded by Napoleon. The land was given to the people and has been broken up over the generations. Pulling your hair out yet? Don't worry, you soon will be!

The permitted yields in Germany seem very high at first glance. Some vineyards can happily double the permitted yields found in, say, Bordeaux. One reason for this is that German vines are some of the healthiest in Europe. Growers are encouraged to replace vines more frequently than in other countries and nearly always use specially bred, virus-free vines and rootstocks.

GERMAN WINE STYLES

Having identified the vineyards and regions that the quality wines can come from, the wines themselves are then classified. This classification, as I have said, is based upon the amount of sugar in the grapes at the time of harvest. The more sugar, the higher the quality. The sugar content is measured in degrees, or *Oechsle*. In a funny, egalitarian sort of a way, this approach means that any vineyard can produce top-quality wines, if their fruit is ripe enough. So, in a good year, a vineyard can make quality wine, but in a lesser year, its wines might only qualify for table wine status.

There are two categories of German table wines

DEUTSCHER TAFELWEIN

This is the lowest classification and must be made from grapes grown in Germany. The wine can show a place of origin, but it has to be one of four areas – Rhein-Mosel, Oberrhein, Neckar, and Bayern – and all the base fruit must come from the area.

LANDWEIN

Nearly the equivalent of the French *I.G.P* classification, *Landwein* has to come from one of seventeen designated areas. It is very rarely used, since, in fact, these two categories only amount to somewhere in the vicinity of 10 per cent of Germany's wine production.

Most wines produced in Germany fall into one of two categories of quality wine. Any hair left?

QUALITÄTSWEIN

This is wine from designated quality regions. It has to be made from permitted grape varieties and has to come entirely from the named *Anbaugebiete*. However, if the grape juice lacks the minimum sugar content, the juice can have some sugar added to it. *Anreicherung* (the French call it *chaptalisation*, after a Dr Jean-Antoine Chaptal, who realised that as far as yeast was concerned sugar is sugar) is only permitted up to this level. Care has to be taken when carrying this out, as clumsy addition can throw the acid/alcohol balance of the wine out of kilter.

PRÄDIKAT WEIN

Any wines with this label will have special qualities or will be of superior quality. This category is subdivided into different grades of *Prädikat*, or certificate. Wines in these classes must come from a single *Bereich* and be made from certain permitted grapes.

The lowest grade is *Kabinett*. This wine is made from ripe grapes, without any special selection. Originally, the term meant that the wine was considered by the winemaker to be good enough to be put aside in his personal cabinet.

Spätlese wines are made from late-harvested grapes. *Lese* is German for harvest, while *Spät* means late. The extra hanging time on the vines allows the grapes to ripen more, not only adding sugar but also extra flavour to the wine.

Auslese wines are made from selected bunches of overripe fruits, some of which may have been attacked by noble rot.

Beerenauslese wines are made from *Beeren* (berries) – that is, individually selected, overripe grapes that may or may not have noble rot.

Trockenbeerenauslese (TBA for short) wines are made from individually selected *Trocken*, or dried grapes. These are single grapes that have been 'dried' by the effects of *Edelfäule*, or noble rot. *Trockenbeerenauslese* is the peak of German wine production. To give you some idea of the sweetness, the grape must, or juice, has the potential, if left to ferment completely, to produce 21 per cent alcohol. Actually, the wines are normally bottled with an alcohol content of 8 to 10 per cent, leaving not only a high degree of sweetness but also high glycerine, giving texture and body to the wine, and such acid levels as to ensure that the wine is not cloying on the palate. The reduced yields, and the gamble of leaving the grapes on the vine for so long, mean that these wines are rare, very expensive, and bottled in half bottles.

The final category of *Prädikat* wines is *Eiswein*. *Eiswein*, or ice wine, uses a different method of concentration than the other categories. Whereas the other *Prädikat* wines use ripeness and noble rot to concentrate the sugars and acidity of the grapes, Eiswein is, literally, made from frozen grapes. By harvesting grapes at a temperature of -5°C (22°F) – pickers struggle in December or January in the dark on steep-sided slopes – and pressing the berries, still frozen, at -2°C (27°F), the winemaker ends up with a concentrated juice and some frozen slush, which is made up from the water content of the juice. This concentrated juice is so full of sugar that it takes weeks to ferment. The result is a concentrated, fresh tasting wine; the grapes are never attacked by noble rot, and so are full of refreshing acidity that balances out the sweet flavours.

Recognising a demand for drier wines, Germany has introduced three new categories specifically for dry wines.

Classic, in principle, is a dry Qualitätswein that is intended to be food-friendly. It needs to be made from classical grape varieties of the region and have a minimum of 12% alcohol by volume

Every *Prädikat Wein* will have an Amsliche Prüfungs number which records the tests it has passed.

(Mosel has a lower limit of 11.5%)

Selection is a Spätlese grade wine that is fermented dry (trocken) from a specific vineyard.

And *Erstes Gewächs* is a 'first class growth' wine from the Rheingau used for top class wines from specific vineyards.

Just to make the whole thing more confusing, the measurements of *Oechsle* for each category are divided into bands, which overlap so one region's *Spätlese* could be another's *Auslese*.

THE REGIONS

Germany's thirteen regions are, roughly, from north to south:

Ahr

Curiously, although this is one of the most northerly wine-producing regions in Europe, this region produces mainly very light red wines from the Pinot Noir grape, known in Germany as the Spätburgunder. These wines are not as deeply flavoured as their Burgundy counterparts.

Mittelrhein

The Rhine of fairytales, castles, and dangerous river currents, the legend of the Lorelei belongs in this region that lies on both sides of the River Rhine. The steep-sided slopes seem to fall right into the Rhine and produce Riesling wines with a racy acidity.

Mosel

This region covers the entire River Mosel, as it runs from the French–Luxembourg border all the way to the Rhine at Koblenz, and includes two tributaries of the river, the Saar and the Ruwer. The soil on the steep slopes is warming slate scree, which gives the wines a steely, slatey, mineral streak. The wines in this area are seldom allowed to ripen above *Auslese* level, and even then, they are not really sweet, but have a honeyed element to those slate minerals.

The steep slopes mean that very little mechanisation can be carried out in the vineyards, but special tractors, or trailers,

Above: This narrow tractor has been specially designed to fit between the rows of vines on the relatively gentle hillside of the red slopes of the Rheinhessen in Germany.

have been developed to run up and down cable rail systems between vertical rows of vines.

The best area is the centre of the region. The middle Mosel runs from just south of Trier down to Zell and includes some of the best, and prettiest, vineyards and villages in Germany. Of course, they also have some of the most abused names as well. Here you will find Piesport and Bernkastel. Both villages have been ruined to a certain extent by the amount of poor wines sold under the *Grosslage* names of Michelsberg and Kurfürstlay respectively. The best wines are made from the Riesling, and almost 60 per cent of the vines planted here belong to that classic variety.

Piesport lies in a huge natural amphitheatre that faces south. The

Left: Vineyards surround the town of Cochem which sits in a south-facing amphitheatre in the Mosel Valley.

opposite bank is much flatter, and this is the source of much of the insipid *Grosslage* wine. However, it does contain some great vineyards, such as Goldtröpfchen, which produce ripe, steely, slightly spicy wines,

Bernkastel is a pretty, picturesque town dominated by the towering slopes of the Bernkasteler Doctor Vineyard that lies behind it. This is one of the world's classic vineyards, producing delicious Riesling wines, some of which need a few years in the bottle to show their full potential.

The area around Graach is almost as good as Bernkastel – look out for the Himmelreich or Domprobst Vineyards on labels – and the villages of Wehlen and Zeltingen both share the Sonnenuhr Vineyard, while the name of Ürzig's top vineyard, Würzgarten, reflects the spicy character that the wines of this village suddenly develop.

The Saar joins the River Mosel above Trier. Here, the grapes sometimes find it hard to ripen, and so a lot of the area's production can end up as base wines for sparkling wines, or *Deutscher Sekt*. Long, warm autumns, however, can ripen the Riesling fruit and produce some wonderful steely, sharp wines, with hints of sweetness. The villages of Serrig, Wiltingen, and Ockfen produce some great honey-and-steel-tasting wines too.

The view of the Mosel valley from above the village of Graach shows the steepness of the slope.

Mainz, at the eastern edge of the Rheingau region, is where the Rhine turns sharply to the left toward Rudesheim.

The cold winters also mean that, if the grower takes the gamble, some great *Eiswein* may be produced in most years, unlike most other regions of Germany.

The Ruwer makes tiny amounts of Riesling wines, as there are only a few south-facing sites on this tributary. A name to look for is that of the Maximin Grunhäus Vineyard.

Rheingau

The Rheingau lies on the 20 miles of south-facing slate and loam slopes which are formed when the Rhine runs east–west rather than south–north. The river of Europe, the Rhine, flows from Switzerland, through Germany and Holland, before emptying into the North Sea, and all of Germany's vineyards and regions are linked to it in some way. It is when it reaches the town of Mainz that it 'hangs a left', because of a huge piece of solid rock at the base of the Taunus Mountains, and forms a perfect south-facing slope on the Rheingau region. And this is where the river does all it can to help produce quality wines before turning right at Bingen and heading north again.

The slow-moving river is wide, and acts as a huge mirror, reflecting the sunlight onto the vines, helping to produce some of the ripest Riesling fruit in Germany, as well as draining the land and carrying away any frosts.

At one time, Riesling wines from this area were more sought after and expensive than the first-growth wines

It may not be the prettiest wine region in Germany, but Pfalz produces more wine than any of the others.

of Bordeaux. It is here that the origins of the German sweet, rich wines began. Schloss Johannisberg sits above the town of Geisenheim. Originally part of the Benedictine monastery, it was 'managed' from Trier by the Bishop. Every year, the Bishop would send out a messenger with the instruction to begin the harvest. One year, the messenger was delayed for a couple of weeks because of an accident. The grapes were left on the vines for longer, and the resulting wines were thought to be superior to the normally harvested wines of the region. The idea of deliberate *Spätlese* was formed.

Geisenheim is also the home of the modern Charta movement, and of one of Germany's biggest viticultural research institutes, where many of the vine crossings that have been foisted upon an innocent wine world have originated. Strangely enough, hardly any of the vines from Geisenheim have found favour in this Riesling-dominated region.

The first major village of the region is Hochheim, and it is the relationship of this village with the UK which led to the great interest in Rheingau wines. In fact, the wines of the Rhine are the only wines, apart from the reds of Bordeaux, to which the British have given a nickname. Hock is a generic term in the UK for these wines. This interest was partly due to the overall interest in all things German after the marriage of Queen Victoria to Prince Albert. The Queen even allowed a local vineyard to be named Königen Victoriaberg, after she visited it.

Further along the slopes are the villages of Erbach, Hattenheim, Hallgarten, and Winkel, before Geisenheim and Rüdesheim bring the slopes to an end. Rüdesheim shows the other important influence of the sun and the river on this area. It is a huge tourist spot, with more faux Bierkellers than should really be gathered together in one town and it has, above the vineyards, a huge monument to the first unification of Germany. Just around the corner from Rüdesheim is the village of Assmannhausen, where red wines are produced from the Spätburgunder or Pinot Noir grape

Nahe

Across the river from Rüdesheim lies the town of Bingen, at the mouth of the Nahe River. The Nahe wine region is surrounded by the regions of the Mosel, Rheingau, and Rheinhessen, and it has been said that the best wines from this area contain the best elements of its neighbours. The wines can combine the floral perfume of the Rheinhessen, the acidity of the Mosel, and the ripe fruits of the Rheingau. The best village has the wonderful name of Schlossböckelheim and is closely followed by the vineyards of the spa town of Bad Kreuznach.

Rheinhessen

As Germany's largest wine region, it is no surprise that Rheinhessen is the home of a lot of the country's production of Liebfraumilch, which is based upon Müller-Thurgau and Silvaner grapes. The law actually forbids the use of Riesling grapes in this wine, although, since Riesling wines reach such a premium on the market, it would be surprising if a grower did add it to the blend.

In common with the Mosel, it has some good village names spoiled by the local *Grosslage*. Nierstein is a strip of angled slopes that runs down the banks of the Rhine and one vineyard name – Gutes Domtal – has caught on so much, that it has become the *Grosslage* name, producing some very ordinary medium-sweet wine. Villages to look out for are Oppenheim and Nackenheim, which produce some stunning Riesling wines. The common factor of these wines is their location on the slopes near the river.

Pfalz

Rheinhessen may be the largest wine region, but this is the largest producer of wine in Germany; a relatively fertile plain, protected from the prevailing weather by the Haardt Mountains. So the best vineyards can produce ripe Riesling wines, which have luscious, exotic, apricot and mango flavors.

Baden's warmer climate produces richer-flavored wines that are normally fermented dry as opposed to sweet.

However, there is also a huge amount of Liebfraumich produced here as well. Try to find wines from Bad Dürkheim, Forst, and Deidesheim.

Baden

Baden lies on the opposite banks of the Rhine from the French region of Alsace. It is a warmer region than the others, so you would expect to find riper flavours. However, the wines from this region tend to be drier than the more northern wines and there is also a larger number of cooperatives producing wines in this area. The Riesling is not, surprisingly, the top grape in this spot. That honour falls to a variety found in Alsace, the Pinot Gris, known as the Ruländer, and the exciting red wines from the Pinot Noir.

Franken

Franken, or Franconia, wines are unusual in Germany in that they are not made from Riesling and are dry. They also come in a distinctive flask-shaped bottle known as a *Bocksbeutel*. Apparently, the shape of the bottle is based upon a goat's scrotum!

The region lies on the River Main, which joins the Rhine at Mainz. The permitted grape variety is Silvaner, and the vineyards tend to be dotted around the landscape in the warmer pockets of this frost-affected region.

The wines have an earthy note and can be incredibly long lived. In the 1960s, writer Hugh Johnson tasted a 1540 Franken wine, which he described as 'delicate and fragrant' for a few moments,

before it disintegrated in the glass. The local name for these wines is *Steinwein*, after the vineyard of Stein in Würzburg.

Württemberg

Based on the River Neckar, which again produces only small pockets of south-facing sites, the production of the Württemberg is small and really only gets drunk by the locals. A lot of the

wine produced is red, made from a grape known as the Limberger, but the best and steepest sites produce Riesling wines.

Hessische Bergstrasse

A tiny area near Worms, Hessische Bergstrasse produces a small amount of wines on the east of the Rhine, mainly from the Riesling grape.

Saale-Unstrut and Sachsen

The last two wine-producing regions of Germany are the newcomers from the former East Germany. Saale-Unstrut and Sachsen lie to the north, and have cold winters and warm summers. Sachsen is also the most easterly of Germany's wine regions.

They produce dry wines from a number of grapes derived from varieties of Riesling and Traminer.

ITALY

The world's largest producer and exporter of wines is finally getting its act together and producing top quality wines as well thanks to adventurous winemakers.

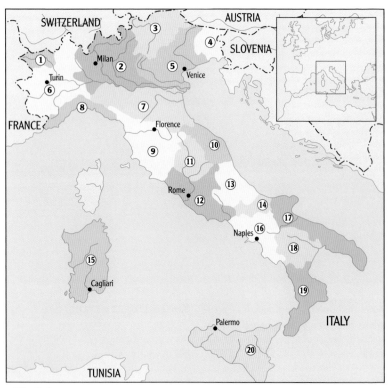

Wine Regions

1 Valle D'Aosta	6 Piedmont	11 Umbria	16 Campania
2 Lombardy	7 Emilia-Romagna	12 Latium	17 Apulia
3 Trentino-Alto Adige	8 Liguria	13 Abruzzo	18 Basilicata
4 Friuli-Venezia Giulia	9 Tuscany	14 Molise	19 Calabria
5 Veneto	10 Marches	15 Sardinia	20 Sicily

Italy produces more wine than any other country in the world and is the largest exporter of wine. Wine *is* Italian culture; no meal is complete without a bottle or two on the table, next to the olive oil, and, unlike any other country, it is covered in vines. Every region has vines planted in it.

What I like about Italy is the fact that so many grape varieties are planted there and only there. While Italy has never produced any of the great classic varieties, it has produced some varieties that are perfectly suited to the local climates,

The rich cuisine of Italy has developed with each region's wines so that they are easily matched.

and which, with modern winemaking techniques, are beginning to make some stunning wines. Having said that, Italian wine could only come from Italy. You will find that there is a common factor of bitter fruits running through most of the red wines, for instance, that is an identifiable Italian style. Very rarely will Cabernet Sauvignon, for example, raise its head and impose its character on the wines of the region.

Italy also has an impressive history when it comes to wine. The Greeks introduced the vine around 800 BC and named the country Oenotria, or Land of Wine. The Romans took the vine with them as they slowly expanded their empire over the length and breadth of mainland Europe and England. But for the remainder of the last millennium, the wines of Italy have, if not stagnated, simply existed.

The Italians, whether in Italy or as emigrants who have moved around the world, are used to drinking a lot of the production themselves. With such a large ready-made market, there was no need to look at quality; it was simply a matter of providing the quantity to meet this demand. That's not to say that there is no quality wine made here, just that there is a vast amount of not-as-good quality wine made and drunk here.

One of the reasons for this lack of quality is that modern Italy is a new animal. Until unification in 1861, this was a collection of principalities, dukedoms,

It is all thanks to the Romans that we now enjoy the fruit of the vine around the world.

and city states. The result of this is that the same grape variety will have a lot of different names, depending on where the vine is grown. In addition, the first national quality system did not come into existence until 1963, and it was not implemented until 1967. Actually, this did not really solve the problem of a lack of quality in Italian wines, because, in order to produce top-quality wines the producers had to, if not break the rules, then ignore them.

ITALIAN WINE LAWS

The classification system, based as usual on the French *Appellation* system, outlined areas of production and defined styles of wines and grape varieties permitted in those areas.

• *Vino da Tavola*. This is the most basic of table wines, or is it? Read on and I hope that this becomes clear.

• *Denominazione di Origine Controllata (DOC)*. There are now over 330 *DOC* wines in existence. When this category was set up, it was meant to represent the pinnacle of Italian wines, and guaranteed the origin of the wine and protected the style produced in that area. Later on, the Italians added a higher category.

• *Denominazione di Origine Controllata et Garantita (DOCG)*. This higher classification was meant to guarantee the quality of the wine as well as the origin. Wines carrying this label must be bottled in the area of production and pass an independent tasting panel before they get a pink or green seal.

But what about that *Vino da Tavola* category? Why did I say that might not be just the most simple of table wines?

Wine producers are an awkward bunch of people. You try to put them in a box and they try to get out of it.

Some Italian winemakers started to introduce grape varieties, such as Cabernet Sauvignon, into their wines and create small amounts of varietal Cabernet Sauvignon wines as well. These did not fit into any *DOC* category, so they had to be labelled as *Vino da Tavola*. No problem, that's the rules. Unfortunately, the wines were good, some of them were very good; so good, in fact, that they sold at higher prices and with more acclaim than the best *DOC* wines. All of a sudden, the wine laws were turned on their head. If you wanted quality wines, look for *Vino da Tavola*! To overcome this, a new category was introduced.

Indicazione Geografica Tipica (IGT) now *Indicazione Geographica Protetta (IGP)* wines lie in between the *Vino da Tavola* and *DOC* categories. It represents a similar wine category to the French *I.G.P.*, but it is also a way of forcing the 'super' *Vino da Tavola* wines into a quality category. Now they have to become *IGP* wines, or get recognition from the awarding body as a new *DOC*.

THE REGIONS

Being such a large country, it is easy to see that there is not only a large variation in climates but also in the soil in Italy. This is reflected in the number of grape varieties used, and, even though you will not find the same correlation between soil and wine styles as you do in France, the adage remains the same: the best vineyards are sited on poorly fertile, well-drained soils. Once again, slopes are best.

Piedmont

Meaning 'at the foot of the mountains', this region in Italy's northwest is dominated by the Alps. The vineyards are split into two distinct areas to the east and south of Turin. Piedmont produces more *DOC* and *DOCG* wines than any other region in Italy, and although a number of decent white wines are made here, this is red

wine country, and the Nebbiolo grape is king.

Barolo

Barolo *DOCG* is one of Italy's great red wines and is named after the village of the same name, which lies to the south west of Alba. Barolo will normally spend two years in large casks, although some

The DOCG vineyards of Barolo lie on the south-facing slopes in the southern part of the region of Piedmont.

Barbaresco

Next door to Barolo is the sister *DOCG* of Barbaresco. This wine is also made from Nebbiolo, but is lighter in style, with more fleshy flavours and raspberry notes. Because it is lighter, it is allowed to be released without so much aging in the cask, so normally the wines are released one year earlier than those of Barolo.

Alba

Much lighter Nebbiolo wines can be found around the town of Alba. These *DOC* wines are simply labelled as Nebbiolo d'Alba. Other *DOC*s to look for in this area are Carema, Langhe Nebbiolo, and Roero.

Gattinara

To the west of Turin lies another *DOCG* wine district, Gattinara, which is also based on Nebbiolo, although, just to confuse you, here it is called Spanna. It is aged for a similar period to Barolo, but Gattinara is lightened by the addition of up to 10 per cent of a variety called Bonarda. A couple of other *DOC*s in this area are Ghemme and Boca, where again the wines, based on the Spanna or Nebbiolo grape, are softened with the addition of some Bonarda.

producers now prefer to use smaller barriques, and one year in bottle before it is released.

Any Barolo labelled *Riserva* will not be released until it is four years old.

The wine is full of dense, tarry, leathery, damson and prune fruits, with a belt of tannin, and alcohol and herbal notes hovering around.

Piedmont reds, however, are not exclusively made from the mighty Nebbiolo. Around the towns of Alba and Asti, the less tannic Barbera grape produces some relatively soft, tobacco, sour raspberry-flavoured wines, while the

Dolcetto grape also produces some good reds in the neighbourhood of Asti. This variety ripens earlier and will produce a wine in places where Nebbiolo won't ripen. Its sweet name comes from the fact that with a low acidity level the wine tastes practically sweet.

Moscato d'Asti and Asti Spumante

There are some white wines produced in Piedmont. Probably the best known are the *DOCG* sparkling wines of Moscato d'Asti and Asti Spumante. Both are made from the Moscato grape, and are aromatic, grapey wines, with a relatively low alcohol content and a resulting sweet note from the unfermented sugars.

The wine achieves its sparkle using a variation on the tank method. The first fermentation takes place in a sealed tank. Then, before this fermentation is complete, the wine is filtered and bottled under pressure, so that the sparkle remains in the wine.

Gavi

The best white wine from the area has to be *DOC* Gavi from the town of the same name. This wine is made from the Cortese grape, which gives it a mineral note that tastes, not unpleasantly, a bit like a stone wrapped in a lemon.

Lombardy

Nestling up against the Swiss Alps in the north of Italy, the region of Lombardy produces some of Italy's finest sparkling wines, made using the traditional method.

Franciacorta sparkling wines are

The region of Asti produces light, sparkling wines from Moscato vines like those above.

based on the Pinot Bianco grape with some Chardonnay and Pinot Grigio and Pinot Nero (Noir) allowed in the blend as well. In addition, there are some still white wines made from Pinot Bianco.

However, this area also produces medium-bodied red wines that are full of colour and flavour. Made mainly from Cabernet Franc and Merlot, these wines can be cherry and raspberry-scented, with grassy notes.

Valtellina

In the north of Lombardy is Valtellina, which has a number of subregions, the best of which are Inferno and Sassella. These *DOC* wines are based on the Nebbiolo grape, but are a lot tougher than their Piedmont neighbors. To the south of the region, you find the *DOC* of Oltrepo Pavese. There are many styles of wine made here, but the best, and most consistent, tend to be the sparkling wines made from the three Pinot varieties of Nero, Bianco, and Grigio, which once again are made by the traditional method.

Liguria

Lying on the north-west coast, Liguria is home to lots of small producers, whose wines are nearly all consumed locally. Probably the best of them come from the *DOC* of Cinqueterre.

Valle d'Aosta

Pushed up against the Alps, this small region – the smallest in Italy, in fact – hardly produces any wine. But the Nebbiolo-based Donnaz is worth looking at, as are the Swiss-influenced Petite Arvine wines.

Veneto

Veneto is in the north-eastern corner of Italy. Lying between Venice and Lake Garda, it goes from one extreme to the other, producing some of the best and, probably, worst wines, though I may exaggerate. The production of this region is based upon four wines: Prosecco, Soave, Valpolicella and Bardolino. Soave is a dry white wine made from the Garganega and Trebbiano di Soave grapes. To qualify for DOC or DOCG status, the wines are limited in the amount of the inferior Trebbiano Toscana grape permitted in the blend. The better wines come from the 'Classico' area around the village.

Valpolicella

Valpolicella's story is a bit like Soave's: lots of overproduction is ruining the reputation of the wine. The main grape is the sour, cherry-flavoured Corvina, but when over-cropped this grape produces dilute, almost flavourless wines. Rondinella and Molinara grapes can be blended in, but even they struggle to improve this wine style. To be honest, poor Valpolicella put me off Italian wines for a number of years.

Then I discovered Amarone. That's Valpolicella, Jim, but not as we know it. It is thought that DOCG Amarone (or the sweeter Recioto version) is the original wine style of the area. This is a 'straw wine' that has been made from grapes that have been dried on straw mats. Traditionally, the whole bunches of grapes would have been laid out on mats in the attic of the winery for around 120 days to dry out. Nowadays, the grapes are dried in temperature and humidity controlled warehouses, but the idea is

Lake Garda lies to the eastern side of the Veneto region, where the large expanse of water influences the climate.

also makes a honeyed, citrus peel and raisin flavoured white Recioto DOCG wine.

Obviously, these wines are not the cheapest in the world, after all, there is so much concentration of the grapes that the final yields are much smaller and this increases the costs, but there are some co-operative produced wines that are less expensive. If you don't want to spend that much money, but want to get a taste of that Amarone effect, look out for the term 'Ripasso' on a label of Valpolicella Classico DOC. After the 'free-run' Amarone wine has been drawn off the vat, the skins and lees are left in place and Classico wines are poured in. Then this wine goes through a mini re-fermentation and takes on some of the elements of the Amarone original.

Prosecco

Recently promoted to DOC and DOCG status, sparking Prosecco is one of the recent success stories of Italian wine. Made in large tanks using the Glera grape, this is a light, fruity, apple and pear flavoured wine that is meant to be drunk young and fresh, without the secondary flavours of Champagne. This however hasn't stopped it becoming a popular alternative, everyday sparkling wine. DOCG wines come from around the village of Valdobiadene.

Bardolino

The third wine of the area is *DOC* Bardolino. This light, almost rosé wine comes from the slopes overlooking Lake Garda, whose huge expanse cools down the area and has an effect on the wine.

the same. When these grapes are pressed, they produce a gooey juice that, when fermented, produces a rich, sour cherry wine with bitter cherry and almond notes fluttering over an alcoholic finish (these wines can easily reach 15 per cent alcohol by volume). You have never really tasted Volpolicella until you try Amarone and again the best examples come from the 'classico' sub-district. Amarone means the 'bitter one' and it is thought that the style was discovered when barrels of the sweeter Recioto style wines accidentally fermented dry. Recioto della Valpolicella DOCG, to give it its proper name, is a Port-like sweet wine that also has a smoky edge that reminds me of an Australian Shiraz – all berries and cherries. Soave

Alto Adige

This area lies to the north of Veneto and is really a bit schizophrenic. It is Italian, or has been since the end of the First World War, but before that was Austrian for over 600 years. The majority of the population still call it Südtirol, and so insist on both Italian and Austrian terms appearing on wine labels, just in case the normal state of affairs is resumed. Fortunately, most of the wines are labelled by grape variety and so this is not as confusing as it might be.

Within the main regional *DOC* are a number of subdistricts, including Santa Maddalena (Sankt Magdalener) and Lago di Caldaro (Kalterersee). The red wines produced here are made from the Shiava grape. The region's white grape varieties tend to be grown on the cooler slopes of the valleys, and this is reflected in the crisp notes on the resulting wines.

Trentino

Within this neighbourhood of Alto Adige, the *DOC* of Teroldego Rotaliano generates a soft, fruity, strawberry red wine, which is made from the Teroldego grape. It is probably the best known wine from this area, though they also make some reasonable Spumante in this area.

Friuli-Venezia-Giulia

Lying between the area of Veneto and the Balkan border, Friuli-Venezia-Giulia can be divided into two main areas: the hills and the plains. The hills produce the best wines, normally white, from this region. Look for the varietal *DOC*s of Colli Goriziano and Colli Orientali.

A total of around twenty different grape varieties are permitted in the region. One of the reasons for this is that the border town of Trieste has had many occupiers, thanks to numerous territorial disputes, and they have all passed through, bringing and leaving different varieties. This is also a reason for a lack of quality in the area; the vineyard owners tend to grow as

many varieties as possible in order to offer as wide a range of wines as possible. The art of matching vine to soil doesn't seem to have arrived here.

Moving south the traveller comes to the central region of Italy, which contains some of the most famous wines in Italy, but they are famous for different reasons.

The Austrian influence of the Südtirol can be seen in the architecture of this picturesque alpine area.

Tuscany

Also known as 'Chiantishire' in the UK, because of the British love affair with the region and its wines, Tuscany is more than just a home to the Chianti *DOCG* wines. It is also the base for a number of young winemakers who are experimenting with new varieties – those super *Vino da Tavola* makers are sometimes simply known as Super Tuscans.

Chianti

Why did these winemakers come into existence? Well, the original *DOC* for Chianti was a bit of a disaster. The habits that were accepted as normal practice in the making of Chianti were based on the customs set up under the city state of Florence in the fourteenth century. The agriculture of the region was mixed, with a lot of tenant farmers growing the grapes, and the area was spread out over a great distance. White wines made from Trebbiano and Malvasia grapes were blended into that produced from the Sangiovese in order not only to soften it up, especially if the Sangiovese was over-cropped, but also to use up the white wine that no one wanted.

When the sharecropping scheme that was in place collapsed, because everyone

were achieving when compared with theirs. But if we consumers get better wine, who cares?

Nowadays, the rules of classification have been changed. Chianti wines must contain a minimum of 90 per cent Sangiovese and Canaiolo with no more than 10 per cent of other grapes, such as the ubiquitous Cabernet Sauvignon. More important, the high-yielding clones have been discouraged and Chianti made from pure Sangiovese is now permitted, resulting in a wine that is full of cherry flavours and smacks of acidity. The higher level Chianti Riserva will spend at least three years in oak and bottle before it can be sold.

At this point, I ought to offer a Chianti warning: quality Chianti comes in a 'Bordeaux'-shaped bottle, with straight sides and distinct shoulders. Decent Chianti does not come in straw-covered *fiaschi*. They may make wonderfully romantic candle sticks, but is it really worth the trouble of drinking the wine?

Once again, the better area is the *classico* area near the centre of Tuscany, but there are also six subregions of Colli Aretini, Colli Florentini, Colli Sensesi, Colli Pisane, Montalbano, and the best area of Rufina.

Montalcino

The Sangiovese grape really comes into its own when it is grown in the town of Montalcino, in the south of the area. Down here, the grape is known as the Brunello, but *DOCG* Brunello di

moved into the cities, the owners began to consolidate the vines into vineyards. Unfortunately, they chose to replant with very high-yielding clones of Sangiovese, which made dilute and virtually tasteless wines. No wonder passionate winemakers and growers rebelled against this and started to work outside the *DOC* regulations, growing new French varieties, reducing yields, and maturing the wine in small barriques, rather than the traditional large casks.

The good news is that the influence of these forward-looking producers has prevailed, perhaps because other producers saw the prices that the wines

Montalcino is pure Sangiovese. By law, it has to spend four years in the cellars (of which at least three have to be in cask) before it is released. The best wines will need more years in the bottle before they are ready. Because this cellar aging is bad for cash flow, producers are allowed to produce an easier, younger brother in the form of Rosso di Montalcino. Made from higher yields of Brunello, this wine only needs to be aged for one year.

Montepulciano

Another top red from this area is the modestly named Vino Nobile di Montepulciano, made from the Prugnolo grape – that is, Sangiovese again. In fact, it was the first wine to be awarded *DOCG* status. There is also a lesser *DOC* of Rosso di Montepulciano, filling a similar role to that of Rosso di Montalcino, to allow producers to sell a wine while waiting for the *DOCG* wine to complete its cellar aging.

Carmignano

The final red *DOCG* wine from Tuscany is probably the least known outside the area. Carmignano is also made from Sangiovese, but up to 10 per cent of Cabernet Sauvignon can be added to give a little finesse to the wines.

San Gimignano

Tuscany also makes a *DOCG* white wine, Vernaccia di San Gimignano, which is made from the Vernaccia grape in the walled town of San Gimignano. This was the first white *DOCG* wine and, in fact, it was also the first wine to be awarded a *DOC*, way back in the mid-1960s.

Vin Santo

Another white wine that is a speciality of the Tuscany region, although it can be produced elsewhere, is the sweet, and deliberately oxidised Vin Santo style. This wine is made from dried grapes in much the same fashion as Veneto's Recioto wines are, except that, as they mature over a number of years, the barrels are not topped up and a controlled oxidation takes place, giving a nutty edge to the wines.

A winter view of the town of Montepulciano, which has been a centre for the production of top quality wines for many centuries.

Emilia-Romagna

Known as the 'fog factory' of Italy, this area is most famous for its Lambrusco, probably one of Italy's best examples of a wine made to go with the local cuisine. The high acidity of this semisweet, low-alcohol, sparkling wine matches the rich Parma hams, Parmesan cheese, and Bolognese ragout of the area.

The wine is made from the Lambrusco grape, and the best *DOC* wines come from the subregions of Sorbara and Grasparossa di Castelvetro. The Sangiovese di Romagna grape can produce some good wines, while other varietal wines from the Barbera and Bonarda grapes develop some interesting raspberry and liquorice flavours. You can also find some dry, white wines in this area, including the undistinguished *DOCG* of Albana di Romagna.

Le Marche

There is a lot of exciting investment going on in this area, resulting in a great improvement in the wines. The best white wine is made from the Verdicchio grape in the towns of Castelli di Jesi and Matelica. If you want red, then the *DOC*s of Rosso Piceno and Rosso Conero are the ones to buy. These wines are made from blends of Sangiovese and Montepulciano.

Lazio

This is the area around Rome but, surprisingly, the wines are not that great. Mainly a white wine area, Lazio's main grape is the Trebbiano, which can make fairly interesting wines, but is normally overcropped, thin, and acidic.

Frascati

The best known wine here is the *DOC* of Frascati. The better versions of this wine have a high proportion of Malvasia in them, rather than Trebbiano. Also from

the area is the interestingly named Est! Est!! Est!!!, which, again, has fallen into the high-yield trap of Trebbiano.

Umbria

Very similar to its neighbour Tuscany, Umbria lacks the moderating maritime influence. The white wines produced here are again based on the Trebbiano, but the better wines of Orvieto will have a proportion of Malvasia and Grechetto grapes blended in as well. There is only really one red wine from this

area, and most of that comes from one producer. The 'owner' of this fiefdom is Lungarotti, whose Torgiano, made from the Sangiovese grape, shows the potential of this improving area.

Abbruzzo

Over on the east coast of Italy is the region of Abbruzzo, which produces some easy drinking, soft reds at very reasonable prices – good everyday drinking wine for when friends come around. The red is made from the Montepulciano grape and can

The rocky town of Orvieto stands above the vineyards, which can produce some exciting dry, white wines.

be full of plums and raspberry acidity. As I said before, do not confuse this grape, or the wine it makes, with Vino Nobile di Montepulciano, which is a wine produced in the village in Tuscany.

As you move south, you come to the blindingly hot 'heel' and 'sole' of the 'boot' of Italy. Here, surprisingly, when you consider the climate, is one of the most exciting areas of Italy, making wine from the indigenous grapes of the region, which have been grown for centuries, but which are finding a new lease on life with modern winemaking and vine-growing techniques.

Molise

This area has long been a vinous backwater of Italy. Not anymore. Biferno is the main *D.O.C.*, producing red wines made from the Montepulciano grape variety.

Campania

Lying on the Bay of Naples, on the slopes of Mount Vesuvius, with all the influence of its volcanic soils, Campania produces some great red wines from the Taurasi *DOCG* These wines, made from the Aglianico grape, must be aged for three years, with at least one year in cask, before they are released.

The best white wines come from the *DOC*s of Fiano di Avellino and Greco di Tufo. Both of these wines are named after the grape varieties used to make them.

Basilicata

Another volcano, extinct this time, is the main geographical feature of this area. Mount Vulture is the base of Aglianico del Vulture, made from the Aglianico grape, and is full of chocolate and bittersweet almond notes.

Calabria

Sitting right on the 'toe' of Italy, Calabria still shows the influence of the Greeks who 'came bearing gifts' of the vine. Gaglioppo produces some full-bodied, red wines in the *DOC* of Ciro, and Greco di Bianco is a

dessert wine made from semi-dried grapes – that Greek influence again – which has an orangy citrus tang on the final note.

Puglia

This is probably where the biggest change has occurred in Italian wines. A lot of Puglia's production used to be used in the north of Italy to make vermouth. Nowadays, this area is recognised for the production of its Primitivo-based wines.

The Primitivo is the Zinfandel of California, and here it produces big,

dense, berry-flavoured, red wines that are sweet and rich.

Another red grape from this region is the Negroamaro. It makes intense red wines with bitter-herbal, chocolate notes. Look for the *DOC*s of Brindisi, Copertino, and Salice Salentino.

Sardinia

This island produces a variety of styles, but the best wines are the white Vermentino di Sardegna and the red Cannonau di Sardegna. Both are named after the grapes from which they are made.

The soil in this vineyard in Sardinia is banked up round the base of the vines to protect their roots from the heat.

Sicily

This island is probably best known for the production of the fortified wine Marsala. However, having received a large amount of European Union investment, Sicily now produces some interesting wines from a combination of classic and indigenous grape varieties. Look out for white wines made from Chardonnay, Cataratto, and Inzolia, and reds made from Nero d'Avola and Cabernet Sauvignon.

SPAIN

A country producing traditional styles of wine, Spain has recently undergone a significant winemaking revolution with new techniques and grape varieties being introduced, without losing its heritage.

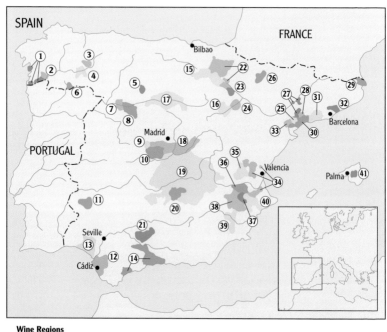

Wine Regions

1 Rias Baixas	9 Cebreros	16 Calatayud	25 Priorato	33 Terra Alta
2 Ribeiro	10 Mentrida	17 Ribera del Duero	26 Somontano	34 Valencia
3 Bierzo	11 Tierra de Barros	18 Vinos de Madrid	27 Costers del Segre	35 Utiel Requena
4 Valdeorras	12 Jerez y	19 La Mancha	28 Conca de Barberá	36 Almansa
5 Cigales	Manzanilla	20 Valdepeñas	29 Ampurdán-	37 Yecla
6 Valle de	13 Condado de	21 Montilla-Moriles	Costa Brava	38 Jumilla
Monterrey	Huelva	22 Navarra	30 Tarragona	39 Bullas
7 Toro	14 Málaga	23 Campo de Borja	31 Penedés	40 Alicante
8 Rueda	15 Rioja	24 Cariñena	32 Alella	41 Binissalem

Spain has a lot in common with Australia. There are extremes of climate in this small country. The centre is arid and desertlike, while the coast is cool to the north but becomes more and more influenced by its neighbour, Africa, as you move south, although there are mountains in the southern region that can be cultivated to create cool areas.

Spain actually has more area under vine than any other country in the world, but rarely suffers from overproduction. Its output is reduced by the effects of that hot climate, meaning that with half as many vines again as Italy and France, it produces only two thirds of the wine that

The vineyards near Jerez stretch into the distance, awaiting their chance to grow and produce grapes for Sherry.

these countries do. Yields are incredibly low because the sun dries out the fruit and the land. This is the only European country that can irrigate its vines and still produce legally recognised quality wines.

As you would expect, the diversity of the climate is reflected in the styles of wines that are produced: from fortified Sherries in the south, to light and full-bodied reds, delicate whites and top quality Cava, or sparkling wines, which are made using the traditional method developed in Champagne and introduced

The architectural influence of Gaudí can be seen in the cellars commissioned from one of his students by Cordorniu.

to Spain in 1872, by José Raventos of the Codorniu Company in Penedes.

For once, it is thought that someone beat the Romans to introducing the vine to this country. It is commonly accepted that the Phoenicians introduced the vines to Spain through trading, and that they actually reached as far inland by river as the area we now recognise as Rioja. Occupation by the Moors seems to have had little effect, with winemaking seen by some as an act of defiance against the Muslim invader. One of the modern influences on wine production was the devastating arrival of *phylloxera* in France.

Bordeaux merchants, looking for a new source of wines to sell, hopped on the train and headed south. When they arrived in Haro, in the Rioja area, they saw the area's potential and got off. These merchants introduced the small 225-litre Bordeaux *barrique* used to age the wine. However, with a slight twist, the Rioja producers prefer to use American oak with its open vanilla and coconut influences, rather than French oak, which tends to be more closed with cedarwood, pencil shavings, and tobacco notes. I once made the mistake of asking a producer why this was so. Was it perhaps a hangover from the Spanish conquest of parts of America? 'No,' he shrugged. 'It's cheaper!'

Recently, there has been a big change in the manner and style of Spanish wines. Traditionally, they were prized for their long periods of oak aging –

the quality system lays down minimum standards, which have to be adhered to if the wine is to qualify for *Reserva* or *Gran Reserva* status. Nowadays, however, a new breed of younger winemaker is producing lighter red and white wines using temperature-controlled, stainless-steel fermentation, with little or no barrel aging, and so leading a world trend in the process.

SPANISH WINE LAW

The Spanish wine classification, like most of Europe's, is based upon the French *appellation* system, which sets out specific areas of production, but there is also a second part, dictating minimum aging periods, which is fairly unique in that it is applied nationally, rather than locally.

• *Vino de España* is basic table wine from anywhere in the country.

• *Vino de la Tierra* is Spain's I.G.P. category for wines from a large geographical area. Wines labelled *Vino de Calidad con indicación* are *Vino de la Tierra* wines that are in the process of being promoted to DO status.

• *Denominacíon de Origen (DO)* is Spain's PDO wine. Currently there are around 60 areas, including the Balearic and Canary Islands, that qualify for this category.

• *Vino de Paga* wines come from individual estates, a bit like Burgundy's *Grand Cru* estates, that are recognised as producing better wines – unlike Burgundy, however, these estates must bottle their wine at the winery. So far, there are 15 *Vino de Pago* wines.

• *Denominacíon de Origen Calificada (DOCa)* is similar to the Italian *DOCG*,

in that it is awarded to wines which can point to a proven history of quality wine production.

Set up in 1991, at the same time as the *Vino de la Tierra* category, to date only two wines have qualified for promotion. These are the premium wine regions of Rioja and Priorat.

Every bottle of *DO*, or *DOCa*, wine in Spain will carry on the back label a seal from the local controlling agency or *Consejo Regulador*. This seal not only guarantees the origin and classification of the wine, but also the type of aging that the wine has gone through. The following requirements are the minimum only and can be exceeded by any *Consejo*.

• *Vino Joven* or *Sin Crianza* are young wines, or wines without age. They will have less than twelve months in wood, if they spend any time in oak, and will be sold straight after bottling.

• *Crianza* red wines will have spent at least six months in oak barrels, followed by another period of bottle aging. They cannot be released for sale until the wines are two years old. White and rosé wines spend the same minimum period in barrels, but can be sold one year after the harvest.

• *Reserva* red and white, and, sometimes rosé, wines are normally the wines of better vintages and will be matured in wood for a minimum of twelve months in the case of the reds and six months for

You can clearly see the chalk content in the soil in these vineyards in Rioja.

the whites and rosés. The reds cannot be sold until they are three years old, the others two.

• *Gran Reserva* wines are only produced in exceptionally good years. Red wines must spend at least two years in casks, before spending a minimum of two years in the bottle. They cannot be released until they reach their fifth birthday. White and rosé wines, on the other hand, can be sold after four years and must spend at least six months in the cask.

As I say, these are the minimum requirements, and many of the regions, especially Rioja, will exceed them.

Northern Spain

Some of the most well-known wine regions of Spain can be found here.

Rioja

This region is the main influence on winemaking in northern Spain. This position of importance is due to the aging and blending techniques, which were developed with the assistance of the Bordeaux merchants, and the main red grapes, which are all traditional and have a long history in the area: Tempranillo, Garnacha (the Grenache of the Southern Rhone), Graciano, and the Mazuelo, which is the French variety Carignan.

Although all these grapes are permitted, most winemakers concentrate on the Tempranillo. This is Spain's premier red grape and, as its name suggests – *temprano* is Spanish for early – it is an early ripening variety.

Rioja itself is in north-eastern Spain and lies on the River Ebro, one of whose tributaries, the Rio Oja, gives its name to the region. It is split into three areas identified by the amount of chalk in the soil: the more chalk, the better the area. The Rioja Alta lies to the west of the main town of Logroño on the south bank of the river.

The climate here is influenced by the proximity of the cool Atlantic Ocean, but it is warmer than the next district, the Rioja Alavesa, which is also to the west, but situated on the north side of

the river, which is cooler and wetter. Rioja Baja lies to the east of Logroño. It is much the flatter of the three regions and is much hotter. The main grape variety grown here is the Garnacha, because of the climate and the clay-dominated soil. Although there are a few single-estate Riojas, classic Rioja is made as a blend of wines produced in all three areas, and much of the production comes from cooperatives.

About 10 per cent of Rioja's production is white wine made from Viura and Malvasia grapes, much less than the 15 per cent of the region's production that goes toward making rosé. It is here that the greatest mind shift has occurred in winemaking. Traditionally, white Riojas were aged in oak barrels for a considerable period of time. Nowadays, you are more likely to find light, fresh citrus wines, which have been fermented in temperature-controlled, stainless-steel vats. Do be aware that some producers still believe in the old ways.

Navarra

This is Rioja's next-door neighbour and, as it has emerged from the large shadow cast by its illustrious neighbour, it has planted a number of classic grape varieties, such as Cabernet Sauvignon and Merlot, in addition to Tempranillo.

Away from the cultivated area of Rioja, the landscape can seem somewhat wild and desolate.

Chardonnay has also been planted here to liven up the white wines.

Aragon

The area leading up to the foothills of the Pyrenees, Aragon is moving towards a lighter style of wine. The best wines from the *DO*s are the reds, but some white and rosé is produced. The most interesting *DO* is Somontano. With its cool climate, it is making some red and white wines from a blend of traditional Spanish and classic international grape varieties. Calatayud is following suit, as its cooperative producers have invested in international expertise in the form of 'flying winemakers' to iron out inconsistencies in their wines from year to year. Other improving areas in this region are the Campo de Borja, making better wines from Cariñena and Garnacha grapes, and the confusingly named Cariñena *DO*, which is made mainly from Garnacha.

The cooler climate of Aragon allows vines to grow more slowly and gives the grapes a longer ripening period.

Cataluña

Lying in the north-east corner of Spain, Cataluña has six regions of interest.

Penedés

This region, and probably one company within it, started the cool-fermentation revolution in Spain. The Torres family was making wine even before 1870, when the present company was set up, but in the 1980s, they began to experiment with temperature-controlled fermentation techniques in stainless-steel vats. At the same time, they also began planting classic grape varieties, such as Chardonnay, Sauvignon Blanc, Pinot

The previous year's growth is still in evidence on these vines awaiting their first prune of the season in Penedés.

Noir, Cabernet Sauvignon, and Merlot, being among the first to do so in Spain. The result has been a range of wines that are a blend of traditional and classic grapes.

By introducing vineyards to the hills behind the region, known as the Penedés Superior, the Torres family also experimented with cool-climate vine cultivation, which is now a permanent feature in a large number of neighbouring vineyards. Down on the coast here, it gets incredibly hot in the summer, so most

One of Spain's most expensive wines, Vega Sicilia has made the reputation of the Ribera del Duero.

of the production is made up of sweet dessert wines, from grapes that have literally shrivelled on the vines. The middle area, in between the coastal strip and the hills, is the traditional quality area. Here, you will find not only the origins of the area's table wine production, but also, around the town of San Sadurni de Noya, Spain's Cava industry.

Cava is not a geographically specific *DO* wine. Other areas, including Rioja, can produce Cava, but it has to be made using the *método tradicional*, or traditional method, brought from Champagne. The red wines of Penedés are the best, but this may be because the vast majority of the white wine production ends up as Cava.

Costers del Segre

Further inland is the *DO* of Costers del Segre, an area based around the town of Lérida. This region is dominated by a single producer. Raimat, or 'red hand', is one of the table wine brands of the Cava giant, Codorniu.

In the 1930s, one of the sons of the

wines, but one to look out for here is the much improving Priorato *DO*, which, by blending in classic grapes such as Cabernet Sauvignon, is now producing complex wines with aging potential.

Ribera del Duero

Some of Spain's best red and white wines are produced over in the north west. Best known for its red wine, Ribera del Duero's status is based on one producer. However, now that more producers are realising the benefits of working in this arid and desolate area, the number of top-quality red wines is growing.

Vega Sicilia is probably the most expensive wine in Spain. It is made from tiny, concentrated yields of Tinto Fino (Tempranillo), and the Bordeaux grape varieties of Cabernet Sauvignon, Merlot, and Malbec. The quality factor in the production of Ribera del Duero wines is the huge temperature difference between day and night. The cold nights preserve the acid levels in the grapes, while the hot days concentrate the flavours and colour in them. If you cannot afford Vega Sicilia, try the wines of Pesquera instead.

Rueda

Downriver, the *DO* of Rueda has been transformed by the arrival of the Rioja house of Marqués de Riscal, precipitating a move from the traditional, heavy, fortified wines to light, dry white wines, made from Verdejo and Sauvignon Blanc or the Vidura grapes.

Toro and Cigales

To the north of the region come the *DO*s of Toro, which could only be Spanish,

controlling Raventos family bought a huge tract of land in this semiarid area for the Spanish equivalent of a song. Thanks to some inside knowledge, he was aware that plans were well advanced to build a canal through this desert. This canal brought with it the water that is still used to irrigate the vineyards here. The wines are made mainly from Cabernet Sauvignon, Tempranillo (known here, as in Penedés, by its local name, Ull de Llebre), and Chardonnay. Most of the other regions in Cataluña, such as Tarragona and Conca de Barberá, produce reasonable, easy-drinking producing big, solid – I am desperately trying to avoid using the word 'bullish' – reds from the local Tinto de Toro (yes, that's Tempranillo, again). The other *DO* is the rarely seen Cigales, where passable rosé wines are made from Garnacha and Tempranillo.

Galicia

Galicia is the bit of Spain that sits on top of Portugal, producing white wines, very similar in style to the Portuguese Vinho Verde wines created just over the border. The main grape variety found here is the Albariño, which makes lightly aromatic wines in the *DO*s of Rias Baixas, Ribeiro, and Valreorras. At their best, these wines can be as fruity and aromatic as the Viognier of the Rhône Valley.

Central Spain

The central area of Spain is responsible for over half of the wine produced in the country.

La Mancha

The dominant *DO* in this area, La Mancha is, in fact, the largest delimited wine region in Europe. It is also home to the world's most widely planted grape variety. What's that? Chardonnay? No, the Airén, of course! Don't worry if you have never heard of it; the vast majority of the production is distilled into brandy.

La Mancha is, of course, the home of Don Quixote and his windmills, but the introduction of irrigation and modern winemaking techniques has completely changed the styles of wines produced in his days. Nowadays, the vines are individually trained low to the ground, so

that the bushy growth can shade the fruit and the ground around the vine to keep the roots cool. Light, everyday drinking wines are the norm here, and long may it continue.

Valdepeñas

In the south of the region lies the quality wine area of Valdepeñas, the valley of the stones. This *DO* is a relatively cooler area, producing red wines from the Cencibel, Tempranillo in disguise again, with sometimes some Airén included in the blend. Look out for the oak-aged Reserva and Gran Reserva styles.

The other *DO*s of the region are producing increasingly better, quality wines, based, in some parts, on the Garnacha and Monastrell varieties. Yecla, Bullas Jumilla, Alicante, and Uteil-Requena all fit into this category, but beware, as a friend of mine found out, the older style of wine can make your teeth go pink!

Southern Spain

The south of Spain is really too hot to produce any table wines, so Sherry is not only the best known wine of this area, but it also ploughs the path that the other areas follow. Montilla-Moriles shares some of the chalk soil of Jerez, but because it is further inland, lacks the cooling sea breezes of Jerez, so the quality does suffer. The wines are made in similar styles to Sherry, such as Fino, Amontillado, and Oloroso. However, the law has given Sherry the unique use of those terms, so Montilla has to revert to the terms 'pale', 'dry', 'medium', and 'cream'. The wines are rarely

fortified and naturally reach higher levels of alcohol.

It is still possible to see the Moorish influence in the town of Jerez de la Frontera in southern Spain.

Sherry

Sherry is the area on the coast, near the port of Cadiz, and to a certain extent it is this transport centre that has helped to spread the word about, and the product of, the region around the world. Sherry takes its name from the corruption of the name of the main town, Jerez de la Frontera, which takes its name from the time when this area was the frontier between Christian and Moorish Spain. Sherry has long been a popular wine in Britain. By Tudor times, inventories of bars in London were listing 'Sherris Sack' wines, and the wine was also referred to by Shakespeare as the drink of Falstaff. This popularity is reflected in the number of English merchants who set up in the area and whose names are still in evidence, such as Harvey, Croft, Osborne, and Sandeman.

For an explanation of how Sherry is produced, see page 140.

PORTUGAL

Long known as a producer of fortified and rosé wines,

Portugal is now gaining a reputation for its table wines.

Portugal's wine trade has long been linked with the U.K.'s, its importance being reflected in the Treaty of Windsor of 1386 and the Methuen Treaty of 1703. Portuguese wines were always the first choice of wines for the English when French wines were "difficult" to obtain—that is, during any Anglo-French war! In the recent past, though, the table wines of Portugal were not recognised as being of any quality. What was there apart from Mateus Rosé? This changed after Portugal joined the

EU in 1986, and an influx of European investment saw temperature-controlled, stainless-steel fermentation introduced.

PORTUGUESE WINE LAW

Naturally, Portuguese wines are classified according to the usual European (French) standards:

• *Vinho de Mesa* is the simplest table wine.

Above: One of Portugal's largest wine regions, Alentejo is not just home to vineyards but also a lot of arable crops.

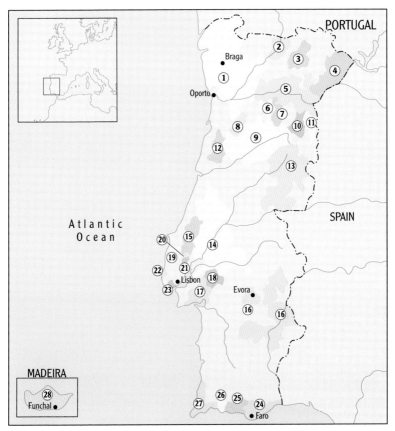

Wine Regions

1 Vinhos Verdes	**8** Lafoes	**15** Estramadura	**22** Colares
2 Chaves	**9** Dão	**16** Alentejo	**23** Carcavelos
3 Valpaços	**10** Pinhel	**17** Setúbal	**24** Tavira
4 Planalto-Mirandes	**11** Castelo Rodrigo	**18** Palmela	**25** Lagoa
5 Port & the Douro	**12** Bairrada	**19** Torres	**26** Portimão
6 Varosa	**13** Cova da Beira	**20** Arruda	**27** Lagos
7 Encostas da Nave	**14** Ribatejo	**21** Bucelas	**28** Madeira

• *Vinho Regional* is the regional equivalent of *Vin de Pays*.

•*Indicaçao de Proveniêcia Regulamentada (I.P.R.)* is better quality than the *Vinho Regional* wines, comes from a smaller demarcated area, but has not yet qualified for the top status level.

• *Denominação de Origem Controlada (D.O.C.)* is the same as France's *Appellation Protégée*.

Northern Portugal

The main climatic influence on Portugal is the Atlantic Ocean, which keeps the country cooler and, very definitely, moister than its Iberian neighbour. To the north of the country, near Spanish Galicia, lies the main *D.O.C.* area of Vinho Verde. Funnily enough, around half of the wine produced in this area is red, not white, although most of it is drunk locally. Where does the "green" come from? It is simply a description of the wine's youth, or "greenness." This wine—the white is made from the Alvarino, the red from Vinhão—is meant to be drunk young (actually, it should be finished as the next harvest is ready), and it will have an attractive, acidic prickle, which makes for a refreshing drink.

Central Portugal

Dão and Biarrada

These areas lie to the south of the River Douro. Traditionally, the wines from these parts were full-bodied and very full of oak. Nowadays, a lot of money and effort has gone into producing light red wines, based on the Touriga Nacional and Baga grape varieties, and they are full of plummy red fruits and herb flavours.

Alentejo

Alentejo wines are nearly all made from local grape varieties, such as Aragonez and Moreto, and the experimental work carried out when this region was an *I.P.R.* has been employed in the juicy, inexpensive *D.O.C.* wines of today.

Southern Portugal

Colares and Bucelas

Around the capital, Lisbon, are two areas that deserve a mention. Colares is actually the sand dunes of the Portuguese coastline. The vines here are not grafted, because *phylloxera* can't survive in the sandy soil, though, to be honest, it is a bit of a mystery to me how the vines themselves can survive in such a dry, sandy soil. The red wines are incredibly tannic, and a small amount of white wine is also produced. You will also find a fortified, sweet white wine, made from Moscatel grapes in a similar style to the *Vins Doux Naturels* in Southern Rhone: Moscatel du Setúbal is a raisiny wine.

The other area, Bucelas, is smaller than Colares, and lies to the north of Lisbon. It produces rich white wines made from the Arinto grape, which are becoming more popular.

Estremadura, Ribatejo and Terras de Sado

Still in the south are the large *I.P.R.* areas of Estremadura, Ribatejo and Terras de Sado, where Australian winemakers have had a great influence on the winemaking techniques used today.

Algarve

The southernmost *D.O.C.* in Portugal is the Algarve, better known for its tourist industry than for its wine. Here, the red wines are made from the Tinto Negro Mole and Periquita grape varieties, and

The terraced hillsides of the Douro Valley are now producing quality table wines in addition to Port.

I am sorry to say that one of the better comments I have heard about the wines of this area is that they "find a ready market with local tourists".

Port and the Douro Valley

One of the most exciting areas in modern Portuguese winemaking is also one of the oldest. The Port region in the Alto Douro was first delimited in 1756, much to the disgust of the English Port merchants, by the Marques de Pombal. But the Douro Valley is much more than the home of Port.

Running westward from over the border in Spain, where it is called the Duero, all the way to the sea at Oporto, the Douro also produces a number of easy table wines as well. The home of much of the rosé production of Portugal, the area, by using modern winemaking techniques, is also creating some exciting, light red wines, made from the same grape varieties as Port, which are softer and much less tannic. The white wines from this area are also attractive, with crisp acidity and fresh fruit flavours.

It is the Alto Douro that is the real home of Port. This wine is really a product of an English market, in much the same way as Sherry, and, in the same way, this is also reflected in the names of the large Port houses, such as Taylor's and Graham's.

The region itself is incredibly steep, with a granite soil which is so hard that the terraces have to be carved out of the hillside with dynamite and bulldozers. For a full description of the way that Port is made, see page 142.

Madeira

This island, off the west coast of Africa, was first discovered in 1420, by a Portuguese seafarer, João Gonçalvez Zarco. Prince Henry the Navigator then appointed him governor and ordered him to plant sugar cane. The name Madeira comes from the Portuguese for "tree", and was used to describe the forests that covered this volcanic isle. In order to plant the cane, Zarco set fire to the woods. Years later, when the fires were quelled, the volcanic soil had been improved by an influx of wood ash.

Madeira's location made it the perfect stopover for sailing ships on their way to the Americas. They picked up casks of wine to trade and use as an anti-scurvy treatment, and soon discovered that, once the wine had been subjected to the tossing and turning of the sea and the heating and cooling effects of crossing the equator a number of times, it actually improved in flavour.

Realizing that employing a fleet of ships continually to ship wine across the Atlantic Ocean and back was extremely expensive and silly, the islanders developed a process to duplicate the voyage without leaving the island.

The wines are made in the normal manner before being fortified. The sweeter styles are fortified during fermentation, in the same manner as Port, while the drier styles are fortified after fermentation is complete. The wines are then stored in wooden casks, in large,

Irrigating these narrow terraces on the island of Madeira can be a feat of hydro-engineering.

heated warehouses, called *estufas*, for around six months, to replicate the ocean voyage. The best quality wines will be heated naturally, by being stored in the "attic" of the winery for a couple of years, before being moved to large casks for twenty or so years of ageing. The effect of this heating is to caramelise the sugars in the wine, which gives the unique burned flavour to the wine. The wines also become oxidised, and this gives the wine its virtual indestructibility.

The styles of Madeira wine are named after the classic wines of the island, and recent legislation has tightened up their usage, and now insists that wines with a variety on the label must include 85 percent of that variety. Sercial is the driest style of Madeira, Verdelho is medium dry, while Bual is medium sweet and is unique in that the vine from which it is produced has hairy leaves. Weird!

Barrels of Verdelho Madeira maturing in the traditional manner on **canteiros**, or racks, in the attic of Blandy's winery.

The sweetest style of Madeira is Malmsey, with its butterscotch, raisin flavours. Shakespeare has it that the Duke of Clarence was drowned in a vat of Malmsey at the Tower of London in 1482. His name is still used by the Blandy company for one of their Madeiras today.

The wines are classified according to the ageing process that they go through. Selected, finest, or choice Madeiras must be at least three years old; Reserve wines must be five years old; Old reserve wines must be ten years old; and Extra Reserve, fifteen years old.

Vintage wines must be made from wines of the stated year and are normally twenty or more years old, the first twenty of which must be spent in casks.

U.S.A. & CANADA

Wines are now produced right across the continent of North America, providing a diverse and mouth-watering range.

U.S.A.

Like most New World countries, the winemaking in the United States got off to a poor start. The fortunate settlers thought that they were lucky when they discovered a native vine that produced grapes from which they could make wines. They were happy, until they tasted it! The American vines made wines that were just too pungently animal and musky for their taste. It was like drinking a fox. Not pleasant at all.

So they sent for some Mediterranean vines, but the foreign climate and pests, including *phylloxera*, were too strong for them, and they soon became diseased and died. Slowly, they began to develop hybrid grapes—the results of crossing European and American vines—and produced some drinkable wines. These

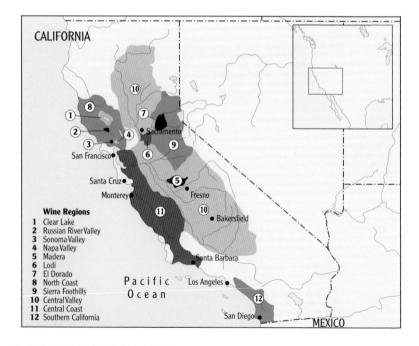

Wine Regions
1 Clear Lake
2 Russian River Valley
3 Sonoma Valley
4 Napa Valley
5 Madera
6 Lodi
7 El Dorado
8 North Coast
9 Sierra Foothills
10 Central Valley
11 Central Coast
12 Southern California

grapes were, and still are, the basis of the wine industry on the eastern seaboard of the U.S.A.

In California, however, the story was different. Not only were the Spanish settlers having few problems planting a European variety known as the Mission, but soon the 1849 Gold Rush brought thirsty miners, demanding wine. A Hungarian, Agoston Haraszthny, imported some European vines into the area, which included some vines from the nursery of the Austrian Emperor Francis I.

These vines formed the basis of the

With its glowing reputation and that of its late owner, the winery of Robert Mondavi attracts a lot of visitors.

fledgeling Californian wine industry. Unfortunately, they soon had to cope with a number of problems. The first was the unwelcome arrival, in 1870, of the *phylloxera* louse from the east coast. Vineyards were soon replanted with grafted vines, but within forty years came the other potentially disastrous period of Prohibition. During the Prohibition period, which lasted until the Volstead Act was finally repealed in 1933, wines

were only allowed to be produced and consumed for medical or sacramental reasons. Beaulieu Vineyards in the Napa Valley only survived because the owner's cousin, Georges de Latour, was Bishop of San Francisco. Many producers went under, or converted their vineyards to the production of table rather than wine grapes, despite an increase in demand for grapes to make homemade "grape juice", The period led to a pattern of alcohol consumption based on beers and spirits, because they were easier to produce illegally. It's hard to hide a vineyard!

Since the end of Prohibition, the production and consumption of wine has increased, and now covers every state in the U.S.A. The majority of America's wine production (some 90 percent), however, comes from California. Other states, such as Oregon and Washington, do have a small share, though.

One of the best areas of production, the Russian River Valley benefits from the cold fogs off the Pacific Coast.

U.S. WINE LAWS

There is a nationwide *appellation* system in place overseen by the TTB. The American Viticultural Area (AVA) scheme identifies geographical areas of quality production.

Unlike the French system, it does not list permitted grape varieties. However, it does state that wines from these areas must be made with at least 85 percent of grapes from that area.

If a variety is named, then at least 75 percent of the wine must be made from that variety, and if the wine label lists a vineyard, then 95 percent of the wine must come from that vineyard. Also, if the wine has a vintage on it, then at least 95 percent of the wine must come from that vintage.

California

The home of American wine, California is thought of as a sunny state, but pockets of it are really cool and are able to produce world-class wines in addition to the everyday, easy-drinking, squashy fruit, "jug" wines, which have made its name across the country.

In the north, around the San Francisco Bay area, are valleys which are cooled by early morning fog banks that roll in from the Pacific Ocean. These fog banks are caused by the cold Alaskan currents hitting warm air. All of the top production areas, such as the Napa, Sonoma and Russian River valleys and Mendocino, are situated near breaks in the coastal ranges. These breaks allow the cold fogs to roll in and cool down the vineyards, and make the sun expend its energy burning off the fog rather than burning the grapes.

The quality of these areas was first recognised on the world stage when Steven Spurrier organised his now famous bicentennial tasting in Paris in 1976. Wines from Stags Leap Wine cellars and Château Montelena, both in the Napa Valley, swept the board in a blind tasting of French and Californian wines, judged by some of France's top experts. Since then, there has been a large number of small, boutique wineries set up in the Napa and Sonoma valleys.

The northern part of California is also the centre of what people call organic wines, but which is, more accurately, wine from organically grown grapes. These are wines that have been made from grapes produced without the use of artificial

The fog has well and truly descended here in the northern half of Mendocino County.

fertilisers, or synthetic and expensive chemicals. Some large wineries are now converting to either organic production, or sustainable production, where the use of chemicals is kept to a minimum. One of the largest wineries to produce wines from organically grown grapes is Fetzer.

When Barney Fetzer was looking for a way to encourage people to drink wine as a social drink, he realised that wine with food was an important way in. He built a restaurant by his cellar door, to give people another reason to visit his winery. The chef he employed wanted a garden to provide fresh produce for the restaurant, and eventually the business demanded that the garden had a full-time

gardener, and the one they employed, by pure chance, was into growing fruit and vegetables organically.

The grape growers and winemakers noticed the quality of the produce and wondered if they could repeat the process in the vineyard. Small sample batches proved a success, and soon the entire Fetzer landholding was being converted to organic production methods. These included planting cover crops between the rows of vines, which included yellow clover, to take nitrogen from the air and inject it into the soil. The cover crops also attract pests away from the vines, as well as the natural predators of those pests. Later on in the growing season, these

Part of the Fetzer vineyard which has established a worldwide reputation for its organic production methods.

Another category of organically grown wines was developed in Europe in the 1920s. Biodynamic wines are made following a system developed by the Austrian, Rudolf Steiner. Once again, the system is based upon creating a healthy balance in the soil. However, there is a less scientific – and slightly more controversial – approach to alternative methods, such as working to moon and tidal cycles. Some people consider the emphasis on natural methods to influence spraying and pruning timings a little too "new age" – like planting manure in the ground in cow's horns from one solstice to the next to concentrate its effect, so that as little as a teaspoon in several gallons of water will have the desired result. The claim is that by following these natural cycles, the plants (vines) will be healthier and the wines better.

crops are ploughed into the soil as a green manure, while the heavy, clay soils are also helped by adding composted grape skins and seeds as a soil conditioner. With birds, hawks and predator wasps all encouraged to nest in the vineyard and live on the pests in the area, the whole regime has the effect of making the vineyard a healthier place in which to work and live, as some of the chemicals normally used can be dangerous if misused.

Organic wines still have sulphur added to them during the winemaking process because of its preservative and disinfecting powers. However, organically grown wines tend to have less sulphur added than most other wines.

California's success is based on a few classic grape varieties that have been introduced over the years. Cabernet Sauvignon, Sauvignon Blanc, Merlot, Chardonnay and Zinfandel are the main varieties, although there are small outcrops of Italian varieties, such as Sangiovese, and some Rhône varieties, such as Syrah and Viognier.

Northern California has just about recovered from a recent attack of *phylloxera*, which was caused by some incorrect advice on the level of immunity to *phylloxera* of a new rootstock. The disastrous AXR1 has slowly been replaced, after the vineyards succumbed to a new strain of this pest.

California made its wines more approachable by labelling the wines by variety. It was not a new idea: Alsace and Germany had been doing it for years, but it was still a revelation. Basically, the wine did what it said on the label. If you wanted a soft red wine, then look for Merlot. Something with more structure? Try Cabernet Sauvignon. Recently, some wineries have begun to develop blended wines, whether a Bordeaux "Meritage" style, or simply a blend of two grapes to make the wines more complex.

Napa Valley

This valley, an hour's drive north of San Francisco, is based on the Bordeaux plan of a single estate with a winery close by. The only real difference, when compared with Bordeaux, is that the vines are quite happily planted on the valley floor, despite the danger of frost. This is overcome by using giant fans or water sprays to protect the young vines. The valley is centred around Oakville and Rutherford. Here, big Cabernet Sauvignon wines are the norm, with some Zinfandels now making a name for themselves. Just up the hill from here is the A.V.A. of Stags Leap, the home of Warren Winiarski's Stags Leap Wine Cellars, and farther on are the other hillside A.V.A.s of Mount Veeder and Howell Mountain.

Sonoma County

The best wineries of this area are relatively new. Until the 1970s, Sonoma wines were used for blending. Now, the best of the wines are dry whites, made in a similar vein to white Burgundies, although they have much more new oak and riper fruit

flavours. The centre of the region is the Sonoma Valley, which runs parallel to the Napa. In fact, the south of the valley is almost shared with the Napa, and it is here that the Cabernet Sauvignon and Zinfandel production is based. Further north, the cooler areas, such as the Russian River and Alexander valleys, are much more Chardonnay influenced.

Carneros

Found to the north of San Francisco Bay, Carneros is cooled by coastal fogs and these, combined with a low rainfall and a clay soil, make it almost perfect for Pinot Noir. The wines lack some of the delicacy of Burgundy's best Pinot Noir wines, but are still very good examples of wines from this grape.

Chardonnay also does well here, as do sparkling wines made from the cool-climate fruit of the area - so well, in fact, that a number of Champagne houses have set up camp here and are using Pinot Noir and Chardonnay grapes in their wines.

Central Coast

South of San Francisco Bay, you will find the Central Coast area, which heads down towards the urban sprawl of Los Angeles. The districts of the Santa Cruz Mountains, Livermore, and Santa Clara do not have a large number of vineyards of quality, so many of the wineries here buy fruit from elsewhere to make their wines. There are exceptions of course, such as Randall Grahm, who produces some stunning wines, inspired by the winemakers of the Rhône Valley and Italy.

Farther south, the cool areas of Monterey County produce remarkable

Pinot Noir wines and Chardonnays. Contrarily, the district of Pasa Robles is not touched by the cooling fogs of the coastline. Instead, vineyards are planted at altitude to compensate. The resulting coolness creates some great Cabernet Sauvignon and Zinfandel wines, with a few growers now experimenting with varieties normally found in the Rhône.

Finally, the Santa Barbara County, Santa Maria Valley, and Santa Ynez Valley A.V.A.s produce cool-climate Pinot Noir and Chardonnay wines. This area became internationally famous as the setting for the film *Sideways*, whose main impact was to cause an increase in the consumption of wine in the USA, especially Pinot Noir.

Part of the Sonoma Valley which is known for its production of Cabernet Sauvignon and Zinfandel wines.

Central Valley

This A.V.A. lies behind a range of mountains, which blocks it off from the cooling coastal fogs. The effect of this is that the area is too hot for great quality wines. However, the large vineyards here, when combined with modern technology, produce huge amounts of drinkable red and white wines.

Central Valley is subdivided into the Sacramento Valley and the San Joaquin Valley, with small areas, such as Lodi, being slightly cooler and, so, better quality. The town of Madera in the San Joaquin Valley produces some top-quality, fortified wines, often using table grapes.

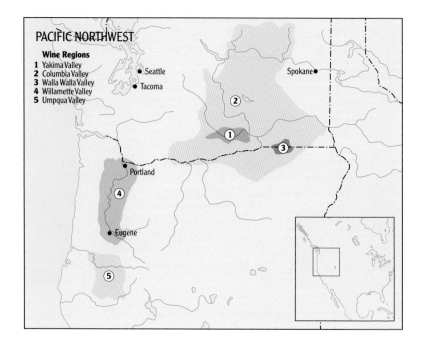

PACIFIC NORTHWEST

Wine Regions
1 Yakima Valley
2 Columbia Valley
3 Walla Walla Valley
4 Willamette Valley
5 Umpqua Valley

Seattle
Tacoma
Spokane
Portland
Eugene

Oregon

A relatively new wine production area, Oregon did not see the first commercial wineries arrive until the 1960s, after the area had recovered from Prohibition.

Its three A.V.A.s, which are all river valleys, are quite small when compared with those of California, and the output from the vineyards tiny. But the quality of the Pinot Noir and Chardonnay wines from the cool areas of the Williamette and Umpqua Valleys, and that of the cool-climate red wines produced from Cabernet Sauvignon and Merlot grapes from the Rogue Valley, is beginning to meet the international standards for these wines.

Washington

The difference between wines from this state and Oregon is due to the climate. That might be a strange statement for people who have been to Seattle and felt that the rain was never going to stop. Surely it is too wet to grow vines. Well, it would be, if it were not for the Cascade Mountains that split the state in half. Basically, the rain stops at the mountains, and the area behind lies in a huge rain shadow, much the same as in Alsace. The land here is almost semi-arid and the vines rely on irrigation. But, being so far north, there is plenty of sunshine from longer days on the slopes with a southern exposure. This produces very ripe grapes, though also, when combined with the cold nights, highly acidic ones.

The growers could have decided to produce large amounts of "jug" wines, as Washington State is, in fact, the second largest producer in the U.S., even though it is a *long* way behind California. However, the growers have decided to concentrate on quality wines from Sauvignon Blanc, Sémillon, Cabernet Sauvignon and Merlot grapes. The main vineyards are in the Columbia Valley, with the sub-districts of Walla Walla and Yakima producing some excellent wines.

A view of the Columbia Valley in Washington where producers are now concentrating on quality wines.

East Coast

The East Coast AVAs now grow a variety of wines. Native American *vitis labrusca* wines abound in New York State, as do hybrid vines, and some European *vinifera* vines. The European vines do need to be located with care, though, as the cold winters can, if the grower is not careful, freeze the sap in the stock of the dormant vine and split it. To overcome this, the growers plant their vineyards near large masses of water, such as the Finger Lakes, Lake Erie and the Hudson River, because the water moderates the extremes of the climate. Recently I have tasted some really exciting Riesling (both dry and sweet), Gewürttraminer and Pinot Noir wines from this region.

Canada

Canada really is a newcomer to wine production. The first commercial European *vinifera* vines were not planted here until the mid-1970s. Before that time, the vineyards were all planted with *labrusca* and hybrid vines. It is one of these hybrids which forms the backbone of one of Canada's most exciting wines. Icewine is Canada's version of the classic German and Austrian Eiswein. Made from Vidal and Riesling grapes, these wines can be created most years, unlike the rare occasions in Europe, and, in fact, Canada is now the largest producer of this wine style. They may lack the intensity of their German counterparts, but they more than make up for that on the grounds of availability and cost.

The Canadian quality system is the Vintners Quality Alliance (V.Q.A.), which sets down the minimum sugar content for the grapes at harvest time—much the same as in Germany—and insists that grapes are sourced from distinct areas. In fact, non-V.Q.A. wines from Ontario can be made from up to 75 percent imported grapes or juice.

British Columbia produces wine in the state's Okanagan Valley, and there is a Germanic influence in the style of wine that it produces. Again, the vineyards of Canada are situated predominantly near large bodies of climate-moderating water, and Ontario is the largest wine producer in the country. The main area in Ontario is the Niagara Peninsula with its good Chardonnay and Pinot Noir.

Harvesting grapes for the delicious Icewine in the Henry of Pelham vineyards in Ontario, in Canada.

SOUTH AMERICA

An area that definitely has a lot going for it, South America shows how much it has gleaned from Europe and elsewhere.

This part of the American continent is probably the most European influenced when it comes to wine styles, even though the wines are definitely not European. The grapes come from European vines, because the Mediterranean wine vine is not a natural resident of this continent. But the climate is so unlike anything that is found in Europe, it raises the question: how can you grow a plant like the wine vine in the tropics and still make very good wines?

The main climatic influence here is the Andes. This range of mountains runs down the region like a spine, dividing the main wine countries of Chile and Argentina, and providing snowmelt water for irrigation. Over the millennia, the rivers formed from this water have carved steep valleys running at 90° to the range, and it is these valleys that are key to the production of wine in this hot area.

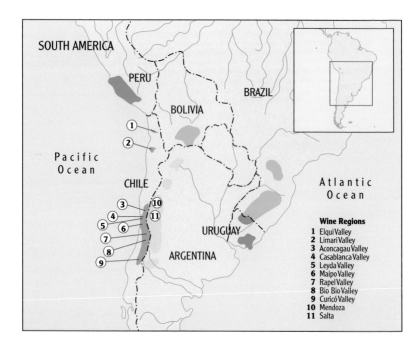

SOUTH AMERICA

PERU

BRAZIL

BOLIVIA

Pacific Ocean

CHILE

Atlantic Ocean

URUGUAY

ARGENTINA

Wine Regions
1 Elqui Valley
2 Limari Valley
3 Aconcagau Valley
4 Casablanca Valley
5 Leyda Valley
6 Maipo Valley
7 Rapel Valley
8 Bio Bio Valley
9 Curicó Valley
10 Mendoza
11 Salta

Chile

This long, narrow country, running down the west coast of South America was first colonised, like most of South America, by the Spanish, who brought the vine with them in the sixteenth century. The original "visitors" were the conquistadors who were searching for the fabled city of El Dorado and its gold. They were soon followed by missionaries, who wanted to convert the "heathen" natives to Christianity, on behalf of the Catholic Church. Wine is an important part of the sacrament, so they obviously brought vines with them.

The natives didn't take too well to either the theft of their gold or being forced to give up their gods and take wine. A common form of revenge during the many uprisings was to pour molten gold down the throats of captured settlers.

Horses for courses – harvest time in Chile is an interesting sight as the Los Vacos vineyards show.

These vines were not the classic varieties that we recognise now. The main red variety appears to have been a very ordinary variety, which today we call the Pias, while the whites were Muscatel and Torrontel. Actually, the Spanish did not encourage wine making in their colony: at different times they banned the export of Chilean wine and even ordered the uprooting of all vines, preferring to ship wine from the vineyards of their homeland than give the colonists the ability to become self-sustaining. Although what the wine would have tasted like after being shipped halfway round the world, I dare not think. Fortunately, the Chileans chose to ignore these orders.

Soon after Chile became independent

in the nineteenth century, the "nouveau riche" of Chile's mineral and guano (fertilizer made from bird droppings) industries began to plant vineyards. The fashion was to travel to France for cuttings and bring back a winemaker as well. One such winemaker convinced the government to set up a nursery to study the effect of the climate on plants, including vines. The Quinta Normal included in its stock some European *vinifera* vines. This was thanks to another Chilean, Silvestre Ochagavia Echazarreta, who travelled to Bordeaux in the 1850s and collected cuttings from some of the best vineyards. Goodness knows how he managed it; I can't see the owners being so obliging nowadays.

But, in one of those coincidences that make you believe in fate, at about the same time that he sailed back to Chile, another ship was leaving New York with some vines that were native to the Americas and were on their way to Kew Gardens in London, to be studied. Unfortunately,

these vines were later sent to France, and, not only were the plants transported, but also a pest, native to that species of vine, which rapidly spread through the vineyards of the world: *phylloxera*!

The idea of fate playing a part only comes to light when you realise that the country that Silvestre was taking his vines to is the only country in the world which has never been ravaged by this pest. Chile is protected by the Andes to the east, the Atacama Desert to the north, the Pacific Ocean to the west, and Antarctica to the south. So it was able to preserve its collection of vines in the vineyards and, of course, the Quinta Nacional. This continues today, thanks to the imposition of a strict plant quarantine system, and means that Chilean vines do not need to be grafted. All of a sudden, it seems like bird droppings—that is the guano industry— saved the wine industry as we know it today! And you can see the strong influence of Bordeaux vines on the Chilean wine industry.

The valley of the River Maipo shows just how desolate and forbidding some parts of Chile can be.

Strange as it may seem, Chile has a perfect climate for growing vines. Actually, it is a huge microclimate, or almost a macroclimate, which is caused by the Andes and those right-angled valleys. The sun heats up the air in these valleys, which rises to the top of the Andes, and then, because this air has to be replaced, since nature abhors a vacuum, the air of the ocean gets pulled in to fill up the void. Normally, this would be cooler than the air on the land because of its maritime influence, but it is chilled by being drawn over the Humboldt Current made up of ice-cold water from Antarctica. Think of it as air conditioning for the vineyards. Of course, the whole thing is reversed at night when the air on top of the Andes cools, becomes heavy, and rushes back down the valleys.

The result of this is that the sun expends its energy on the cold air, rather than heating the grapes, and so creates a longer, cooler, ripening period in the vineyards, allowing the flavours to develop in the grapes.

Chile's wealth, derived from its huge mineral reserves including copper, has ensured that it has the most stable economy in South America and this has allowed the winemakers of Chile to explore new regions and plant new vineyards. They are also quick to learn from others.

When the Chileans were stumped as to how New Zealand Sauvignon Blanc wines were so much crisper than theirs, they simply visited the regions and discovered how cool they were in comparison to their own Sauvignon Blanc areas. This, amongst other things, has driven the Chileans to discover newer, cooler areas further north and nearer the coast. They are also beginning to concentrate new plantings on the slopes of existing valleys rather than the easier, but more fertile valley floors.

CHILEAN WINE LAWS

These are not so strict as in other countries, since terms such as *reserva especial* appear to mean little, and producers may use various terms to denote their best wares. Having said that, if the words *especial*, *reserva*, or *gran reserva* are on the label, the wine must come from a single estate. Normally, these wines show that they have been made from selected grapes, with lower yields and that they will have spent more time in wood, which is most likely to be in the form of newer barrels than the normal wines of the estate.

If a wine is labelled with a varietal name, then it must contain at least 85 percent of that grape, and if an estate is named, then the wine must have been grown, produced and bottled there.

THE REGIONS

The wine regions of Chile have recently been classified into five distinct areas, of which three are the most important. They are Aconcagua, the Central Valley and the Southern Region. The others are mainly used for table grapes and the production of the local Pisco brandy, and I have it on good authority that this should be avoided in all cases.

Aconcagua Valley

Aconcagua Valley is north of the Central Valley, a huge plain that lies between the Andes and a low range of coastal hills. Running north–south for about 600 miles around the city of Santiago, the centre of the valley is where wine grapes are grown.

The Aconcagua Valley is hot, but manages to produce some world-class premium red wines from Cabernet Sauvignon at the Errazuriz estate, and especially from the Don Maximiano vineyard, which is named after the founding father of the company. Merlot and Carmenère are grown here as well, and the region is also proving an exciting experimental area for Syrah. In the sub-region of Casablanca, which is cooler and nearer the sea, you will also find some sublime Chardonnay and Sauvignon Blanc wines.

Few vineyards would have to put up with the rather prickly problems which this one in the Aconcagua Valley has to!

Central Valley/Valle Central

The Central Valley region itself is based around the best-known wine valley in Chile, the Maipo, which lies just south of Santiago and is where the modern, post-Spanish wine industry began. Its convenient location meant it could provide a workforce and water for irrigation as well as the land for the vines.

The nearby Rapel Valley used to sell a lot of its grapes to Maipo vineyards, but is now selling a lot of wines under its own name. Farther south are the Maule and Curicó Valleys, where cooler climates produce good Cabernet Sauvignon and Chardonnay wines, as well as Sauvignon Blanc and Merlot.

Elqui Valley

What do astronomers, James Bond and winemakers have in common? The Elqui Valley and the Atacama Desert. Here, the most northerly vineyards of Chile back onto the Atacama Desert, the driest and most cloud-free place on earth. So cloud-free that there are eight international observatories here, one of which was "blown up" by Daniel Craig in his second outing as Bond. Those same clear skies help ripen the fruit, but the cold night air rolling down from the desert and peaks of the Andes each night also preserves the acidity in the grapes. The result is wines with a clean, fresh taste.

Originally the grapes from this region were used to produce Pisco, Chile's grape spirit, but in the late 1990s the first wine vines were planted and wines from this region are already winning gold medals around the world. A number of producers grow grapes here, but only one, the pioneer in the valley, Vina Falernia, has a winery on site.

Limari Valley

A bit further to the south and nearer the coast lies the Limari valley. Here the vines benefit from the cooling Camanchaca fog in the morning, cooling sea breezes in the afternoon and a dry climate where what little rain does fall, falls in the winter when the vines are dormant. The result is a cool-climate region with a long, slow growing and ripening season especially suited to red wines such as Syrah, Carmenérè and Cabernet Sauvignon

Leyda Valley

Another new area situated near the coast, Leyda is getting cool-climate wine specialists hot under the collar. It's situated at the end of the San Antonia valley on the "wrong" (ie Pacific) side of the coastal ranges, and eyebrows were raised when vines were first planted here by the aptly named Vina Leyda wine company in 1998. They probably went past the hairline when an eight-kilometre water pipe had to be laid to irrigate the vines. But now everybody seems to want a piece of this wine heaven. Cooled by sea breezes chilled by the Humboldt current and with an annual rainfall of only 250mm, this area is being touted as Chile's equivalent of New Zealand's Marlborough region, with great potential for aromatic white wines and cool-climate loving grapes such as Pinot Noir. I have tasted some really exciting wines from

this area, especially Sauvignon Blancs, Chardonnays and Pinot Noirs.

Southern Region

The Southern Region is mainly given over to the Pias grape variety. Strangely, most of the wines made from the classic varieties of grape end up being exported and the locals have to make do with this fairly ordinary wine. But new plantings of Pinot Noir in the Bio Bio area are proving very interesting, as the cooler climate helps bring out the best in this cantankerous grape variety.

I can't leave Chile without talking about Carmenérè. Once one of the permitted varieties in Bordeaux, it was thought lost when it wasn't replanted after the *phylloxera* epidemic, until it was discovered in field blends of Merlot vines in Chile. Obviously, the vines had got mixed up in the past and been thought of as the same grape variety— well, almost. The Chileans realised there was something different about some of the Merlot vines, but could not work out what it was. They just realised that this "Merlot" was better, and, since the local Chilean dialect apparently doesn't have an adjective for better, they simply repeat the word. Hence Carmenère was known as "Merlot Merlot". I can just imagine the confusion in the vineyards.

Since it has been recognised as a distinct variety, the Chileans have been working at understanding Carmenère, and some interesting, savoury wines are now appearing on the market. But a lot is still mixed in blends of Chilean Merlot wine.

Argentina

There are a couple of reasons why we are only just discovering the wines of Argentina. The first is political: the wines were just beginning to become popular at the beginning of the 1980s, when the Falklands War began. But the second is that the Argentineans seem to have a huge capacity for drinking their own wines; at the last count, they were each knocking back some 90 litres of wine a year—that's 120 bottles!

Lying on the other side of the Andes, Argentina is a land of opposites when compared with Chile, and again, it is all due to these mountains. The huge rain shadow of the Andes means that areas, such as Mendoza, have not had any rainfall in ten years, but the Andes are also the area's saviour because the vast snow fields provide more than enough water to irrigate the vineyards. By planting on the mountains, the growers can also overcome the heat of the sun without a cooling breeze. The vineyards of Mendoza lie at an altitude of over 1,200 metres—that's a mile high! I always feel that the vines in this area probably need oxygen as much as irrigation.

Of course, it is not as simple as that. When rain does fall from the skies in Mendoza, it is in the form of hailstones the size of golf balls, which, in the summer, can smash entire vines and dent cars. To protect the vines, nets are suspended over them and, in extreme cases (as it is very expensive), planes are hired to "seed" the clouds and persuade the hail to drop elsewhere. As for the cars? I want to come back as a Mendoza panel beater in my next life.

The usual irrigation system used in Argentina is, in many cases, the older method of flood irrigation, as opposed

Oak barrels with lots of promise in the cellars of the Nieto y Senetier bodega in the Mendoza region in Argentina.

and is generally not thought of as a great grape. It is the main variety of Cahors and is a real minority grape in Bordeaux. In Argentina, however, the wine produced from it is filled with all sorts of dark, ripe fruits: damsons, spicy blackcurrants, and floral, violet notes leap out of the glass.

There is no real national classification system in Argentina, so look for the producer that you know and trust.

THE REGIONS
There are two main regions in Argentina that are producing good wine.

Mendoza
Mendoza, high up in the foothills of the Andes, is the main wine area of Argentina, with somewhere in the vicinity of two-thirds of the country's wines being produced in this area. The higher, cooler parts produce the more delicate white wines, whereas the lower, warmer Maipu area produces the beefy red wines, which are made for Argentinean beef and growing gauchos.

The best Torrontés wines come from north of Mendoza, in the Salta and La Rioja regions. Here the highest vineyards in the world, at around 3,000 metres, provide the cool climate and exposure to the sun to ripen the fruit slowly.

The South
In the south of the country, the Neuquén and Rio Negro areas are beginning to produce lighter wines, mainly white, from Chardonnay, Torrontés and Sauvignon Blanc varieties.

to drip. It can be really confusing to see a vineyard filled with water, so that it resembles a paddy field. After a few hours, however, the water has soaked in and all is back to normal. This system was originally built by the native Huarpes Indians before the arrival of the Spanish.

Argentina also differs from Chile in the type of vines that are grown here. A large influx of Italian immigrants has resulted in a number of Italian varieties, such as Sangiovese and Nebbiolo, being planted. But it is a Spanish white grape and a French red that are proving to be the stars of Argentinian wines. Torrontés is the second grape variety of Galicia, in northwestern Spain, after Albariño, and in Argentina it produces lightly aromatic, slightly spicy and muscatty wines. Malbec is the red grape of Argentina, which comes from the southwest of France

The Rest of South America

Many other countries in South America produce wines, most of which doesn't make it outside of the borders.

Brazil

Brazil actually makes more wine than Chile, and is second only to Argentina in the volume produced by South American countries. The humidity in this former Portuguese colony is the main problem when it comes to vine growing, encouraging, as it does, rot and moulds. Serra Gaucha, lying in the south of the country on the coast by the Uruguayan border, is the main region of production. Here the vineyards are situated high up in the hills to combat the worst of the heat. The Italian heritage of this region means that a lot of tank-method sparkling wine is produced, but the table wines show a more international outlook with Chardonnay and Cabernet Sauvignon joining the traditional Italian varieties.

Uruguay

Uruguay produces intense red wines, from another grape variety that comes from southwest France. The Tannat was introduced by Basques, who seem to have

One of the growing number of vineyards near Santana do Livramento, in Rio Grande do Sol in Brazil.

had a great influence in most of the wine countries of South America. In France, with the exception of the A.P. Madiran, the Tannat is sneered at, and used purely as a blending grape, but here it is given a free reign and shows what it is capable of.

Mexico

Mexico produces a surprisingly large amount of wine, but a lot of it is not very interesting, and a large amount of it goes into the production of brandy.

You will find some good red wines from Baja California, especially those made from the Petite Sirah, which is probably a disregarded southern French variety called the Durif, which was created by crossing a little known variety Peloursin with Syrah, though there are also some wines made from Cabernet Sauvignon, Merlot and Zinfandel. The extra ripening produces meaty, dense red wines with blackberry flavours.

There are a few vineyards in Peru, Ecuador, Colombia and Bolivia. Most of the production, however, ends up in the local Pisco brandy.

AUSTRALIA

Now setting standards as far as the world of wine is concerned, Australia's wine industry owes its origins primarily to a canny Scot by the name of James Busby.

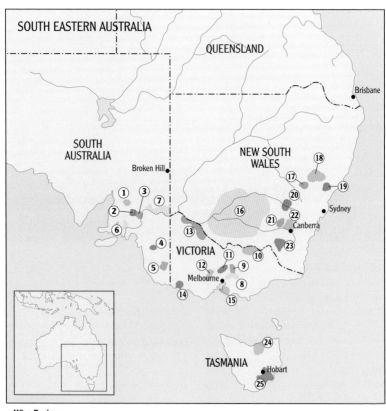

Wine Regions

1 Clare Valley	7 Riverland	13 Murray Darling	19 Lower Hunter Valley
2 Barossa Valley	8 Yarra Valley	14 Henty	20 Cowra
3 Eden Valley	9 Goulburn Valley	15 Mornington Peninsula	21 Hilltops
4 Padthaway	10 Rutherglen	16 Riverina	22 Canberra
5 Coonawarra	11 Macedon Ranges	17 Orange	23 Tumbarumba
6 McLaren Vale	12 Bendigo	18 Upper Hunter Valley	24 Pipers River
			25 Hobart

Château Tahbilk in the Goulburn Valley in the Victoria area is now a national monument as well as a thriving concern.

Imagine this: it is January 26, 1788, and you have just disembarked from the First Fleet, the first convoy of convicts sent from Great Britain to the new penal colony of Australia. Once everyone has landed, what do they do? Build a prison? Catch some food? No, they plant some vines! The first vines in Australia were planted in the grounds of the governor's residence, which is situated in what is now the Rocks area of Sydney.

Unfortunately, these vines were used to a moderate European climate and were soon suffering from rot and new diseases, which they had never been exposed to before, so they soon perished. Replacements were rushed out from the Cape of Good Hope, and the first crop was recorded in 1791. As the colony expanded to Parramatta, Tasmania, Hunter Valley, Victoria and the Swan Valley in Western Australia, commercial winemaking became an important industry.

One of the founding fathers of the wine industry was a Scot, James Busby, who had spent several months studying viticulture in France before emigrating in 1825. On his arrival in Sydney, he was granted some 2,000 acres, along the Hunter River, which he named Kirkton. He wrote a manual on the practices and procedures for growing vines and making wines in New South Wales, which contains a saying that could be the anthem of winemaking in Australia: *"The man who could sit under the shade of his own vine, with his wife and children about him, and the ripe clusters hanging within their reach, in such a climate as this, and not feel the highest enjoyment, is incapable of happiness, and does not know what the word means."*

He taught viticulture at a local school, but his most important contribution to the wine industry in Australia came in 1831, when he returned to Europe and collected some 680 vine cuttings to take to Australia. On his return, this collection was planted in the Sydney Botanical Gardens, and many of the important vine varieties of today's Australian industry can be traced back to it. Unfortunately, the collection was later broken up, with some of the vines being sent to Kirkton and others to the Botanical Gardens in Adelaide. But without the vision of James Busby (who wanted Australia to be "England's Antipodean Vineyard", a vision that is probably true today) the industry as we know it might not exist.

From early on, Australian wines were winning international awards. In 1873, a wine from Geelong in Victoria was awarded Best Wine in Show in Vienna, Austria. But this early success was short-lived, mainly because *phylloxera* arrived in Victoria in 1877 and soon devastated the vineyards. It did not reach all parts of this large continent, though, and some areas of Victoria and New South Wales, as well as the whole of South Australia are still *phylloxera*-free. As a result, South Australia dominated the Australian wine industry, as production in Victoria fell and new production areas came online. Even today around 50 percent of Australia's wine still comes from that state. The other reason for the short-lived, early success was the change to fortified wine production in northern Victoria.

The modern Australian wine industry owes its origins to the influx of European immigrants after the Second World War. They brought with them a wine culture that was based upon drinking table wines with meals. This, combined with the introduction of modern, temperature-controlled fermentation techniques, changed the styles of wines that could be, and needed to be, produced. The development of the wine cask, or "bag-in-the-box" wine, showed that Australia could produce inexpensive, everyday drinking wine, better than everyone else.

These original wines were regional, or even interregional blends, because the Australian winemaker did not care about, or believe in, the French concept of *terroir*. They believed that the grape is much more a representation of the climate rather than the soil it is grown in. The most popular *appellation* in Australia, for example, is Southeastern Australia, a huge area that covers all of New South Wales, Victoria and South Australia! Having said that, they are coming around to the idea, especially as they look for cool-climate sites to produce lighter and more elegant wines, that location, if not soil, is important, and smaller areas are gaining recognition.

The success story of Australian wine was built on the premise of supplying wines that the consumer wanted, at a reasonable price. This fantastic idea—making wines that people actually wanted to drink, at a price they could afford—worked well for them for a number of years, with the big wine-producing companies merging to become even bigger or getting taken over by bigger companies themselves.

Recently, though, they have struggled to keep the price of their wines down. The Australian economy has not been as badly hit as some by the recession and the result is that the Australian dollar has kept a lot of its value. Even very successful brands such as Yellow Tail have been hit by a big drop in export sales as their wines become relatively expensive in a price-driven market. This has led to a division in the wines produced in Australia at the moment. To my mind they are producing some of the best AND worst wines they ever have.

The big companies are now starting to break up, with Foster's for example devolving all their wine brands into a new company called Treasury Wine Estates, and Constellation Brands (once the largest wine company in the world) selling its Australian and some USA and South African brands to Accolade Wines and moving out of the European market altogether. However, even these smaller, but still sizeable, producers are driven to cut production costs to meet price targets on some of their brands. On the other hand smaller, independent and more boutique family producers are differentiating themselves in the marketplace by charging more but concentrating on the product rather than the price.

Wine Australia, the government agency set up to support Australian wine exports, has recognised this and begun to change the emphasis of its marketing, promoting the regional diversity of the wines as opposed to the bulk Southeastern Australia approach of the past. So perhaps again we shall see Australia as a land of wine opportunity rather than a source of supermarket specials.

AUSTRALIAN WINE LAWS

There is an *appellation* system of sorts in place, but it is more a business arrangement to allow Australia to sell more wine in the European Union than a serious attempt to categorise wines. The general *appellation*, and the equivalent (though perhaps of better quality) of France's *Vin de France*, is Produce of Australia. Southeastern Australia is as described above, and the State of Origin definition divides and subdivides the wine states into zones, regions and subregions.

Also included in this arrangement was an agreement to phase out the use of "generic" European wine names on Australian wines, so nowadays the terms Burgundy, Champagne, Port and Sherry, for example, have been dropped.

There are a few vineyards in the hot areas of Queensland and the Northern Territory, but the prize for Australian wine folly must go to the vineyard in Alice Springs, right in the centre of the continent. Irrigation keeps the vines alive in this desert, and the vines have to be picked very early, like New Year's Day, otherwise they overripen.

New South Wales

Hunter Valley

This is where it all began, as it was really the planting of the Hunter Valley in the 1820s which developed the wine industry in the area. Hunter Valley is not the best place to plant vines. It has a subtropical climate, which really brings the rain at the wrong time of the growing season, and, having been caught in one of those short, sharp storms, I wonder how the vines survive. The only positive aspect of such

a downpour—I couldn't see out of the car to drive—was that the heat was such that the grapes were dry soon afterward.

A cool climate it ain't, and this is reflected in the styles of wines. You very rarely find Pinot Noir or Riesling here. No, this is the land of fat Chardonnay, big Cabernet Sauvignon, sweaty, leathery Shiraz, and, most exciting of all, oily Sémillon.

This unoaked, dry wine is made only by a few of the growers, and is not really commercially viable, but it is as unlike any other Sémillon produced today as it could be. As it ages, it turns into a toasty, honey monster of a wine, which annoyingly tastes as if it has spent its entire life in wood. I don't know how they do it, but long may they do so.

Cowra and Orange

These two small areas can be found up in the hills of the Great Dividing Range. Orange, especially, is finding a name for itself as a cool-climate area. It has spring frosts, and even suffers from vintage variation, because it can be difficult to ripen the fruit some years. It sounds so European! The area is producing some exciting Chardonnay and Cabernet Sauvignon wines, with definite cool-climate flavours, if in small quantities.

Mudgee

Now producing some rather interesting red wines from Cabernet Sauvignon and Shiraz grapes, the warmer, drier climate of Mudgee meant that the wines produced here used to be blended into Hunter Valley wines to improve them, if the harvest had been too wet. Now, they are sold under their own name.

Riverina

Riverina is the bulk wine-producing area of New South Wales. Or it used to be. Nowadays, some winemakers are reducing the yields, by turning down the irrigation a bit, to produce better-quality wines. The original name of the area was the catchy Murrumbidgee Irrigation Area —you can see why they changed it—but there are some serious wines produced here, including De Bortoli's *botrytised* Sémillon, Noble One, which, year in and year out, gives the wines of Sauternes and Barsac a run for their money.

Canberra

Technically, this is the wine area of the Australian Capital Territory, but since land cannot be bought inside, it is actually outside the borders. Unfortunately, the area suffers from frosts because it is so far inland, but winemakers are producing high quality cool-climate wines from a range of red and white varieties such as Riesling and Syrah that are worth hunting out.

The Tyrrell's Vineyard in the Hunter Valley in New South Wales where Murray Tyrrell has set standards for Pinot Noir.

Hilltops

Situated half-way between Sydney and Canberra, this high-altitude area in the Murray-Darling Basin, whose vineyards are situated between 450 and 600 metres above sea level, is fast gaining a reputation for premium red wines made from the Cabernet and Shiraz grape varieties. First planted by Croatian gold miners in the 1860s the region failed to attract attention until new investment in the 1970s. The altitude results in a high diurnal temperature between midday and midnight. This change in temperature preserves the acidity and freshness in the grapes and wine. One of the vineyards in this area has another claim to fame: not content to plant grape varieties that originate in France, they have managed to attract a young French winemaker as well.

Victoria

Once the largest wine-producing state in Australia, due in no small part to the gold rush of the 1850s, Victoria lost its status when *phylloxera* devastated the vineyards. In fact, the government of the day ordered all the vineyards of Geelong and Bendigo to be uprooted and burned. Soon there were only vines in the northeastern corner of Victoria, which were concentrating on fortified wine production, and some small plantings in the Goulburn Valley, just north of Melbourne. Included in these plantings was the vineyard of Château Tahbilk, the winery of which is now a national monument, and, because of the sandy soil, is still *phylloxera*-free. The result of this is that it has some of Australia's oldest vines, at around 150 years old. The small numbers of these remaining vines produce low yields of intensely

Yarra Valley

This area, to the east of Melbourne, is a relatively cool-climate area, which produces delicious Pinot Noir and Chardonnay wines, as well as top-quality sparkling wines, using the traditional method. Moët & Chandon have an outpost of their empire here, in the form of Domaine Chandon, a high-tech winery producing great sparkling wines. At the other end of the spectrum, the valley's warmer locations generate some deeply flavoured Cabernet Sauvignon.

Mornington Peninsula

To the south of Melbourne lies the Mornington Peninsula, which is full of boutique wineries. The maritime-influenced climate is cool, but frost-free. Look out for the Pinot Noirs from here.

Glenrowan, Rutherglen and Milawa

North of the Goulburn Valley are the warmer areas of Glenrowan—where the infamous bank robber, Ned Kelly, was captured—Rutherglen and Milawa, where some of the finest fortified wines of Australia are produced. Made from Muscat and Muscadelle grapes, these wines, which used to be labelled as Port, have intense butterscotch flavours, and are made from grapes that have been allowed to dry and shrivel into raisins on the vine.

These areas also produce strong Shiraz wines, but the best wines come from vines planted up in the cooler hillsides, such as the King Valley and Whitlands, where Brown Brothers produce some premium Chardonnay and minty Cabernet Sauvignon wines.

The Yarra Valley produces both good whites and reds from Pinor Noir, Chardonnay and Cabernet Sauvignon.

flavoured wines. Tahbilk also produces a hefty-flavoured, peach-dominated Marsanne wine along with its well-known neighbour, Michelton.

A smaller area to the north of Melbourne is the Macedon ranges. This area produces light and elegant wines from a range of small, boutique wineries.

Tasmania

This is probably the coolest wine-producing area in Australia. Piper's Brook was selected by Dr Andrew Pirie for his vineyard, because research proved that the sunlight levels and temperature were very similar to those found in Burgundy. As you would expect then, the best wines are made from Pinot Noir and Chardonnay. The problem is that, in cooler years, it can be hard to ripen the grapes. To use these underripe grapes, Tasmania has developed an excellent sparkling wine industry, with help, originally, from the Roederer Champagne house; some large producers of sparkling wines on the mainland source grapes from here to supplement their own.

Over the years, winemakers have found some sun traps on the island—the Tamar Valley near Launceston is one example—where Merlot and Cabernet Sauvignon vines can also ripen. Freycinet, which lies on the east coast, south of Bicheno, is also warm, and has enough shelter to ripen grapes, as do the warm Coal and Derwent valleys north of the state capital, Hobart, and they produce some intense Pinot Noir and Cabernet Sauvignon wines in sheltered corners, especially from the Moorila Estate and Domaine A vineyards.

Most of the production is from boutique wineries, with Chardonnay,

seen today in the names of some of the producers: Peter Lehmann is a fifth-generation Barossan, for example, but the names of Henschke, Seppelt and Gramp also show the families' origins.

A few years ago, the Barossa Valley was so out of fashion, it was believed that the vineyards would soon vanish. The Shiraz grapes were being dried for English muffins because no one would buy the wine. The same went for the German-influenced white wine made from the Riesling grape. Then, suddenly, people began to discover the intense Shiraz wines made from forty- and fifty-year-old vines, and realised that the cooler valleys in the hills of the Barossa Valley, especially Eden Valley, could produce stunning Riesling wines and cool-climate Pinot Noir and Chardonnay wines.

It was not only the original Silesians who built wineries, though. English immigrants also settled in the Barossa Valley. Names such as Thomas Hardy and Doctor Penfold are still carried on the labels of the companies that they set up, while the Smith family built the Yalumba Company, which is now the largest family-owned winery in the country.

Riesling and Sauvignon Blanc wines among their output.

South Australia

The vineyards for this region are all crammed into the southern corner of the state. The region is home to the largest wine companies in Australia, as well as numerous medium and boutique wineries.

Barossa Valley

One of the largest production areas in the country, the Barossa Valley was settled in the late 1800s by Silesian immigrants, who were escaping religious persecution in Germany. These origins can still be

Clare Valley

Further to the north is the Clare Valley, which was discovered by an explorer called John Horrocks, who gave some of the first vines to George Hawker to plant. Unfortunately, John did not live to see the beginnings of the Clare Valley wine industry, as he was shot soon afterward… by his camel! Together with the nearby Watervale area, the Clare Valley is now home to a variety of wine styles. These vary from intense reds, based on the Rhône Valley grapes of Shiraz (Syrah) and Grenache, to light, dry Rieslings (there were some German immigrants in this area, as well as in the Barossa Valley, although most of the early immigrants here were Irish), Sémillons and Chardonnays.

Southern Vales

To the south and east of the state capital, Adelaide, lie the Southern Vales. This area includes the McLaren Vale and Adelaide Hills. The McLaren Vale is cooled by coastal breezes, whereas the Adelaide Hills have the altitude to cool the vineyards down.

The entire area produces some cool-climate wines: Chardonnay and Sauvignon Blanc in the Adelaide Hills, and Rhône reds and whites in the McLaren Vale, although Chardonnay and Cabernet Sauvignon also do well, when in the right location. The wineries of Petaluma, d'Arenburg and Wirra Wirra are all worth looking out for.

This area, unsurprisingly, contains the first vineyard planted in South Australia. John Reynella planted Château Reynella in 1838, and one of his workers was Tom Hardy, who soon planted his own vineyard. The BRL Hardy company, part of Accolade wines, is still based at Château Reynella.

It is also in these southern suburbs of Adelaide that the house and original vineyard, planted in 1844, of a young English doctor, Christopher Rawson

Château Reynella was the first vineyard to be planted in South Australia and it is now the HQ of Accolade wines.

Penfold, is situated. Grange Cottage is situated on the Magill Estate, which, even then, was recognised as a quality piece of prime land. The doctor planted vines because he recognised the healthy benefits of wine. However, he was so busy, that his wife, Mary, soon took over the winemaking operations. The first wines produced were fortified ones, and this is reflected in the name of Penfold's modern fortified wine, Magill. But the estate also gave its name to Australia's most famous wine.

Grange, originally Grange Hermitage, is a wine inspired by the visit of Penfold's then chief winemaker, Max Schubert, to Bordeaux, in 1951. Schubert had seen the Bordeaux winemakers use small French oak barrels to produce powerful wines, capable of long-term ageing, but which came from much-reduced yields when compared to the Australian norm of that time. He believed that a similar style of table wine could be produced in South Australia.

When he returned to the Penfold's vineyards, he found some new American oak barrels, which were cheaper than those from France, but he had great problems sourcing quality Cabernet Sauvignon. In the end, relying on Antipodean inventiveness, he used Shiraz—there was more of it, although it was used then purely to make a wine for fortifying. The grapes were sourced from vineyards all over South Australia, including the Grange vineyard, and when the first vintage was tasted, the winery's owners told him to forget it. They were

in the business of making fortified wines and this did not fit in.

Max quietly ignored them and persevered with small batches. After five or so years, the wines changed completely as they matured in the bottle. At the same time the market began to look for table wines. Once the early vintages that Max had hidden around the winery were tested again, an Australian classic was born.

Coonawarra

This is probably Australia's most distinctive piece of *terroir*. Growers have recently gone to court to define the boundaries of the area, much in the manner of a French *appellation*. What is

it that makes this area unique? The soil. A cigar-shaped patch of flat soil, about 21 by 2 kilometres, lying to the southeast of Adelaide.

What made it so interesting was the colour; it was bright red—Terra Rossa. Eighteen inches below this iron-rich soil is a ridge of limestone, which makes for perfect drainage, leading to a shallow water table, meaning that there is a constant supply of pure water.

It was in 1861 that John Riddoch arrived and set up the Penola Fruit Company to plant vines. Shiraz and Cabernet Sauvignon wines did especially well, and, in fact, Coonawarra Cabernet Sauvignon is now recognised as a world-class wine.

Western Australia

A long way from anywhere, and very hot, Western Australia is well and truly cut off from the vineyards on the other side of this great continent. It meant that settlers here had to make their own wines.

Swan Valley

The location of these vineyards was chosen for reasons of convenience, rather than because anyone took the time to search for what we would now consider to be the best conditions for grape production. In other words, they planted around the corner from the first settlements in the Swan Valley.

With all the heat, sweet wine was the forte of this area, but a trial batch of dry Chenin Blanc wine surprised local producers with its quality, and placed Western Australia's name on the country's wine map. The Houghton Wine Company developed this dry, white wine, turned it into a standard-bearer and labelled it

Houghton's White Burgundy, even though the grapes in the blend had never seen Burgundy in their life. The end of generic labelling, however, has meant that the wine is now called HWB.

Margaret River

Nowadays, the best wines come from the much cooler southern coastal areas. Margaret River, first planted in 1966/67, is cooled by breezes off the Indian Ocean. The pioneers here were Dr. Tom Cullity, with his Vasse Felix estate, and Diana and Kevin Cullen on their own estate. Even though this region and the nearby Great Southern Region only produce three percent of Australia's grapes, they account for over 20 percent of Australia's premium wine market.

The region produces wines that are very similar in style to Bordeaux. Well, it is on the coast, generally has the same temperature as the French region and an

The Leeuwin Estate in the Margaret River region which produces some of the best wines in Western Australia.

overall climate similar to a dry Bordeaux vintage. So, as you would expect, Cabernet Sauvignon and Merlot do very well here, producing minty wines with eucalyptus notes. Shiraz from this area can also be rather good, but sometimes the climate is a little too cool to bring out the best in this variety. Dry white wines made from the Sauvignon Blanc and Sémillon varieties also do well here— what did I say about Bordeaux?

Great Southern Region

This area was first set out when the Mount Barker area was planted in the late 1960s, and the vineyards slowly expanded. Don't be fooled by the size of the area. The vineyards are, if not few and far between, spread out a lot. And that sums up the wines here. The industry is based on lots of small, top-quality, boutique wineries, so a lot of the wines do not get out of the state, let alone the country.

Look out for cool-climate white wines from this region—the Frankland river area produces award-winning Riesling and Sauvignon Blanc wines in addition to cool Cabernet Sauvignon and Shiraz wines. However, like their neighbours in Margaret River, they have to be careful about the clones of Shiraz they plant and make sure that they are early-ripening.

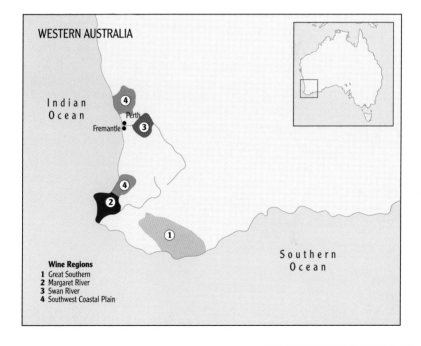

WESTERN AUSTRALIA

Indian Ocean

Perth

Fremantle

Southern Ocean

Wine Regions
1 Great Southern
2 Margaret River
3 Swan River
4 Southwest Coastal Plain

NEW ZEALAND

From small beginnings via faltering steps, New Zealand's

wine industry is now gathering acclaim around the world.

The amazing thing about New Zealand wine is that it is made in the first place. In 1919, New Zealanders almost voted for prohibition, and, until the late 1960s, you could not buy wine in a restaurant. Wineries could not sell wine in amounts less than 25 litres, and it was 1990 before you could buy wine in a supermarket.

In addition, during an attempt to revive the industry in the 1960s, a consultant was brought in for some

NEW ZEALAND

Wine Regions
1 Northland
2 Bay of Plenty/Waikato
3 Auckland
4 Gisborne
5 Hawkes Bay
6 Wellington
7 Nelson
8 Marlborough
9 Canterbury
10 Otago

Indian
Ocean

Pacific
Ocean

Auckland

Wellington

Christchurch

The rolling vineyards of Hawkes Bay on the east coast of the North Island are among the best in New Zealand.

expert advice. Unfortunately, the consultant came from Germany and was a champion of the crossings being developed there. His recommendation? Müller-Thurgau!

This was never going to get New Zealand wines a place on the international stage. Fortunately, some enterprising winemakers also planted Sauvignon Blanc, Chardonnay and Pinot Noir vines, and it was the pungent, Sauvignon Blanc wines that first took the world by storm.

New Zealand has a cool, maritime climate, but it also has a high level of sunshine. Those features, combined with very old, poor soils, produce the perfect conditions for growing grapes. The cool winds mean that the grapes can hang longer on the vine, until they are fully ripened, without losing acidity.

The first vines were planted by James Busby - yes, the same one who set up the Australian industry, in 1833. He had been sent to New Zealand as the first British

resident, and was responsible for signing the Treaty of Waitangi with fifty Maori chiefs, which meant that the islands became a British colony.

North Island

This is where vines were first planted in New Zealand, and it is still where most of the wineries are located. Gisbourne and Hawkes Bay, on the east coast, produce good Chardonnay, and are beginning to get a name for red wines from the Pinot Noir, and, in the right locations, Cabernet Sauvignon, Merlot and Syrah.

The area around Auckland has a lot of wineries, but most of the fruit is now shipped in from other areas, while Martinborough uses its cool climate to produce some excellent Pinot Noir wines, which have some of the silkiness and elegance that you expect to find in Burgundy.

South Island

A relatively new wine-producing area, South Island is dominated by the Marlborough region in the northeast corner. In 1970, there was not a single vine planted in this area, just lots of sheep. But then, in 1973, the Montana Wines, now called Brancott Estate after this vineyard, invested here because Hawkes Bay was just too expensive. It was a gamble, but, wow, has it paid off!

Some of the 400 acres that they bought, they planted with Sauvignon Blanc. Hindsight being twenty-twenty, this was an inspired decision. The first vintage produced lean, zippy, gooseberry and asparagus fruit, quite unlike anything produced in the Loire Valley. A very rare thing had happened: a new wine style had been born. Nowadays, Marlborough is nowhere near as cheap as it was, but it is recognised on the world stage as a quality Sauvignon Blanc wine producer and it is now a sheep-free zone. New plantings of Riesling and Pinot Gris are also proving interesting, but it is highly unlikely that they will replace the Sauvignon Blanc.

The main factor in the success of Marlborough is the sheltering effect of the mountain range behind it, which keeps the rain away, leaving sunshine and cool breezes to do their magic. Other areas on the South Island include Nelson, Canterbury and Waipara. These regions are producing increasing amounts of Chardonnay, Sauvignon Blanc and Pinot Noir. Central Otago in the very south is cooler and drier and is now the home of some world class Pinot Noir wines.

Net-covered vines sit in a Marlborough vineyard—one of the most successful wine ventures in recent years.

SOUTH AFRICA

Almost an "old" New World country now in terms of

winemaking, South Africa has much to offer the wine lover.

South Africa is unique, in that it can point to a specific date for the birth of its wine industry. The original Dutch governor, Jan van Riebeeck, first planted grapes in 1654. Like most of the New World settlers, he was looking to find a control for scurvy. On 2 February 1659, he was able to record in his diary, "Today, God be praised, wine was pressed for the first time from Cape grapes." Soon afterwards, another governor, Simon van der Stel, planted Muscat vines on his Constantia estate, near Table Mountain, in an area that was to be named after him.

Constantia wines from Stellenbosch were just what the European doctor called for. They were rich and delicious, and were soon recognised as one of the world's great wines. Later, French

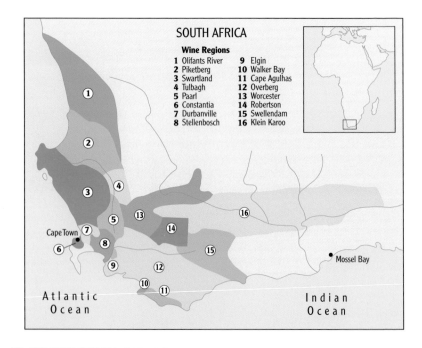

SOUTH AFRICA

Wine Regions

1 Olifants River	9 Elgin
2 Piketberg	10 Walker Bay
3 Swartland	11 Cape Agulhas
4 Tulbagh	12 Overberg
5 Paarl	13 Worcester
6 Constantia	14 Robertson
7 Durbanville	15 Swellendam
8 Stellenbosch	16 Klein Karoo

Cape Town

Mossel Bay

Atlantic Ocean

Indian Ocean

Huguenot refugees came and planted vines on a more commercial basis, allowing the wines to be traded through the use of passing ships on their way to the Dutch East Indies and Europe.

A view over the Klein Constantia estate to False Bay in the Cape Province in South Africa.

But 1886 saw the arrival of *phylloxera*, with the normal crisis that ensued. Once grafted vines arrived in the Cape, a huge replanting scheme was instigated. The predictable result of this was a glut in production, a problem that was not rectified until the arrival of the *Kooperatiewe Wynboures Vereniging* (*KWV*), or Cape Winegrowers Co-operative, in 1918. The *KWV* soon became the industry in South Africa: it set prices for grapes, controlled the vines, and their clones, that could be planted, became the official control board for the business and marketed the country's wine to the rest of the world, in addition to being a large producer in its own right.

To be honest, the *KWV* did the job that it was set up to do. A market was found for all the grapes that previously had been thrown away—a lot went into the production of brandy—but the way

that it approached the problem would eventually cause as many problems as it solved. Rather than reduce quantity and improve quality, it found a market for its wines, and stopped any expansion of vineyards and planting of new varieties.

This stranglehold continued as the market for South African wine was reduced by the imposition of anti-apartheid embargoes, leading to its withdrawal from the international scene. But this coincided with the largest, most radical shake-up in the history of winemaking: the arrival of Australian wines and the modern techniques that we take for granted today. The KWV is now a private company and has a heavily reduced influence on the South African wine industry.

When apartheid came to an end, the South Africans did not really know how much the wine world had moved on. They soon learned, but it is only now that the fruits of that learning curve are coming

Vineyards in the wine ward of Franschoek in the district of Paarl, the home of the K.W.V.

to the fore. Clones of classic vine varieties were hard, if not impossible, to come by. Growers insisted on picking red grapes too early, when they were underripe, giving a green, leafy note to the wines, and winemakers tell me that this is still the hardest change to implement.

The tendency has been to pick early, because the grapes can become overripe almost overnight and lose a high proportion of their acidity, so the growers play it safe and pick "green". This was especially so with South Africa's own grape variety, Pinotage. Pinotage is a crossing that was developed in South Africa in 1925, by Professor Al Perold at Stellenbosch University. This crossing of Pinot Noir and Cinsault, if picked too early, can have leafy, raspberry notes, with volatile acidity, but when left on the vine, develops wonderfully intense mulberry and dark, smoky fruit flavours.

SOUTH AFRICAN WINE LAWS

South African wines were first classified in 1973, and again in 1993. The vineyards of South Africa are divided into regions, districts and wards, and the origin is guaranteed by the addition of a Wine of Origin Seal that is placed on the neck of the bottle. Any wine naming a single grape variety must contain at least 75 percent of that variety (85 percent, if the wine is exported), and the same percentage of wine from a vintage, if the vintage is named on the label. If an estate is named, then all of the wine must come from there.

WINE REGIONS

Most of South Africa's wine regions are clustered around the southern tip of the country. Here, the growers can take advantage of the cooling sea breezes, which are affected by the ice-cold, Benguela current that comes up from Antarctica, creating the cool climate essential for wine production.

Other, hotter regions rely on irrigation to make bulk wines—that is, wines for fortification or for distillation into brandy.

The vineyards of Vriesenhof lie in the foothills of the Helderberg, just inside the area of Stellenbosch.

Stellenbosch

Stellenbosch is the area for South African red wines, and while it is not that cool there, it has a long mountain range, which can be used to plant the vines at altitude, to find cooler, moister climates. Helderberg and Simonsberg are the two wards inside Stellenbosch.

Durbanville

Lying next to Stellenbosch, Durbanville is now recognised as a quality production area, especially of Sauvignon Blanc and Cabernet Sauvignon. The best Cabernet

Sauvignon wines come from an area of shale in the Malmesbury area.

Paarl

Inland, behind Stellenbosch, is the region of Paarl. This is, as you would think, a warmer region, but it still makes some surprising Sauvignon Blanc and Chardonnay wines, in addition to the reds that you would expect to find. The ward of Franschhoek, which is the area where the French Huguenots settled after being thrown out of France, is an especially good area.

Constantia

This area lies on the other side of Stellenbosch, in the "hook" of land around Cape Town. This is where the Constantia estate was first planted, and one of the new estates in the area, Klein Constantia, has begun producing a dessert wine as a homage to the wine that made the area famous. The area is also well-known for the Dutch-influenced architecture that abounds in the wineries of the region.

Worcester and Robertson

The Worcester and Robertson regions lie much further inland, and rely on massive irrigation schemes to produce bulk wines and wines for distillation. Some areas of Robertson are beginning to be recognised as having potential for Chardonnay and Sauvignon Blanc, grown on a lime-stone soil.

Overberg

Two new areas that are really showing great potential are the neighbours of Elgin and Walker Bay, lying around the town of Hermanus in the southerly region of Overberg. For more information about these cool areas and their production of Pinot Noir, Pinotage, Chardonnay and Sauvignon Blanc wines see page 302.

Swartland

A fairly large area on the west coast of South Africa, this region is centred around the towns of Darling, Riebeek and Malmesbury. There is little natural rainfall here, so the area relies on irrigation, and it produces wine, mainly from the Chenin Blanc grape, as well as some Sauvignon Blanc and Pinotage.

Tulbaugh

What goes against the grain here is that this rather warm region has seen a partnership between the Champagne house of Mumm and winemaker Nicky Krone at the Twee Jongegezellen estate that has produced a brut sparkling wine, made in the traditional method, from Chardonnay and Pinot Noir grapes. In order to achieve the correct ripeness in the grapes, they are harvested at night.

Wellington

This relatively hot region, only 45 minutes from Cape Town, used to be the centre of South Africa's fortified wine production. As the demand for these wines has declined, however, the winemakers have turned their hands to brandy and table wine production. Big, bold Cabernet Sauvignon-based wines from this area are beginning to get an international following,

The cellars of the Twee Jongegezellen estate owned jointly by Mumm and Nicky Krone in the region of Tulbaugh.

Post-Apartheid

Soon after South Africa re-entered the world of wine after years in the apartheid "wilderness", producers realised that modern wines differed completely from the styles of wine they were producing. Knowing that they had a lot of catching up to do, they looked at the modern, clean, fruit-driven styles being produced in New Zealand and Chile and tried to work out how they could produce similar wines.

They soon realised that to produce modern white wines, especially, they needed cooler vineyards and so looked further south than they had previously thought it possible to grow vines. They found that the south coast of the country was cooled by breezes coming off the Bengula current which begins in the South Atlantic and runs along the South African coast.

Elgin

One of the first of the new areas to be developed was Elgin. As the South African economy contracted, many nationalised industries began to suffer. One of these was the Forestry Commission, and in Elgin they helped their ex-workers set up a fruit-growing co-operative with the assistance of a group of mentor growers. The quality of the fruits produced by the Thandi (pronounced Tandy) Co-op began to attract the attention of winemaker Paul Cluver. Under his mentorship, vines were planted and the first wines produced in the late 1990s. The results were impressive. Thandi soon became the first Fairtrade wine brand in the world and other growers moved into the region.

One winemaker I spoke to told me that he'd purchased land in Elgin after tasting fruit grown there by his neighbour, "and since he was a terrible grower, I knew that I could do better".

The Thandi company has gone from strength to strength and in 2009 moved away from its supported assistance status to become an independent company. It is one of the wine stars among the government's BEE or Black Empowerment Enterprises. These enterprises range across all industries and are designed to encourage the native workforce to become involved in the running of the companies they work for. We now see more winemakers and owners coming from the native population. A BEE company set up by Charles Back's Fairview company called Fair Valley employed Awie Adolf as one of the first black winemakers and all of the profits from the company are invested in the local community.

Awie Adolf, winemaker at the Fair Valley wine company.

Walker Bay

Right down on the south coast is the district of Walker Bay. Getting direct breezes off the sea, this area is beginning to make a name for itself producing cool and crisp Sauvignon Blanc as well as Pinot Noir wines.

Within the Walker Bay region is the picturesque district of Hermanus. Here the cool waters not only prevent frost but also attract large numbers of Southern Right whales into the bay during the breeding season. The road from Hermanus leads to the romantically named Hemel-en-Aarde or Heaven on Earth valley. Here the cool breezes lengthen the growing season, allowing more time for the flavours to develop in the grapes. Look out for world-class Pinot Noir and Chardonnay wines.

Cape Agulhas

Not far from Hemel-en-Aarde we finally we come to the newest and most southerly wine region in South Africa, Cape Agulhas. Here two oceans, the Atlantic and the Indian, meet and the coastline is dotted with shipwrecks to demonstrate how treacherous the waters are. Dangerous they may be, as shown by the picturesque red-and-white-striped lighthouse, but this is the coolest wine region in South Africa. I once tasted a Shiraz wine made there and it was wonderfully fragrant and elegantly smoky. Already winning awards, this definitely is a region to look out for.

AUSTRIA

Once the centre of the Austro-Hungarian Empire, Austria
has long been producing quality wines with a significant
European influence and a touch all of its own.

The main influence on the wine
styles of Austria comes from the
country's nearby German neighbours,
whose own wine laws have helped shape
Austria's wine legislation. But one must
look east, to the countries Slovenia
and Hungary, to see the origins of the
spicy flavours found in the glasses of
Austrian wine.

AUSTRIAN WINE LAWS

Germanic in origin, the classification of
Austrian wines is sufficiently different
to make you truly frustrated. There are
four regions or zones: Niederösterreich is
the largest, and covers the north of the
country; Burgenland runs down the border
with Hungary; Styria lies toward the south;
and, finally, Wien, or Vienna.

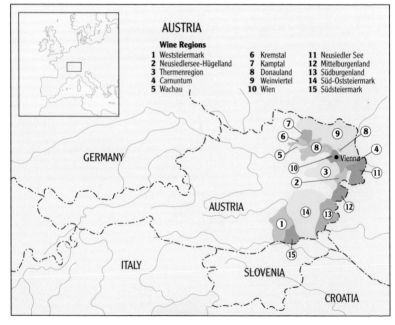

AUSTRIA

Wine Regions

1	Weststeiermark	6	Kremstal	11	Neusiedler See
2	Neusiedlersee-Hügelland	7	Kamptal	12	Mittelburgenland
3	Thermenregion	8	Donauland	13	Südburgenland
4	Carnuntum	9	Weinviertel	14	Süd-Oststeiermark
5	Wachau	10	Wien	15	Südsteiermark

Captivated by the breathtaking scenery of Austria's mountains, many people are unaware of the country's wine.

Tafelwein is the basic level of wine, followed by *Landwein*, which is hardly ever seen but is almost the equivalent of *I.G.P.* Then comes *Qualitätswein*, which includes *Kabinett* (a dry style). *Prädikatswein* is the equivalent of the German *Prädikat* wine level with a few subcategories:

• *Spätlese*
• *Auslese*
• *Beerenauslese*
• *Ausbruch*, which was originally made by adding fresh grape must to the fermenting juice of botrytis-affected grapes. This method was developed, and is still followed, in Hungary, for the production of Tokay Aszú. Nowadays, Austrian wine law says that this wine must be made from overripe and/or *botrytised* grapes.

• *Trockenbeerenauslese*
• *Eiswein*
• *Strohwein*, or straw wine, which is made from grapes which have been dried on straw mats for three months. This concentrates the sugars, flavours and acids in the grapes.
• *Districtus Austriae Controllatus (D.A.C.)*. Latin for 'Controlled District of Austria', this new wine category is a PGI which recognises the concept of

terroir and specifies specific varieties for qualifying regions. At the moment there are eight D.A.C. regions in Austria.

One of the biggest changes in Austrian wine production came about as a result of a disaster that could have wiped out the whole industry. In 1985, it was found that some unscrupulous producers had artificially sweetened their wines by adding diethylene glycol. Despite urban myths that this had killed people, the substance is harmless, although illegal.

The effect of this is that the new wine laws are some of the most exacting in the world, and have meant a huge increase in demand in Austria for dry wines.

The climate in Austria is much more continental and warm—verging on hot—than it is in Germany. This is reflected in the different grape varieties that can ripen here. Cabernet Sauvignon, Chardonnay and Sauvignon Blanc all make an appearance here, but the local star is Grüner Veltliner, which produces light,

steely Rieslings, while Thermenregion, as its name suggests, is a hot region, full of spa towns. It was a centre of sweet and semi-sweet wines until the change of fashion post-1985.

Burgenland

Burgenland has four regions, two of which are heavily influenced by the climatic effect of the Neusiedlersee. This large lake cools these regions down and produces early morning mists, which encourage the growth of *botrytis cinerea*. The two zones, called Neusiedlersee and Neusiedlersee-Hügelland, lie on opposite sides of the lake. Most years, noble rot wines can be made, and they still have an international reputation, since it was the cheaper wines that were adulterated in the wine scandal. The village of Rust, near the Hungarian border, specialises in *Ausbruch* wines, while elsewhere in Burgenland you can find some intense red and white wines.

Styria

Lying to the south of the country, Styria produces lean-and-mean dry white and rosé wines that are perfectly suited to the modern palate. It is subdivided into three zones: Südsteiermark, Weststeiermark and Süd-Oststeiermark.

Wien (Vienna)

Finally, Wien comprises the vineyards around Vienna. Most of the wine produced here is drunk locally in little wine inns, or *Buschenschenke*, of an evening along with a serving of schnitzel.

peppery wines, and the best examples of it can withstand some ageing.

Niederösterreich

Translated as "Lower Austria", Niederösterreich is subdivided into seven regions, the largest of which is the Wienviertel, but the best of which are Kamptal and Kremstal, which make good Grüner Veltliner wines. The Wachau lies on slopes overlooking Europe's other important river, the Danube, producing

THE REST OF THE WORLD

Included here are those countries that make wine, whose
reputations may be that of a rising star, or in some cases of a
falling one. They may also not necessarily export any of their
production in the way the major wine countries do.

wines are struggling to regain their place on the supermarket shelves.

Bulgaria

This was one of the few countries not to suffer too much from a lack of investment during the rule of the Communist regime. For many years, the large co-operatives took a more commercial attitude toward vine planting and grape purchasing. In the 1960s, they began planting French varieties, such as Cabernet Sauvignon and Merlot, and thought far enough ahead to train the vines so that they could be harvested by machine. Unfortunately, the money ran out when they came to buy the tractors, but they had got vineyards full of quality vines and lots of cheap labour.

In the early 1980s, the jammy, black currant and berry wines arrived in the U.K. market, and, within a few years, Bulgarian wineries were the fifth largest suppliers of wine. Soon after, however, the central planners changed the market. President Mikhail Gorbachev began a programme to reduce alcohol consumption in the Soviet Union, vineyards were uprooted, wineries closed and the economy collapsed.

A few producers managed to survive through all this doom and gloom, however, and with the help of Western investment and flying winemakers, they are producing soft, juicy, red wines from some indigenous grapes, such as the Mavrud and Gamza, as well as those classic varieties that first made their name. The producers in the region of

Eastern Europe

The first group of countries fall into the last category that I mentioned. A few years ago, the wines of Eastern European countries were rather popular. Nowadays, after the collapse of the Communist bloc, the resulting loss of a major market, and, therefore, the lack of investment (some of which had started before the fall of the Iron Curtain), and the ravages of war, in some cases, these

Suhindol, for example, have privatised the government-controlled co-operative and are trying to break into the international market again.

Hungary

This is a country with a real wine heritage, as evidenced in some of the grape varieties it uses and the international recognition of its most famous dessert wine. There is an obvious Austrian influence here, a legacy from the days of the great Austro-Hungarian Empire, which is shown in the plantings of Olaz Rizling (Austria's Welschriesling —it's neither Welsh nor the Riesling of the Rhine, but never mind), Zöldveltelini (Grüner Veltliner) and the red grape

Kékfrankos (Blaufränkisch). There is also a smattering of classic French varieties.

The best-known red wine is made from the Kékfrankos grape, with the addition of some Kadarka, and is called Bull's Blood, or Egri Bikaver. But, overall, Hungary's most famous wine, and the one that has attracted the most foreign investment since the collapse of the Communist state, is a dessert wine from the Tokaj region, known simply as Tokaji Aszú, or Tokay Aszú. The permitted grape varieties used for making this wine are the Furmint and Hárslevelü, and it is made from a combination of a dry base wine and a paste derived from botrytised, or Aszú, fruit. The botrytised fruit is measured in baskets, or *puttonyos*; the more *puttonyos*

on the label, the sweeter the wine. Once the paste has been added, the wine is left to mature in barrels for up to three years before being bottled. The resultant wines are butterscotch-sweet with orange-marmalade notes on the finish. Tokaji Aszú Essencia is made with pure Aszú fruit and is so sweet that it has been known to age for centuries in the bottle, gaining the reputation as the wine of the czars.

Romania

For years, people have been talking about the potential of Romania as a wine producer, but to date they have not been able to attract the same levels of investment as other countries of the former Communist bloc. The botrytised, sweet white wine of Cotnari is a traditional wine that can still be found here, while you will also find some wines made from Pinot Noir.

Slovenia

Part of the former Yugoslavia, Slovenia was the quality wine-producing region of that country. The main influence on Slovenian wines is Italy, which is hardly surprising given that it is located right next to the Italian border and the region of Friuli-Venezia-Giulia. In fact, some of the vineyards are actually an extension of the Colli vineyards of Italy.

There is quite a lot of stainless-steel winemaking equipment used in this area, because the old Communist regime did allow a small amount of private enterprise among the producers. As a result, you can find some clean, crisp wines among those produced.

Croatia

The best vineyards of Croatia lie on the Dalmatian coast, especially on the Istrian Peninsula. Croatia is also the home of the grape variety that is thought to be the original parent of the Californian Zinfandel, the Crljenak (difficult to pronounce, I know), which was identified using DNA fingerprinting at the University of California, Davis.

The other countries that have emerged from the war-torn former Yugoslavia also produce wines, but small yields and high prices mean that they have yet to reach the international market. Slovenia was by far the best of them in this industry, and it will take a long time for the rest to catch up.

Georgia

Here, we approach the "cradle" of wine: the place where the vine was first cultivated. This is supported by evidence gathered by scientists, who dated grape seeds found in Georgia at somewhere between 7000 and 5000 B.C. Nowadays, Western investment, combined with local support and Australian winemakers, has begun to resurrect the wine industry.

Indigenous grapes, such as the Saperavi (one of the few red grapes to have a coloured juice), are making some very approachable, big wines full of earthy, red-berried flavours. Georgia also produces crisp, dry and aromatic white wines from the Rkatsiteli and Mtsvani grapes. Look out also for 'orange' wines which are white wines made with long skin contact.

Tasting the wine in the mould-covered cellars of a Tokaji Aszú vineyard in Hungary.

The Mediterranean

The Mediterranean Sea has long provided a cooling influence on the countries around its coastline, creating a climate that is suitable for growing vines. It was from here that traders took the vine around the then-known world—from Greece, all the way to modern Spain—without falling off the edge!

Greece

That the Greeks have a wine industry is not surprising: any student who studied classics will have read about it, and any tourist will have drunk it. No, the surprise is that, despite many years of neglect and concentration on the domestic Greek market, Greek wines are rushing to catch up with the rest of the wine industry, and are gaining all the time.

Some of the reds can still be far too tannic; one mouthful and it feels like someone has walloped you in the face with an oak stave. But investment in the wineries, with stainless-steel vats to control the fermentation temperatures, is resulting in softer, more juicy red wines made from local grape varieties, such as the Xynomavro and Agiorgitiko (also known as the St. George). It's definitely an up and coming area.

Of course, you cannot forget—especially if you've tasted it—the distinctive wine, Retsina. Nowadays, this wine is made from the Savatiano grape, with some pine resin added before fermentation. However, this wine style owes its origins to the early wine traders.

The Greeks soon learned that wines had to be sealed to keep them fresh. The only method available to them was to float pine resin on top of the wines in their storage amphorae. This stopped the wine coming into contact with the air, but as the wine was shaken up during its transport, it absorbed some of the resin. Hey presto! A wine style was born.

Retsina is by no means the only white wine made in Greece, and you can also find some dessert, Muscat wines from the islands of Samos and Patras.

Cyprus

Cyprus has suffered over the centuries from colonial occupation, which has suppressed any attempt to make quality table wines. For a long time, a tax break, earned through its membership of the former British Empire and the subsequent Commonwealth, meant that inexpensive, fortified wines from Cyprus were popular in the U.K. That market was then extended through the export of concentrated grape juice for the production of so-called British wines in the U.K. itself. Cyprus still produces a local, fortified wine called Commandaria, and it is this which gives a hint to the possibilities of Cyprus wines.

Turkey

The vast majority of the grapes that are grown in Turkey are table grapes and for the production of raisins. Hardly any of them end up in wine bottles, and generally that is no bad thing. There are one or two producers who are trying hard, but, if I am honest, they have a long road to travel.

Lebanon

To all intents and purposes, wine in

Lebanon means the Bekaa Vallay, and the Bekaa Valley means Château Musar, which is owned by Serge Hochar. Actually, there is another quality producer in the valley, Château Kefraya, but it is Musar that has brought this area to international notice.

I once tasted a thirty-year-old example of Château Musar and have to admit that I placed its combination of Bordeaux and Rhone Valley grapes squarely in the Medoc in Bordeaux. Serge would have been proud of me! Cabernet Sauvignon, Syrah and Cinsault never taste better together than after fifteen or twenty years in a bottle of Château Musar wine.

Stories abound about the problems that Château Musar faced during the long Lebanon civil war, when the vineyard was on the front line and tanks were parked between the rows of vines at harvest time. The fact that, during that long struggle, Château Musar only missed two vintages says a lot about the resilience of Serge Hochar and his workforce.

Israel

Although this country has been making wine since biblical times, most of the production is consumed by the home market. A lot of the production is, of course, kosher. This means that the production of the wine has to be carried out under the supervisory control of a rabbi and only by practising Jews.

Algeria, Morocco and Tunisia

These North African countries still show the influence of their former colonial masters, the French. For a long time, Algerian wine was, allegedly, imported to France for the purpose of "beefing" up underripe wines from Burgundy. Now, these countries produce a small amount of wine to sell for themselves. Recently, a Sicilian company set up a vineyard in Tunisia and is producing a wine using modern techniques that shows potential.

Western Europe

Switzerland

In some ways, the Swiss wine industry is similar to the English wine industry— demand far outstrips supply, which means that very little Swiss wine is seen outside the country and it is expensive. In fact, the only people who tell me that Swiss wine is not expensive are the Swiss!

The cost of the wine is not surprising when you consider a couple of things: first, the cost of living in Switzerland is high, and workers in the vineyards have to be paid enough money to be able to afford to live there. The second thing is the fact that the vineyards are all on steep, sometimes terraced, slopes. This helps improve the exposure of the vines to the sun, and the good drainage and the rain shadows created by the mountains also contribute to the growing conditions, but while it is all very pretty, it is not cheap to operate.

Despite the traditional picture of snow-covered Alps, in reality, the lakes in Switzerland all help to moderate the climate, by raising the temperature a degree or so, and the rivers also help with frost control.

Most of the vineyards lie in the French-speaking cantons, although

some wine is grown in the German- and Italian-speaking areas as well. The main grape variety grown here is the white Chasselas grape, the Swiss being the only winemakers to produce an interesting wine from it. Other varieties, such as Petite Arvine, or Humagne Blanc, are only really grown in Switzerland, but, in addition to these, you will find a number of classic varieties, such as Pinot Noir, Merlot and Gamay.

The majority of the wine comes from the French-speaking area of Valais on the slopes of the Upper Rhône Valley, with their southern exposure. Here, the Chasselas is known as the Fendant. The region also produces some red wine, called Dôle, which is made from a blend

Despite its troubles, Israel still manages to make wine for local consumption, most of which is kosher.

of Gamay and Pinot Noir that is similar to Burgundy's Passe-Tout-Grains wines, and some rich, dessert wines made from the Petite Arvine grape.

Vaud, Geneva and Neuchâtel all produce Chasselas-based wines, with the last two also making a pale rosé, or *oeil de perdrix*, wine from the Pinot Noir.

The German-speaking regions produce a lot of Müller-Thurgau-based wine—well, Dr H. Müller, after whom the grape is named, came from this area, so in some respects, this is their grape. As you would expect, there is a German influence on the style of wine made here. In fact, the neighbouring countries all tend to influence the wine styles of the regions nearest to them. The Italian cantons seem to concentrate on producing Merlot-based, light red wines, the best of which come from the region of Ticino.

England and Wales

Wherever the Romans invaded they brought with them a culture of wine-drinking, firstly by importing wine from home, then by planting vineyards. Britain was no different.

Archaeologists have found evidence of Roman vineyards as far North as Grimsby. Yes, you read that correctly... *Grimsby*! North Thoresby to be exact. Having lived in the area, I'd say there must have been a mini-heatwave then. The wine they would have made however would bear little resemblance to the wines we know today. It would have been quite cloudy, sweetened with honey and flavoured with herbs and spices.

When the Romans left, the vineyards would have continued to produce wine, with ownership slowly moving to the monasteries where wine would be made under the direction of trained winemakers and used to help fund the monastery.

Winemaking continued on this small scale until 1584 and the dissolution of the monasteries by Henry VIII. This act effectively destroyed English winemaking, with only one or two vineyards struggling on until the First World War when sugar rationing stopped all production.

Fast forward to 1952 and an ex-military attaché to Paris, Sir Guy Salisbury-Jones,

with some advice from the Champagne house Pol Roger, plants an acre of Seyval Blanc hybrid vines on a south-east-facing slope on his property at Hambledon in Hampshire. In 1954 he harvests his first crop and so begins the renaissance of English winemaking.

Since then it has developed from a cottage industry, with farmers planting vines on spare plots of land, to a business that produces millions of bottles of wine a year. At the last count there were over 350 vineyards in England and Wales, although many of them are very small and send their grapes to larger vineyards with wineries to be made into wine. The star of English wine production has to be dry, crisp white table wines made from German crossings such as Bacchus and Kerner, although there is a small amount of Chardonnay produced as well. Some red wines are produced but the grapes have to be suited to the climate. Pinot Noir and the German Dornfelder variety do well, with the Dornfelder's dark skin adding a depth of colour to the wine.

However, it is for sparkling wines that English wines are gaining their international reputation and it is no coincidence that the most planted varieties at the moment are Chardonnay, Pinot Noir and Pinot Meunier.

Even with the benefit of the warm Gulf Stream on the south and west coastline, our general climate is a bit too cool to fully ripen most red grapes. But sparkling wine production needs grapes that are slightly under-ripe and acidic, and the cool English temperature preserves the acidity in the grapes.

The soil along the south coast of England is part of what is known as the Franco-British Basin. This is a bed of limestone and chalk that extends from the Champagne region of France all the way west to Cornwall, before heading south to the Cognac region and back to Champagne.

It was only in 1994 that the first vineyard dedicated to sparkling wine production was planted in the UK. Ridgeview was soon joined by companies such as Nyetimber, Chapel Down and Camel Valley, amongst many others. In blind tastings, Ridgeview, Nyetimber and Camel Valley regularly beat Champagnes and are all award-winning producers in their own right.

So our best producers sit on the same soil, use the same grapes and traditional winemaking method and share a similar climate to Champagne. No wonder they do so well. Who knows, with climate change, we might one day turn full circle and be looking out for Château Grimsby on our wine lists once again.

China

When I wrote the first edition of this book I have to admit Chinese wine was a bit of a joke. Our local Chinese restaurant would stock wine called Great Wall, and it wasn't very good. Although there was evidence that the Chinese had been making wine from grapes over 4,000 years ago, they had long since concentrated on drinks made from grains such as rice and other fruits.

All this slowly began to change in the 1980s when the Chinese government, concerned about the amount of spirits being consumed, began a programme to encourage grape wine consumption instead and state-owned companies like China Great Wall Wine Co. were set up.

Today China is the eighth-largest wine-producing country in the world and is projected to be the sixth-largest by 2016. Although most of this wine is consumed in China, its wines are winning international awards in competitions like the *Decanter* World Wine Awards and the International Wine Challenge. You will even find Chinese wines stocked

a joint venture with Rémy Martin, while the owners of Château Lafite-Rothschild have invested, with partners, in a new 25-hectare vineyard in the Penglai peninsular in Shandong province.

The current star of Chinese wine is Chateau Changyu. This massive producer (thought to be in the top 10 producers by volume in the world) has set up a number of joint ventures with European and Canadian producers across China. In the north they produce ice wines in association with the Canadian company Aurora; further south Bordeaux company Castel has helped develop a Cabernet Sauvignon vineyard; and in the west the Austrian producer Lenz Moser is also helping produce a Cabernet Merlot wine. Chateau Changyu's latest investment is a huge "City of Wine" in Shandong. This 400-odd-hectare site will include not only a winery and vineyard but also a research centre, wine trading centre and a holiday resort. Wine is obviously becoming big business in China.

The strength of the Chinese economy in the past few years, combined with this interest in fine wines, has also resulted in Chinese investment in European vineyards. The regions of Bordeaux and Burgundy especially have seen Chinese entrepreneurs and investors purchase châteaux and domaines as they come on the market—and in some cases sending the entire output to the Chinese market. This just goes to show that we are all share the same dreams; when we make it big, we all want to own a vineyard.

by some of the most traditional wine merchants in the UK.

One of the driving forces of this boost in quality was the increased popularity of top-quality French wines in China as the country became more affluent. Basically these wines became status symbols to be seen drinking and to be given as gifts. To help gain access to this market, wine companies developed joint ventures, not only to ensure distribution of their wines but also to produce wines in China. Dynasty wines in Tianjin, for example, is

As with any food or drink that is packaged, the label on a wine bottle can never tell you exactly how the contents will taste, or whether you will like it, but it should point towards what you can expect in terms of quality. Just remember, wine producers are no different from any other goods manufacturers; they want you to buy their wares, so don't be fooled by a pretty-looking label or bottle: it's no guarantee.

Wine bottles may have up to three labels: one on the front of the bottle, which tells you details about the wine inside; one on the back, which usually adds a bit of background about the wine's origins and may offer suggestions as to what food to serve it with and possibly one on the neck of the bottle, which will probably tell you no more than the producer's name or the vintage of the wine. The front label is undoubtedly the most important.

WHAT'S ON A LABEL?

Well, rules vary from country to country, depending on their system for assessing the quality of wine (see Wine Around the World), and producers may have to put different labels on bottles for export, to meet the importing country's regulations. (This is especially true with wines exported to the European Union which must show the country of origin, the quality level, the address of the producer and/or importer, the volume and alcoholic strength of the wine, the fact that it contains sulphides/sulphur, a "lot" or bottling batch number and, finally, the contents of the bottle, i.e. red or white wine. After these compulsory requirements, everything else is voluntary, including the wine's name.) But almost every country

will require labels to carry some of these items, such as the alcohol percentage in the wine, the amount of wine in the bottle and the country of origin. After that, it will depend on the producer and the individual country's rules. This optional information, as far as Europe is concerned, can include the number of units in the bottle, a health warning regarding the harmful effects of alcohol consumption and whether the wine is suitable for vegetarians or vegans.

There are three main types of labels, where one particular feature is predominant: the variety of grape, the region, or the producer, though it's fair to say you will see many variations on these, "hybrids" if you like, which develop as the wine becomes more established.

VARIETAL LABELS

First used by the Wente family in California in 1936, varietal labels state little more than the bare minimum required by law and focus on the type of grape used to produce the wine, such as Shiraz or Cabernet Sauvignon. You will find these labels mainly on wines from countries such as the U.S.A., Australia, New Zealand and Argentina, but they can be found on European wines such as those from Alsace, in France, Germany and Austria.

When the use of these labels became widespread in the U.S., the Bureau of Alcohol, Tobacco and Firearms (B.A.T.F.), now the Alcohol and Tobacco Tax and Trade Bureau (T.T.B.), stepped in to provide regulations to govern the use of such terms, so that the wine must contain a certain percentage of the grape stipulated (see page 258), which has increased over the years, although good producers would always have used something nearer to a 100 percent of the grape in question. And there is a similar system in Australia, overseen by the Australian Wine and Brandy Corporation.

The label to the left may look very simple, and it would be easy to assume that this is the front label of the wine, but, in fact, it is the back label. The producers decided to put a nice-looking label on the back, which is usually the one that gets presented to customers, while the front label shows all the information that is legally required. As you can see, the wine is made from Sauvignon Blanc grapes and the producer has added the brand name, Cloudy Bay.

REGIONAL LABELS

This type of label is found principally on wines from the "Old World" countries,

They may be continents apart, but the labels above and below show how the name of their region is important—the one above for commercial reasons and the one below because it is a delimited area in France.

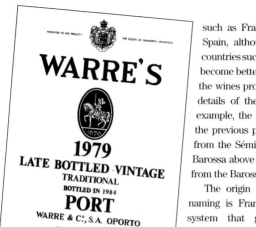

Some established producers, such as Warre's, will show the year their company was established as a mark of reliability, while other producers show the awards they have won, as with the Spanish label below.

such as France, Germany, Italy and Spain, although as various areas in countries such as the U.S. and Australia become better known, so the labels on the wines produced there are carrying details of their region of origin. For example, the label on the top right of the previous page shows a wine made from the Sémillon grape, but the word Barossa above it indicates that it comes from the Barossa Valley in Australia.

The origin of this type of regional naming is France and the *appellation* system that governs the country's production of wine. For instance, if a white wine in France is labelled as a Mâcon-Villages, it means that it has come only from a designated group of villages within the Mâcon region of Burgundy. Or, if you see an Italian wine named Barolo, it has to have come from the Barolo region in the Piedmont area.

In the U.S.A., the *appellation* is known as an A.V.A. (American Viticultural Area). The A.V.A., awarded by the T.T.B., , may be a state, or a county, and if it is used on a label, the law requires that 75 percent of the grapes used must come from the A.V.A. named. Then, if a vineyard is also named, it must be wholly within the A.V.A. and 95 percent of the grapes used for the wine have to come from that vineyard.

One thing that can confuse the wine buyer is the "borrowing" of certain French wine regions' names, such as Chablis and Sauterne (yes, it is missing an "s"). It became common practice in the U.S.A. and Australia to use these names to describe different types of wine, such as Chablis for a medium-dry white, or Champagne for a sparkling wine, or Burgundy for a medium-bodied red. These wines have no connections with the wines from those areas in France, and they cannot be exported to Europe carrying those names, as trade agreements limit their use. Nowadays, if you purchase a generic-labelled wine in the U.S.A., you may also see the term "Meritage", which implies that the wine has been made in the style of a red Bordeaux wine, using the same grape types as would be found in that region of France.

PROPRIETARY LABELS

The more individual the wine, the more proprietary labelling is added to the territorial designation, which is when you will see the name of a Château or particular producer. Basically, it's no different from any brand name usage. Though, if the name is well-established as well as respected, it indicates that the wine will be of good quality, if not top-notch, as in the case of the Piper-Heidsieck Champagne label below.

Just as in the Old World, labels in the New World countries increasingly include regions or appellations and the producer's or the brand's name, such as Mondavi and Bonterra (for wines made from organic grapes) in America, and Tyrrell's and d'Arenberg, in Australia are now respected worldwide.

These are examples of labels from producers whose names are known worldwide and who are known for the quality of their wine.

LABEL EXAMPLES

It's impossible to show every type of label available, but the following are indicative of what to look out for, and the features that appear on each are explained, so that, hopefully, when you go out to buy your next bottle of wine, you will know what to look for and what to avoid!

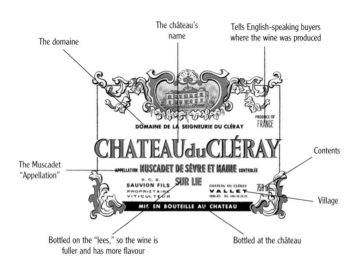

The domaine

The château's name

Tells English-speaking buyers where the wine was produced

PRODUCE OF FRANCE

DOMAINE DE LA SEIGNEURIE DU CLÉRAY

CHATEAU du CLÉRAY

APPELLATION **MUSCADET DE SÈVRE ET MAINE** CONTRÔLÉE

SUR LIE

Contents

The Muscadet "Appellation"

S.C.E. **SAUVION FILS** PROPRIÉTAIRE VITICULTEUR

CHATEAU DU CLÉRAY **VALLET** LOIRE-ATL. TEL. (40) 36.22.55

750 mL

Village

MIS EN BOUTEILLE AU CHATEAU

Bottled on the "lees," so the wine is fuller and has more flavour

Bottled at the château

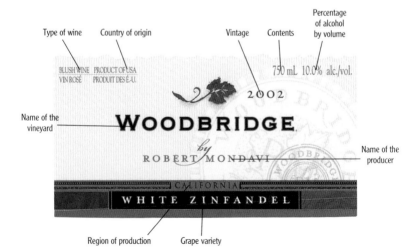

Type of wine

Country of origin

Vintage

Contents

Percentage of alcohol by volume

BLUSH WINE VIN ROSÉ

PRODUCT OF USA PRODUIT DES É-U.

750 mL 10.0% alc./vol.

2002

Name of the vineyard

WOODBRIDGE

by

ROBERT MONDAVI

Name of the producer

CALIFORNIA

WHITE ZINFANDEL

Region of production

Grape variety

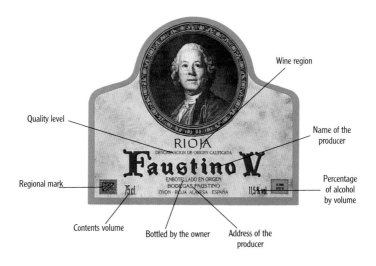

Wine region

Quality level

Name of the producer

Regional mark

Percentage of alcohol by volume

RIOJA
DENOMINACION DE ORIGEN CALIFICADA

Faustino V

EMBOTELLADO EN ORIGEN
BODEGAS FAUSTINO
OYON · RIOJA ALAVESA · ESPAÑA

75 cl.

11,5% vol.

Contents volume

Bottled by the owner

Address of the producer

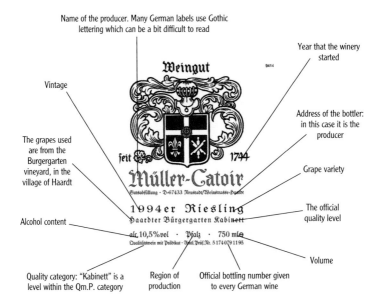

Name of the producer. Many German labels use Gothic lettering which can be a bit difficult to read

Year that the winery started

Vintage

Address of the bottler: in this case it is the producer

The grapes used are from the Burgergarten vineyard, in the village of Haardt

Grape variety

Alcohol content

The official quality level

Quality category: "Kabinett" is a level within the Qm.P. category

Region of production

Official bottling number given to every German wine

Volume

Weingut

9414

seit

1744

Müller-Catoir

Gutsabfüllung · D-67433 Neustadt/Weinstrasse-Haardt

1994er Riesling
Haardter Bürgergarten Kabinett

alc. 10,5% vol · Pfalz · 750 mle
Qualitätswein mit Prädikat · Amtl. Prüf.Nr. 5 174 079 1195

CHAPTER 8

SERVING WINE

OK, it's not rocket science, but knowing how to serve a bottle of wine so that you present it to its best advantage should add to your enjoyment of it.

The best way to serve wine is to keep it simple. There are a few rules to observe, and they have nothing to do with snobbery but are all about showing the flavours and the appearance of the wine to their best advantage.

The first thing you need is a good corkscrew, and it is worth finding one that suits you. Some people also like to use a foil cutter, but you can remove the foil just as easily using a knife or the point of a corkscrew. Take care when choosing a corkscrew, as not all designs are equally efficient, and many everyday wines now come in bottles with synthetic corks, which can be quite difficult to shift.

OPENING THE BOTTLE
The ideal corkscrew is one with an open screw that spirals around empty air, rather than one where the spiral has a central

Corkscrews come in many styles today, but an open screw, such as the "waiter's friend" at the top, not only grips the cork better but folds up to fit easily in a pocket or bag.

column. An open screw grips the cork far more securely, while a corkscrew with a central column is likely to pull right through old and fragile corks.

There are many designs of corkscrew on the market, most of which employ a lever of some kind, for making the task of extracting the cork easier. A very simple design is the 'Screwpull', which has a screw coated in non-stick material. When screwing it into the cork, lift the lever or keep turning in the same direction, and the cork will rise up the screw. The Waiter's Friend, a favourite with restaurant sommeliers, is also effective once mastered. Finally, the simplest, albeit least elegant, option is just a screw and a handle, which involves holding the bottle steady between your knees while pulling to extract the cork.

in a glass doesn't matter: just fish it out with a knife or your finger.

Not all wines require a corkscrew. Metal screw caps, championed by New Zealand producers, are increasingly gaining favour, especially with producers of aromatic wines. These make an extremely effective airtight seal, and can simply be screwed back on again if you do not finish the bottle. But beware, once the seal is broken the wine will deteriorate in the same way as a bottle sealed with a cork.

Sherry, and some other fortified wines, use stopper corks, which you can pull out with your fingers. And Champagne, of course, requires a different technique completely.

The trick to opening Champagne and other sparkling wines is to get them properly cold first—they will fizz up

WHAT TO DO IF THE CORK BREAKS OR TEARS

Inevitably, there will be an occasion when the cork breaks or splits inside the neck of the bottle as you are trying to open it. Depending on how firmly the cork grips the glass, you can either push it into the bottle with your finger, or try to remove it with a narrow blade. If the result of either operation is many pieces of cork in the wine, then you may need to filter it through muslin into a jug or decanter. The odd bit of cork

less when the cork pops—and ensure that the bottle is not shaken. Place the bottle upright on a table and remove the foil capsule. Loosen the wire cage and remove it. Be careful from now on, don't point the bottle at anyone (including yourself) and keep your hand over the cork. Now, take a firm hold of the cork in one hand and twist the bottle with the other and let the pressure ease the cork out of the bottle. The cork shouldn't 'pop' out (bad manners, old boy!). And remember to have a glass ready in case the wine does foam out of the bottle.

If the cork is very stubborn, and some can be, then wrapping a cloth around it can give you a better grip. If the cork does break, then you have no option but to use a corkscrew in the normal way— easing the remaining cork out slowly, in order to let the gas escape gradually.

When you pour Champagne, have your guests tilt their glasses towards the bottle at an angle of 45°. That way, they get more wine and less froth, with less risk of the froth rising up and running over. Remember, the winemaker has spent years putting the bubbles in the wine—don't lose them straightaway.

THE RIGHT GLASS

The question of which glass to serve wine in is an important one, and, again, the principle is to show the wine to best advantage. Any decoration on the glass itself—cutting, gilding, painting or colour

Below: Riedel designed these glasses with specific shapes to emphasise the aromas and flavours of specific grape varieties.

—is superfluous. The ideal glass is plain and made from the thinnest glass possible because this is the most pleasant to drink from.

`Make sure the glass is big enough. Small glasses are unsatisfactory for most wines: you need to be able to get a decent serving in, without filling the glass more than one-third. Leaving this much space will enable you to swirl the wine a little before tasting it; again, it's all about showing the wine off at its best.

The Austrian Riedel glass company have developed a range of glasses which are suited to specific grape varieties or wine styles. You might think that this is perhaps a bit pretentious, after all a glass is a glass, but using the 'correct' glass does seem to make a difference. However, if you do not want to invest in 'special' glasses, here are a few simple guidelines to help you choose the best glasses:

• Champagne or sparkling wine glasses, should always be tall, narrow flutes rather than flat saucers. (The latter allow the sparkle to dissipate too quickly.)

• Standard tulip-shaped glasses for red and white wine. You need bigger ones for red wines to allow the aromas to settle on top of the wine in the glass.

• If you're fond of Fino sherry, you'll need some small tulip-shaped glasses, which will also do for Port.

You may want a decanter. The purpose of decanting is twofold: to allow it to breathe faster and more effectively and to separate wine from its sediment. Even young red wines will improve if they are decanted, and they always look better served this way.

When buying a decanter, choose

whatever you like the look of. There are many unsuitable wine glasses on the market, but all decanters do the job, although some do the job better than others by incorporating more air into the wine as you pour. The decanter shown on this page may look exotic, but it will improve the flavours of many wines.

One thing to bear in mind, however, is to consider how easy any decanter will be to lift and pour when it's full of liquid. If the neck is difficult to grip, or it becomes terribly heavy, you may want to think again.

DECANTING WINE

It is traditional to decant reds, but actually almost any wine may be decanted; in the nineteenth century, it was common to decant whites and even Champagnes as well. There are some cases where it is better to decant a wine, however, and this is a question of judgement. For example, a fine red, designed for long ageing, might well benefit from decanting if being drunk in its youth: the interaction with air will help release bouquet and flavour. Decanting will help mimic the effect of ageing that the wine has not yet had. An older fine wine, on the other hand, may well have thrown a deposit in the bottle, and will need careful decanting as a result. Vintage Port, for example, should always be decanted for this reason. Tawny or other sorts of Port do not generally need decanting.

The question of when to decant is harder. Remember that exposing the wine to air mimics the effect of ageing: the wine will gradually increase in aroma and flavour, but then it will fade. Decant it too soon before serving, and, if it is an old wine, it may be starting to fade just as you serve it. Too late, and it may not have reached its peak when you serve it (a lesser problem by far). If it goes on improving in the glass, fine. If it dies in the glass, you've had it. The best advice, therefore, is to decant no more than an hour before serving, and less in the case of old or fragile wines.

To decant a bottle of wine, all you need is a steady hand, a candle flame or table lamp, and, of course, a decanter.

Open the bottle carefully, taking care not to shake it. If you're able to leave it upright overnight, so much the better: this will ensure that any deposit has settled nicely. Extract the cork smoothly. Tilt the bottle as gently as you can, aiming for a smooth, steady flow that avoids stirring up the deposit. By positioning a light source—a lighted candle or a lamp—behind the bottle, you'll be able to

Left: This decanter is designed to incorporate air into the wine as it is poured into the glass. It looks to me like a pig's tail!

see how the deposit is advancing down the bottle. Stop pouring before it escapes.

If a wine surprises you by having sediment when you hadn't expected it, and you have already served it, all you can do is pour all the wine into a jug, take it away, and filter it through a muslin-lined funnel, before serving it again. Beware—don't use a paper coffee filter. This will add an unpleasant flavour to the wine.

SERVING TEMPERATURES

It is possible to buy wine thermometers, which tell you exactly what temperature a red Bordeaux should be, or a red Burgundy, but most people with busy lives do not have time for such detail. The crucial points to remember are that, if wine is too cold, it will have little flavour, with tannic reds tasting very hard in particular; and, if it is too warm, the alcohol will be too volatile, and it will taste soupy and unrefreshing. Remember, too that, once a wine is poured, it's easy to warm it up (just cup your hands around the glass), but virtually impossible to cool down. So slightly too cold is better than too warm.

White and rosé wines should be served colder than reds, and lighter wines should be served colder than bigger, richer, weightier ones. The box above gives ideal temperatures, where you will see that young, light reds, like Beaujolais, are

Ideal Serving Temperatures

Sweet whites	3–5.5°C (38–42°F)
Champagne and sparkling wine	4.5–9°C (40–48/9°F)
Dry whites	5.5–10°C (42–50°F)
Bigger whites, Chardonnay, light reds, Beaujolais, Loire reds	10–12°C (50–54°F)
Bigger reds, Burgundy, Chianti	12–16°C (54–60°F)
Shiraz, Barolo	13–17°C (56–62°F)
Vintage Port, red Bordeaux, Cabernet Sauvignon	16–19°C (60–66°F)
Normal home refrigerator temperature	3–7°C (38–44°F)
Ideal cellar temperature	10–13°C (50–56°F)
Normal room temperature	upwards of 17.5°C (63°F)

best slightly chilled. This makes them particularly attractive as summer wines.

The coldest temperatures in the box are achieved by putting the bottle in the door of the refrigerator for a couple of hours; the warmest ones by leaving the bottle at room temperature.

Standing a cold bottle by (or even on) the stove is unsatisfactory as a way of warming it quickly, and a fine wine may be damaged by such treatment. It is better to decant the wine into a decanter or jug that has been warmed by filling with hot water. Standing a warm bottle in a bucket of ice and water is the quickest way to cool it.

WHEN TO SERVE
The order in which wines are served is traditionally white before red, light before heavy, and dry before sweet. This is partly because one's palate adapts most easily to this order: tasting a light red after a sweet white is difficult, whereas the reverse is not. But it also reflects the order in which food is traditionally served (fish before meat, for example). Food is not always so straightforward, however.

For example, you might serve chicken liver pâté, followed by roast cod. The pâté would normally require a sweetish

This type of bottle stopper is particularly effective for keeping the bubbles in bottles of Champagne that have been opened.

spicy white—perhaps an off-dry Alsace Pinot Gris—and the cod needs a drier wine.

If that is the case, try to find a fairly weighty, dry white to go with the cod; a wine that won't be overwhelmed by the Alsace Pinot Gris that has gone before. An Alsace Riesling might do the trick, or a lightly oaked Chardonnay.

Similarly, if your menu requires you to serve a red before a white, then do so—but make it a light red and a big white.

When it comes to cheese before a dessert, and vice versa, there are in fact several arguments. The logic behind serving cheese before a dessert is that you finish up the red with the cheese and then have a sweet white with the dessert. The reverse is more difficult, since a tannic red will not taste pleasant after a sweet white.

LEFTOVER WINE

If, as often happens, you have some wine left over at the end of the evening, there are various ways of keeping it.

A Vacuvin removes the air from the bottle, leaving a vacuum above the wine, and preserving the wine from oxidation. It also can remove some flavour and aroma, however.

Canisters of inert gas are sometimes available: a squirt from one of these will do a better job. But actually, just putting the cork back in and putting the bottle in the door of the refrigerator is pretty effective, provided that you plan to drink the remainder the next day.

For leftover Champagne or sparkling wine it is advisable to use a Champagne stopper, available from many wine stores—I'm sorry to say that placing a silver spoon into the bottle has no effect whatsoever. This can be clamped onto the bottle securely, and keeps the fizz in, protecting the wine from oxidation. You won't be able to get the original cork back in the bottle, and an ordinary cork will shoot out under the pressure of the carbon dioxide.

Left: If you are only keeping your opened bottle of wine for a day or so, sticking the cork back in and putting it in the fridge will help keep it fresh.

CHAPTER 9

WINE AND FOOD

Food and drink go together, whether it's bread and water or the finest Grand Cru and a great roast.

FOOD AND WINE MATCHING

Food and wine were made for each other. Remember, for a long time wine was safer and better for you than water so it makes sense that they should develop a relationship.

Food and wine will interact with each other and each change the way other tastes. Balancing a wine with your food choice can really take advantage of this effect and result in a heightened gastronomic experience.

As with most things in life, people have developed rules to guide you through the maze of possible matches. But I only have one rule and that rule is… there are no rules! If you find a match that works for you, then that is a perfect match.

Obviously I don't just want to push you in at the deep end and leave you on your own, so there are a few guidelines. But because, like all tastes, food and wine matching is so subjective, the final choice is yours.

So, how does food and wine matching work? Well, just like wine tasting (see page 30) we "taste" using the olfactory bulb. Your palate, again, will only recognise the basic blocks of sweetness, bitterness, saltiness, acidity and umami, so a good match will depend on how these elements work together combined with your tolerance levels of these "flavours".

Every time you place some food or wine in your mouth your palate adapts to the levels of sweetness, acidity etc. and the flavour of the next thing on your palate will be affected by that change in perception.

Sweet foods, for example, will make wines appear to taste more bitter and astringent and even less fruity; for this reason a dessert wine needs to be sweeter than the dish it is matched with.

Bitter foods make a wine taste more bitter. So whilst the food may be pleasantly bitter and the wine displays a balanced bitter note, when put together the two will combine to show an unpleasant level of bitterness. To make this element more complicated, we all find different levels of bitterness attractive (do you remember a time when you found black olives too bitter?) so here the best match is totally subjective and only you can be the judge of what is the right combination for you.

Salt in food has a strange effect on wine. In the food it is used to enhance the flavour, but with wine its effect is to make the body of the wine appear fuller,

Previous page: A glass of unoaked Chardonnay goes well with seared king scallops.
Left: Roasted lemon chicken could be accompanied by a wine made from an oak aged Chardonnay.

Above: Desserts need a lot of thought; here it is not just the flavour of the wine that has to be taken into account, but also the sugar level. If the wine is not sweet enough, the dessert will make it taste too acidic

whilst at the same time it reduces the perception of bitterness and acidity on the palate. Think of how soft a bitter red wine can taste when matched with a mature cheddar and you will see what I mean.

Acidity in food increases your perception of acidity so wines will appear less acidic, sweeter and fruitier. You need to be aware, however, that wines with a low level of acidity might appear flat and flabby when paired with the same dish.

Umami is a strange thing. It is more of a sensation than an actual flavour. It is best described as savouriness and is hard to isolate. It is incorporated in foods rather than an isolated flavour. Pure sweetness can be represented by sugar, salt by salt etc., but it is hard to find umami rather than umaminess. Foods that contain umami include asparagus, cooked mushrooms, parmesan cheese and Marmite. As you can imagine, these are not the most wine-friendly of ingredients. This is because umami makes wines taste more bitter, astringent and acidic.

The final "flavour" that has to be taken into account with food and wine matching is spice, especially chilli spice. Now this is really a personal thing because the main effect of chilli spice on wine is to increase your perception of alcohol. Combine this with the fact that the alcohol increases the burning effect of the chilli and it puts a whole new spin on the word Phaal! Other effects of chilli are the reduction of the sweetness and fruitiness of a wine. This is why low-alcohol, fruity wines such as German Rieslings from the Rheingau and Pfalz go well with hot curries.

Now, if it wasn't complex enough, there are another few things you should think about before opening that bottle of wine or starting to prepare that dish.

WHAT COMES FIRST? THE WINE OR THE DISH?

Actually, it doesn't matter. Do you have a special wine that you want to open? Then think of a dish that will match. Having a special dish? Then think what wine will work best. It's really that simple.

LOCAL WINES WITH LOCAL DISHES

On the face of it, this makes perfect sense. Over the years, the wines produced would be developed in such a way as to match the local cuisine—if only because if it were a bad match no one would have bought the wine. A classic example of this is the acidic Sauvignon Blanc wines of Sancerre with goat's cheese. Here the yoghurty acid in the cheese softens the wine and makes it seem more fruity. If you visit Sancerre you will see small alpine goats running through the vineyards.

But what about Bordeaux with its myriad styles of wines? Roast lamb and Sauternes, anyone?

And what about Asian cuisine, which has developed in its own way with no local wine production to support it? Here it really is a matter of personal taste, but the guidelines above should help you.

Below: Game and poultry dishes, such as this honey-glazed organic duck breast, can take a more robust red wine like a Sangiovese.

DO I MATCH THE FLAVOURS IN A DISH OR CONTRAST THEM WITH MY WINE CHOICE?

The idea of matching a flavour is one of the most common in food and wine pairing. A smoky, spicy dish and a smoky, spicy wine for example. It might work but more often won't. The number of times people try to convince me that Gewürztraminer wines are a match for curries won't change my opinion that they're not. The important thing is the interaction of the primary flavours. The luscious texture of a Sauternes means that it will match the fatty texture of foie gras whilst at the same time the high level of acid in the wine stops everything from cloying on the palate. The structure is as important as flavour when it comes to food and wine matching.

"WHITE WINE WITH FISH, RED WINE WITH MEAT"

A classic rule from the past that still echoes today. The problem with it is that, whilst there is a grain of truth to it, everything has changed. Not only are

Below: Matching a wine with Asian-influenced dishes, such as this Thai green chicken curry, is not easy, but some of the whites from New Zealand make good choices.

the wines we drink today different to the wines of the past, so are today's fish and meat dishes.

In the past most fish dishes would be made using white fish such as sole. Nowadays if you go to a fish restaurant you are more likely to see "meatier" fish such as tuna, swordfish, salmon or mackerel on the menu. With the first two a rosé or light red wine might work well. It is the umami sensation of fish which tends to make red wine taste bitter, so a more full-bodied red could appear too bitter when matched.

With oily salmon and mackerel, a wine that is too acidic might overpower the oils and make the fish lose texture. Here an oaked white wine will match the texture instead of smashing it.

Again, the principles above mean that colour and flavour are not the only factors to take into account. The interaction of the primary flavours can be more important when enhancing the experience.

DIFFICULT MATCHES

Some foods are recognised as being "awkward children" when it comes to matching with wine. But a little bit of thought might bring them off the "naughty step" and back to being happy family members.

Tomatoes have a reputation as wine "killers", especially for reds, but Italians do not seem to have a problem find a match, red or white. Why? It is all to do with the flavours in a tomato. Yes, they are sweet; yes, they are juicy; but they also have a high acid level and this will make a wine feel less acidic and more fruity. Italian wines tend to have a high

natural acidity so, although they will feel less acidic, they won't fall into a "flabby" soft state when matched with tomato. The same will go for any wine that has a high natural acidity, like a Sauvignon Blanc or dry Riesling.

Chocolate doesn't so much "kill" a wine as simply overpower the palate. Once you eat a piece of chocolate, everything you eat for a few minutes after will also taste of chocolate. This is because cocoa fat dissolves just below body temperature so it coats your palate and very little can get through that. (By the way, it is thought that this change in texture is one of the reasons that we like chocolate so much. That and the endorphins, of course.) This is why restaurants will normally serve chocolates with coffee, the heat helps to dissolve the fat and wash it away. The good news is that alcohol has the same effect. Next time you are indulging in a chocolate dessert, try accompanying it with a fortified wine and see what happens. Of course, the normal rules still apply. The wine has to be sweeter than the chocolate. Beware of any red wine with a high tannin bitterness—this will be exaggerated by the bitter element of the chocolate.

So the answer to food and wine matching is that there is no perfect answer. Even if someone recommends a classic pairing such as Port and Stilton, you might find that you prefer a different Port to your partner simply because your sensitivities and preferences are not the same. No one is wrong, everyone is right. Unless they disagree with me, of course…

CHAPTER 10

STORING WINE

Storing wine properly can make a lot of difference, no matter whether you have one bottle or several cases.

Anyone who buys wine regularly is faced with the troublesome problem of how to store it. Troublesome, because wine is both bulky and fussy about its conditions; and while it is not necessary to worry too much about ambient temperatures and darkness for wine that is to be drunk within a matter of weeks, anyone planning to keep it for longer—a year or more—should be prepared to pay attention to the basics.

THE IDEAL CONDITIONS FOR STORING WINE

The temperature should be constant, varying only between 10 and 15°C (50 and 59°F). Humidity should be between 60 and 80 percent. There should be darkness. There should be reasonable ventilation, and no strong smells. There should be no vibrations. And, most important of all, the bottles should be stored horizontally.

It is not always easy finding these conditions in the average home. Most modern houses are far too warm and far too liable to temperature fluctuations to house wine happily. (If you have a proper cellar under your house, then you are one

Right: Immaculately kept cellars can be beautiful in their own way, as this one in Spain shows. The only thing is, though, you have to be careful how you take the bottles out!

of the lucky few.) You may well have a cupboard that is ideally dark, could be ventilated, and is odour-free. But if it is hot on a summer's day and cold on a winter's night, it will not be perfect. And if it is near hot-water pipes, it could well prove disastrous.

CREATING MANAGEABLE CONDITIONS

Of all the factors listed above, temperature and darkness are the most important, and temperature in particular. Warmth over 15°C (59°F) will make your wine mature faster—you might think this rather useful, of course, but if you are storing fine wine, you might, over a period of years, lose a little quality, a little finesse. Wine will certainly reach its peak and fade faster. Moreover, the hotter the temperature, the more likely the wine is to suffer: allow your wine to get very hot—say on a hot summer's day—and you risk corks being forced out by the expansion of the wine, with consequent seepage and oxidation. You also risk maderisation from the heat.

The ideal storage space is a spare bedroom with a northern exposure, where you can keep the heating to a minimum in winter. Failing this, a cupboard under a staircase can be good, but watch out for hot-water pipes; a garage will work, but might need some heating in winter; a loft or attic—unless it is very well insulated—is even more subject to temperature fluctuations than the rest of the house; a

garden shed offers no protection against temperature changes. Avoid any spot near a radiator, hot-water pipes, a boiler, an oven, a refrigerator, or any other source of heat.

Light can destroy a wine, and most wines are bottled in coloured glass for this very reason. Allowing your wines to acquire a good thick layer of dust might help, too. Bright sunlight must be excluded from your bottles, and this is easily achieved by draping a dark cloth over the wine rack if there is no cupboard available. As in the case of temperature, the harmful effects of light will be felt only slowly, but they will be felt.

Humidity is important because it helps keep the corks in good condition and prevents them drying out—dry corks shrink, letting wine out and air in. Placing a bowl of water in the room will help raise the humidity, or, if you've settled on a garage for storing your wine, a layer of sand or gravel on the floor, kept sprinkled with water, will work perfectly.

Humidity brings its own problems, with the deterioration of labels among them. They can look wonderfully pretty on the dining table—everyone will think the wine is at least a hundred years older than it is—but if they become difficult to read, their picturesque quality may lose its appeal. If you are storing seriously fine wine, with an eye to future sale, it is important to keep the labels in good condition: some buyers won't consider wines with imperfect labels.

Ventilation helps to keep humidity from soaring (or indeed plummeting) and keeps smells at bay. It has never actually been proved beyond doubt that smells can affect wine adversely, but nobody is willing to take the risk. It is unwise to expose wine to chemical smells in particular. If you're storing wine in a garage, check what else is stored there.

The same goes for vibration. It is always said that a cellar should be vibration-free, but no real proof seems to exist. Many traditional London wine merchants have cellars under railway arches, which can hardly be vibration-free. This is probably the least of your concerns—nevertheless, try not to store wine next to a washing machine or dryer.

Keeping bottles horizontal is easy: there are many bottle racks on the market, and most are inexpensive. Many can be custom-made to fit a space. Bottles fitted with screw caps do not need to be kept lying down, however, nor do fortified wines, with the exception of vintage Port. In fact, the latter often come with a dab of white paint on the bottle, so that you can keep them lying in precisely the same position all their lives, and so not disturb the deposit.

In fact, you should disturb fine wines as little as possible. It doesn't matter with everyday wines, which get thoroughly shaken up being delivered to the store and then taken to your house. But fine old wines do seem to suffer, and almost go into shock when subjected to a journey.

CREATING IDEAL CONDITIONS

The easiest way to create the right conditions for storing wine is to buy a temperature- and humidity-controlled, wine cabinet. These plug into a normal electric socket and come in various sizes; the smallest are about the size of a small

One of the most important things is to remember to store bottles which are sealed with a cork horizontally in order to keep the cork moist. This does not apply to those bottles which have a screw cap.

refrigerator, and the largest are the size of a room. They are not cheap, but they are efficient, look good and give you easy access. They can be heavy when full, so make sure your floors can take the strain, and the motors can be noisy—a point to consider if you put it in a living area.

An alternative, if you want your wine at home, is to convert a room, installing insulation and humidity control. This might be a practical solution if you have a useful builder, or a talent for home improvements: insulation materials, such as foam boards, are useful here, but be careful to choose an air-conditioning unit that is suitable for wine storage: many dry the air too much to be ideal. Bear in mind, also, that you may need to heat the area in winter, as well as cool it in summer. Remember to exclude light, but do not block up air vents: you need ventilation.

A more permanent solution is to dig a cellar under your house. This requires the services of a surveyor and builder, and is not something to be undertaken lightly; there is no doubt that a traditional underground cellar is the best of all options, however, if your wine justifies the expense. If money is no option, then your cellar can be state-of-the-art, with beautiful polished hardwood storage, a professional tasting and decanting area, and computer-controlled temperature, light and humidity.

If you don't want to go to those lengths, you can buy a semi-made-to-measure

jeroboams, and the like. Bigger bottles are ideal for long-term storage, but will not fit into standard bottle racks and you will have to build or buy special racks. And you will need a system of labelling your bins or racks, so that you can see which wines are where without disturbing them.

version: the Spiral Cellar is a concrete-lined system, designed around a spiral staircase that you access via a trapdoor in a floor. It is not a cheap option, but your wine will be convenient.

If you are designing your own wine cellar, then you should think about whether you want bins or racks with holes for individual bottles. Bins take a minimum of twelve bottles each, and are more economical of space, but less convenient if the bottle you want happens to be at the bottom of a stack. In traditional wine producers' cellars, bins are the norm, but then space is not at a premium in such cellars, and if there is only one bottle left of a vintage, it gets a bin to itself. You might prefer simple shelves: if you are storing wine with a view to future resale, then these can be a good option, since you will want to keep your wines unopened in their original wooden cases. Think, too, about the space required for big bottles: magnums,

Left: If space is a problem, you need to find an alternative way of keeping your wine. This cellar designed around a spiral staircase hidden by a trapdoor is ideal.

STORING WINE IN A WAREHOUSE OR WITH A WINE MERCHANT

If you do not wish to build a cellar, or convert somewhere in your house, then you have no option but to store your wine in somebody else's cellar. To store fine wine with a friend requires a high degree of trust, and you might prefer to pay a fee to a professional to do it for you. Basically, you can store it with the merchant from whom you bought it; or you can deal with a warehouse directly. Either way, there will be an annual per-case fee. If you are likely to need access to your wine at short notice, this is not the most convenient way to keep it: you will need to make an appointment, and give plenty of notice, before collecting it. So it is only suitable for wine you want to lay down for a matter of years.

If you do choose this route, however, try and visit the warehouse before entrusting your wine to it; if you are only planning to store a couple of cases, this might not be possible, but you should do all you can to check on the efficiency of the management. You also need to be certain that the place is secure from theft, with locks, window bars and a good alarm system. All cases should be marked with their owner's name, and the warehouse should have papers detailing ownership of all cases. You should also keep papers detailing your wines at your house, in case problems arise.

If you are arranging storage with your wine merchant, then you should be just as rigorous in ensuring that your cases are marked with your name, and that you both have papers detailing your title to the wine. Wine merchants can go bankrupt, and you need to be sure that you would get your wine if this should happen. Check the insurance position before you go ahead. Is insurance included in your fee, or do you have to arrange for it yourself? (Insurance is also something to consider if you are storing a lot of wine at home.)

You will find some wine merchants have arrangements with their customers whereby they offer a certain amount of secure storage in a warehouse, for customers to fill as and when they like. This can be very convenient, provided you are happy to be tied in to buying from the same merchant every time.

TAKING STOCK

If you have the wine, you might as well have the computer software to go with it. A number of programs exist, which enable you to keep track of your wine, wherever it is. You feed in the details of your wine and where it is stored, and as you drink it so you adjust your records. Such programs also come with features like vintage charts, tasting notes and advice on ageing, to help you decide

Below: Every wine lover's dream would be to have a cellar, such as this, where they not only have room to store their wine but also room enough to decant it when necessary.

when to drink your wine, but the main attraction seems to be the clever things you can do: charts, graphs and all manner of computer tricks.

In any case, you'll need to keep some sort of record. A cellar book is the traditional way, entering the details of the wine, and recording when it was drunk, and on what occasion. This sort of record also gives you the opportunity of relishing how little you paid for a wine, and how much it is worth now—by no means the least of the wine collector's pleasures.

CHAPTER 11

NEW WORLD vs. OLD WORLD

It is possible to teach old dogs new tricks, or should the young pretenders be taking note of their elders?

Before we compare the Old and New Worlds of wine, it might be a good idea to agree on a definition of what constitutes the "Old" and "New" worlds.

Does the New World comprise the lands that humans have taken the wine vine to, in other words, the countries that *vitis vinifera* is not indigenous to? Well that definitely identifies the Americas, Australasia and South Africa. But it could be argued that it also includes parts of France and Italy outside the area of the Caucasus Mountains where the wine vine was first identified and cultivated.

Most people accept that the "New" World consists of the lands, well colonies really, set up by European explorers from the fifteenth century onward. This makes some producers, especially those from South Africa, claim that they cannot be "New" World producers because they have been making wine for three hundred years. Hardly new, I agree, but when you think that the French and Italians have produced wine for nearly two millennia, they're still the new boys on the block.

OLD HABITS DIE HARD

It used to be fairly simple to compare the winemaking of "Old" and "New" World producers. The "Old" world producers had their hands tied by restrictive legislation,

which, by protecting the production of wines in a traditional style, also managed to stifle experimentation and encouraged a lazy attitude in producers who were forced to make wine in the same manner as their forebears.

Change was frowned on; "if it ain't broke, don't try fixing it" appeared to be the prevailing attitude. The mindset of all concerned in the production of the wine—from the bureaucrats devising and policing the classification system to the producers and merchants—was that this was the way to make the best wines in the world, and that was enough. Who cared that the flavours that were described as *terroir* were actually winemaking faults? If all the wine was sold, what was the problem?

TIME FOR A CHANGE

The "New" world producers, on the other hand, were scientific in approach, innovative, competitive and had a single, overall aim: to make good wine with sweet, fruit flavours that people enjoyed drinking, no matter where it came from. If the better fruit was a state away, then they would go get it and bring it to their winery. In other words, satisfy the consumer.

Experimentation was the route to progress. What would happen if the grapes

Previous pages: Stainless-steel vats in use in Spain.
Above: Vineyards in the Côte d'Or in Burgundy in France.

were picked at night? Why couldn't the juice be fermented in stainless steel? What would happen if the fermentation was kept cool and took a bit longer? How would this or that variety stand up to barrel maturation?

So it seemed "'Old' world staid; 'New' world modern and exciting," was the situation. But of course it wasn't that simple, and it never has been.

MARKET FORCES

It is true that, at the less expensive end of the wine market, the "New" World producers were using every trick in the winemaker's handbook to produce fruit-driven, easy-drinking wines with oak flavours, even if the wine had never seen a barrel in its life; whereas the "Old" World producers seemed to be stuck in a deep rut of thin and acidic wines. However, at the middle and upper end of the market, there were New World producers who were picking the best, traditional practices of the "Old" World and applying them to their wines.

So you would find wines coming from vineyards that were densely planted in the first place to cut the yields, which were then further reduced by "dry farming", that is, there was no irrigation, in order to produce concentrated flavours in the berries. The bunches of grapes were then harvested by hand and gently transported to the winery to damage the fruit as little as possible, and this also enabled the pickers to discard damaged, or rotten, berries before they got to the press. In other words, the producers of these wines were using the techniques developed over centuries in the "Old" World to produce top-quality wines in their own country.

Take the Australian wine Grange, for example. Max Schubert, who developed the wine, was inspired after a visit to Bordeaux in the 1950s. Or the collaborative project between Robert Mondavi and Baron Philippe de Rothschild in the Napa Valley, Opus One. Both these wines combine the best of both worlds to produce top-class wines with an international following.

OLD DOGS AND NEW TRICKS

Of course, the same is happening in the "Old" world; many of the younger generation of winemakers have travelled the world's wine regions and have returned to the family home filled with new ideas. They have planted new vine varieties and made wines that don't fit into the recognised scheme of things, which consequently have to be sold in strange and different categories.

Some of these wines are beginning to develop a following, perhaps not as strong as some of the "New" World wines, especially those cult wines produced by small, boutique wineries in areas like California, but a following nonetheless. Look at Le Pin, from Pomerol, in Bordeaux. Prior to the 1982 vintage bursting onto the wine scene, very few people had heard of it. Then the owner, Jacques Thienpont, produced a concentrated, powerful wine with lots of new oak flavours battling

with rich Merlot grapes. Using only the best grapes and making some six hundred cases a year, he created an instant classic, and the price shot through the roof.

For every Le Pin, there are, naturally enough, a number of wines that haven't changed, that still rely on finesse and structure to deliver a wine style that has hardly changed over the centuries. But even some of these wines are benefiting from a "tweak" here and there in the techniques used to produce them.

The big danger is that we may get a homogenisation of wine styles and end up with an international style of wine. And, in some cases, that is beginning to happen. It is now not as easy to recognise, say, Cabernets from Chile, as opposed to those from the Napa Valley, or Coonawarra. But there are still enough wines, passionate winemakers and legislators to ensure that this does not, and cannot, happen. The saving grace of the French *appellation* system, and its fellow wine laws, is that they have preserved wine styles from different regions and prevented the globalisation of their vineyards.

In summary, it is probably true to say that it is a state of mind that defines an "Old" and "New" World style, as the better producers cherry-pick aspects of each other's winemaking culture in order to help them to produce the best wines that they can. The great leveller in this argument is, of course, the climate that the vines grow in. Grapes grown in warm, or hot, climates will very rarely taste the same as cool-climate fruit grown in more marginal vineyards. Pinot Noir, for example, is always Pinot Noir, but great Burgundy is a wine!

EUROPEAN WINE LAWS

When we look at the wine legislation of Europe, which controls all wine produced in and imported to Europe, we find the basic DNA is that of French wine laws that date back to the seventeenth and eighteenth centuries. In fact, if you look at many a country's wine legislation around the world you can see elements of European wine laws that have been "cherry-picked" and "shoehorned" into a shape that suits that country. So even today the French can claim to be the centre of wine production because most countries still look to them for inspiration.

European wine law is based on the concept of "place" rather than "product"— not that silly when you think that vineyards have to be located *somewhere*, but this idea can trace its origins back to the French notion of *terroir*. You can read more about this on page 153. As noted there, the present system has maintained the diversity of French wines, but it has also stifled experimentation.

In short, countries like Chile may have stolen a march by being able to plant what they want, where they want, to see what happens. France on the other hand will never know, for example, where the next great Sauvignon Blanc region might be because they are not allowed to plant it any further north or east of Touraine in the Loire Valley. Is the Muscadet region really too cool for Sauvignon Blanc vines?

Even with all these strictures it is important to point out that, in common with almost every set of wine laws around the world, European wine laws are not a guarantee of quality. Terms such as *Appelation Contrôlée (AC) or Denominazione di Origine Controllata (DOC)* simply state that the wine or food (the system does not just classify wine) comes from a certain area and has been made following certain rules.

Recently the European Union sought to harmonise the legislation within member states and brought out two new terms that you may find appearing on wine labels, although it seems that wine might be able to continue to use the existing terms as well:

PROTECTED DESIGNATION OF ORIGIN (PDO)

To qualify for a PDO a wine must show that it has qualities and characteristics that are due to its region of production and that it is produced exclusively within that region.

This means, for example, that all French Appellation Controlée, Italian DOC and DOCG and German Prädikat wines are included in this category. You may soon see the initials AC on a French bottle of wine change to AP (Appellation Protégée).

PROTECTED GEOGRAPHICAL INDICATION (PGI)

This is the grade below PDO and to qualify the product (wine in our case) must come from an area that has a specific quality which can be attributed to its geographical origin. It does not have to be specifically produced in that region, however. Cabernet Sauvignon can come from many places, but Cabernet Sauvignon IGP Pays d'Oc can come only from that region.

Wines in the French Vin de Pays and Italian IGT categories fall under this designation.

Research into the effects of alcohol continue, but sometimes a little of what you fancy does you good.

It is only very recently that the beneficial—and harmful—effects of wine have been studied scientifically; and these studies come after a period when wine, and alcohol in general, was widely regarded automatically as harmful. For most of human history, however, wine has been seen as one of the most healthy substances available to humanity. Indeed, until at least the eighteenth century, wine was considered a great deal safer to drink than the local water in much of Europe. In some parts of the world, this is still the case.

A HISTORICAL OVERVIEW

The benefits of wine were recognised early. Wine was used as a base for medicines by the ancient Egyptians and Sumerians as early as 2000 B.C.; somewhat later, around 450 B.C., the great Greek doctor, Hippocrates, recommended wine as a disinfectant in its own right, and as an essential part of the diet. Some 600 years later, Galen, the most celebrated doctor in the Roman Empire, honed his skills on wounded gladiators, and found that wine was the most effective disinfectant available for treating their horrendous wounds. It should be remembered that distillation had not yet been invented, so pure alcohol was not available to these physicians. Anyway, modern research has proved that wine is

Below A glass of wine when out relaxing with friends is no bad thing, but remember not to drink and drive.

actually a better disinfectant than spirits, and contains antibacterial agents that spirits lack. It is worth bearing this in mind, even today, when visiting parts of the world where the water might not be safe to drink.

The Jewish Talmud shares the view of wine as a medicine: "Wine is the foremost of all medicines," it says; "wherever wine is lacking, medicines become necessary." The Islamic world, which produced many of the great physicians of the early medieval period, also used wine for medical purposes, although, since the drinking of wine was forbidden, then as now, it could only be used externally.

In medieval Europe, local medicine tended to be the responsibility of monasteries, and here again wine was widely used; indeed, monks were in the lead when it came to nosing out good sites for vineyards. Monastic plantings are at the heart of many a classic wine region, including Burgundy and the Rheingau. It is pleasing to think that patients were not only given a daily ration of wine, but that the wine might well have been rather good. One hospital in Germany provided each patient with ten pints a day, each: enough to keep a whole family happy.

It wasn't until the late nineteenth century that attitudes about wine and other forms of alcohol began to change. The disinfectant properties of wine were still recognised—as late as 1892, when there was an outbreak of cholera in Hamburg, wine was added to the water to make it safer to drink—but wine as a recreational drink increasingly came under attack. Temperance societies preached the virtues of total abstinence, Prohibition hit the U.S., and the role of wine in medicine diminished with the development of a new generation of drugs. By the 1970s and 1980s health campaigners were increasingly focusing on the ill effects of wine, and it seemed to many that the neo-Prohibitionists were winning.

KNOWN BENEFITS OF ALCOHOL

Until, that is, 1991, when the television programme *60 Minutes* turned the then current wisdom on its head. The show outlined something called the French Paradox—that the French seemed to eat a high-fat diet, while having only a low rate of coronary heart disease. This was absolutely contrary to everything the medical profession had preached, high-fat foods being more or less equal to alcohol in the list of deadly sins. The doctors behind the research had come up with a J-shaped graph showing rates of heart disease fell by nearly a third with moderate wine consumption, only to rise again with very heavy consumption.

Sales of red wine in the United States quadrupled almost overnight. There have been further studies of the effects of wine on health since, and the general verdict seems to be pretty consistent: moderate drinking is good for the heart. Defining moderation has been more problematic: one to two drinks a day is a common rule, though specific definitions vary. In the United Kingdom one glass of wine measures 175 ml, and is considered to contain two units of alcohol. In Britain, a unit of alcohol is taken to be 10 ml of pure alcohol; women are advised to have no more than two or three units a day,

Above: If you are going to have a glass of wine, then it is always better to drink it with a meal of some kind.

while the figure for men is three or four units a day. Compare this with France, where a unit of alcohol is considered to be 15 ml and men and women should not exceed three units a day. For women who are pregnant or breastfeeding, these limits drop to zero to prevent any damage to the baby. That said, my mother told me that if I was unsettled she would have a glass of sherry before feeding me to help me drop off to sleep. That might explain a lot!

No two people are identical, however, and individuals should take into account their age, build and general health; each person's genetic inheritance also affects how they deal with alcohol. And women and men do not metabolise alcohol equally: it is not just a question of size. Different levels of stomach enzymes mean that women absorb more alcohol from the same intake.

Research into the effects of wine and other forms of alcohol is ongoing, and brings both good and bad news for the drinker. Most media attention has been focused on the effects of wine on the heart, and here the news seems to be almost entirely good, provided consumption of wine is moderate. The significant reduction in the rate of heart disease—by almost a third—seems to be because wine encourages the formation of high-density lipoprotein (HDL) cholesterol, which, in turn, clears the blood of the artery-blocking plaques formed by low-density lipoprotein (LDL) cholesterol. Alcohol also has an anticoagulant effect, which makes blood clots less likely.

IN MODERATION

This anticoagulant effect lasts only twenty-four hours, however, which is why regular moderate drinking is the key, rather than binge drinking. The latter is universally recognised as bad, leading to all sorts of health problems, including strokes, while not offering the protection of a regular couple of glasses of wine with a meal.

The phenols in wine, particularly red wine, also have a part to play in protecting against heart disease. These phenols, in particular, resveratrol, have antioxidant properties, which help to prevent the formation of LDL cholesterol; it may well be that resveratrol is central to the beneficial effects of red wine on the heart. A recent study also suggests that red wine can stimulate an enzyme, which, in turn, increases levels of nitric oxide; this can help to lower blood pressure and inhibit plaque formation in arteries. Another recent study has indicated that moderate drinkers have lower levels of C-reactive protein (CRP)—which is a predictor of cardiovascular disease—than those who drink only occasionally or not at all.

Most attention has focused on red wine as a heart protector; white wine, beer and spirits do not seem to have the same effect, although further research in the future might contradict this.

Above: A glass of red wine has been shown to help women combat the risk of heart disease after menopause.

THE POTENTIAL HARM OF DRINKING ALCOHOL

The bad news for women is that, although red wine can help protect against heart disease after menopause, until then there does seem to be a slightly increased risk of breast cancer from drinking wine.

Research on other cancers is still ongoing, and findings are generally bad. Wine consumption has an association with cancer of the oesophagus, a smaller association with cancer of the stomach, and a smaller still association with cancer of the colon. In laboratory tests, resveratrol has been shown to protect cells from cancer, so one might hope that the good effects of resveratrol in red wine might counteract the bad effects of alcohol; but wine is a complex substance, with complex effects.

Wine's effect on strokes has also come under close scrutiny recently. The latest verdict is that moderate drinking—two or three drinks per day—seems to reduce the risk of ischemic stroke, the kind caused by a blood clot, although heavy drinking—exceeding the daily limits—increases that risk. Again, we have that J-shaped graph, with moderate drinkers coming off better than non-drinkers, while heavy drinkers come off worst of all. It is this that makes the medical profession nervous about endorsing the health benefits of wine—that and the known effects of drinking and driving, underage drinking and binge drinking. All these cause enormous social problems; and drinking by pregnant women comes in for particular criticism. Excessive drinking in pregnancy can result in foetal alcohol syndrome, with its associated low intelligence and abnormal facial features.

For the elderly, regular moderate wine consumption can help improve memory and help ward off dementia. Wine drinking also seems to be good for the eyes in old age: again, it might be the antioxidant and anticoagulant properties of wine that help keep the eyes in good condition. Postmenopausal women may find that moderate wine drinking helps keep osteoporosis at bay, though, as usual, heavy drinkers show the opposite effect, with a greater risk of fractures.

One of the most common ill effects of wine drinking is a headache, with red wine taking the blame for many a migraine. Although research is continuing, wine, in moderation, is increasingly seen as being part of a healthy lifestyle, along with exercise and a balanced diet.

CHAPTER 13

ORGANIC/BIODYNAMIC/ NATURAL WINEMAKING

Winemaking, especially on a large scale, can be harmful to the environment. Moulds, rots and pests need to be controlled, yields need to be maintained and the easiest way to achieve this is to use industrial fungicide and pesticide sprays and fertilisers.

Unfortunately these chemicals are not selective, and overuse can result in harm to friendly insects and natural yeasts. So environmentally aware growers are turning to other growing methods to limit the effect of vineyards on the environment.

SUSTAINABLE AGRICULTURE

Known as "Lutte Raisonee" in France, this system minimises the use of chemicals in the vineyard. Before, growers would have a programme of spraying that was carried out as a preventative measure. Sustainable growers monitor the state of the vineyard and only spray when it is necessary to control a problem. This reduces the environmental impact but still allows the grower to intervene when necessary to protect the crop.

Some wineries are also moving towards becoming carbon-neutral—pretty hard when you think of the amount of carbon dioxide created by yeasts during the fermentation process.

One winery in New Zealand has gained certification through a number of means. They have reduced the weight of their bottles, they have installed wind turbines and solar panels, they recycle

Above: These vines in Champagne have small packets of pheromones hanging from wire to stop insects laying eggs on them.

water for irrigation, use recycled glass and cardboard in their packaging and, my personal favourite, have installed a flock of Baby Doll miniature sheep in the vineyard to keep the grass and weeds under control without using machinery. Why miniature sheep? To stop them reaching up and eating the grapes, of course!

There are more environmentally friendly ways to grow grapes. A grower's choice can be decided by a passion and belief in preserving the environment.

ORGANIC VITICULTURE

It is important to point out that there is no such thing as an organic wine, simply because no one can define an organic winemaking process. No, when people talk about organic wine they are really talking about wines made from organically grown grapes, although you may also find that the winemaker may use less sulphur in the winemaking process.

To grow organic grapes you cannot use any artificial insecticides, herbicides or fertilisers. There are a number of organisations that certify the process used in vineyards to guarantee that the grapes are organically grown and there is normally a three year "crossover" or qualification period where the grower will follow organic practices before the vineyard is classed as organic. This allows time for any chemical residue to leech out of the soils and vines.

What are the accepted organic practices? Well, instead of insecticides growers can encourage natural predators of the pests into the vineyard. For

Above: This cockerel and his chicks 'rule the roost' in 'his' organic vineyard in Chile, eating bugs and fertilising the soil.

example ladybirds, if encouraged to stay by creating the right environment, will eat thousands of aphids a day, while predator wasps can lay their eggs inside the larvae of other pests which when hatched will live off the larvae. Chickens can also be used to control beetles and other insects (and they can help fertilise the soil—enough said).

Instead of herbicides, plants can be used to control the growth of weeds between the rows of vines. The flowers of these plants can help to attract the predator insects into the vineyard.

Industrial fertilisers can be replaced by composts made from winemaking residue such as grape skins. Plants, such as clovers, between the rows can also inject nutrients into the soil and

Above: A couple of the around 1,000 geese employed at Cono Sur's Chimbarongo vineyard to eat insects such as the Burrito. Their love of grapes however, means that they are barred for the three months before harvest.

when cut back in the summer can act as "green" compost.

All of these practices are aimed at improving the quality of the soil and attracting insects and worms into the vineyard to increase its viability.

BIODYNAMIC VITICULTURE

Biodynamics could be described as "Organics Plus". It takes all the precepts of organic farming, including the replacement of industrial herbicides, pesticides and fertilisers, but adds to that a belief in philosophy, herbal preparations and the influence of the cosmos—a sort of spiritual mysticism if you like, very "New Age".

The origins of biodynamic viticulture can be traced back to 1924 and the Austrian philosopher Rudolf Steiner, who noticed a deterioration in the health of crops and farm animals affected by industrial fertilisers. The practices are now certified by the Demeter organisation, amongst others.

Two of the most controversial practices of biodynamics are the homeopathic use of nine preparations. These include preparation 500, where cow manure is buried over winter in cow horns, and preparation 502, where Yarrow flowers are placed in a stag's bladder which is then hung up in the summer sun, buried over winter before being dug up in spring and the contents, after being removed from the bladder, mixed into the compost. Unlike the cow's horn the stag's bladder is not reused.

A teaspoon of the cow manure is mixed with 60 litres of water and after stirring (apparently you have to change the direction of the stirring every few minutes) is sprayed over the soil in the afternoon.

The other contentious practice looks at the cosmic influence on the plant and its fruit. The biodynamic calendar is not the simple one that we look at daily in our diaries; this calendar also includes the lunar cycle. The belief is that since lunar and other astrological influences will affect the soil, so planting, composting, spraying and harvesting times should be controlled by these influences as well. However, to my knowledge, no one has to dance naked around the vines.

Biodynamic growers are passionate in their conviction that these practices produce better, healthier grapes and it is true that wines made this way can and do taste better. But, and it is a big but, since there is no way to measure the influence of the moon for example, I am not sure if the wine is better because of the biodynamic principles, or the passion and care of the growers and winemakers.

"NATURAL" WINES

This is a relatively new concept and if you thought that biodynamics was contentious, you ain't seen nothing yet!

Firstly, let's get rid of the contention. No one can agree what is a "natural" wine. There is no definition. The producers agree that "natural" wines are made with little or no chemical or other intervention. But that's about it. And whilst I agree with some of their thoughts, some of the comments about "natural" wines just make my blood boil.

Yes, use natural wild yeasts rather than laboratory-developed ones Yes, grow organically or biodynamically. Yes, don't adjust the acidity or add sugar to the grape juice. Yes, don't manipulate the wine to adjust the alcohol level. But no sulphur? The wine won't keep for longer than a few months. No new oak barrels? That's a flavour policy, not a belief. No irrigation of the vineyards? Well, goodbye Spain, the USA and most of South America, Australia and South Africa amongst others.

Some of the producers I have met are reasonable people who want to make the best wine they can with the minimum of intervention. They want to make the grape and the *terroir* shine through and I can follow their thoughts and enjoy their wines. Others, though, seem to be wine "zealots" who want to take us back to the dark ages. They accept faults because the wine is "natural." Producing some of the worst wines I have ever tasted, but enthusing over the fact that this is how wine used to taste hundreds of years ago.

A nice academic exercise but not really relevant to today's wine market, where purity of fruit and flavour is important.

I'm sorry to say this, but at its worst you can simply replace the word "natural" with "bad", and that is no help to a consumer who is looking for wines made with a thought to the effect its production has had upon the world we live in. As the late Australian winemaker Len Evans once said, "Life is too short to drink bad wine."

To me, the case for "natural" wines is still not proven. Until there is a definition of the process and producers who put beliefs before ability are weeded out, it is a case of buyer beware and try before you buy.

CHAPTER 14

VINTAGES

WHAT IS VINTAGE WINE?

When most people think of "vintage" wine, they usually associate it with newspaper headlines, saying a case of Chateau This or That 19XX has been sold at auction for thousands and thousands. In fact, the term "vintage" simply refers to the year a bottle of wine was produced, or rather, the year in which the grapes used to make it were harvested, and actually not all wine is vintage wine— for example, Champagne is mostly non-vintage, because much of it is blended with wines from different years to ensure a consistent taste and quality, likewise Sherry.

The majority of wine is drunk maybe two to three years after it has been made, but many people buy wine as an investment and not just for consumption, so having some kind of guide as to whether one year was better than another is of help to them and to those who occasionally want to splurge on something a bit special.

One thing to bear in mind, though, is that wine can vary, not just from region to region, but also from one area to another within a region. Also, in a year that is generally considered indifferent, a producer of quality wine may still produce something that is decent enough to drink, while a poor producer will just produce a poor wine.

Charts normally tell you about the quality of a wine, rather than whether a wine is ready to drink or not. That's why the following charts are slightly different. They aim to do two things: first, to give an idea as to the quality of a wine and, second, to show how good a wine might be to drink, since some wines really do need to stay in the bottle for a while to mature, whereas others are best drunk young.

Of course, the only true test is to taste the wine oneself, and how hard is that?

VINTAGE CHARTS

Key:

0 = Poor   1 = OK   2 = Above average   3 = Good   4 = Very good   5 = Excellent

I = Ready to drink   ✓ = Can drink, but will improve with keeping   — = Keep a little longer | = Probably past it

YEAR	11	10	09	08	07	06	05	04	03	02	01	00	99	98	97	96	95	94	93	92
France																				
Bordeaux Red	4I	5I	5I	4I	3I	4—	5—	3✓	4—	3✓	4✓	4✓	3I	3✓	2I	3I	4✓	2I	2I	2I
Bordeaux White	4✓	3I	3—	4✓	3✓	4—	4—	3✓	4—	2✓	4✓	4✓	2I	4I	2I	3I	3I	3I	2I	2I
Sauternes/Barsac	4—	4—	4—	3—	4—	4—	3—	2✓	3—	4✓	5✓	3✓	4I	3✓	4I	5I	3I	2I	1I	1I
Burgundy Red	4I	4—	4—	3I	3—	3✓	5—	2✓	4I	4✓	4✓	4✓	4✓	3I	3I	4I	4I	3I	4I	4I
Burgundy White	4I	4—	4✓	3—	3✓	4✓	4✓	3I	3I	4✓	3✓	3✓	4✓	3I	3I	4I	4I	2I	2I	3I
Chablis	4I	5I	3✓	4✓	3I	4I	3I	3I	4I	5I	3✓	3✓	3✓	3I	4I	5I	4I	2I	2I	2I
Alsace	4✓	5✓	4✓	4✓	5I	3✓	5✓	3I	3I	5I	3I	3I	3I	3I	4I	4I	4I	2I	2I	1I
Loire Red	4I	4I	3—	3—	3✓	3✓	4✓	3I	3—	3✓	4✓	4✓	3I	4I	5I	4I	4I	3I	2I	2I
Loire White	4I	5—	4✓	4✓	4✓	3✓	5✓	4I	4I	4I	4I	4I	4I	3I	5I	4I	4I	3I	2I	2I
Champagne	n/a	3I	3—	4—	3—	4—	4✓	4✓	3✓	5✓	2✓	3✓	4✓	4✓	3✓	4✓	4✓	2✓	3I	2I
Rhône Red	4—	4—	4✓	3I	3I	4—	4✓	3I	4✓	3I	3✓	4✓	3I	4I	3✓	4I	4I	3I	2I	2I
Rhône White	4I	4—	3I	3I	3I	4I	4I	4—	3I	3✓	3✓	4I	4I	4I	4I	4I	3I	3I	1I	2I
Beaujolais	4—	4—	5✓	4✓	3✓	4✓	4✓	3I	4I	3I	3✓	3✓	4I	4I	4I	3I	5I	1I	3I	3I

# Key:
0 = Poor   1 = OK   2 = Above average   3 = Good   4 = Very good   5 = Excellent

I = Ready to drink   **✓** = Can drink, but will improve with keeping   **—** = Keep a little longer   **!** = Probably past it

YEAR	11	10	09	08	07	06	05	04	03	02	01	00	99	98	97	96	95	94	93	92
Germany																				
Rheingau/Rheinhessen	4I	4I	3I	4I	4I	5I	4I	3I	4I	4I	4✓	3✓	4✓	3I	5I	3I	4I	3I	4I	
Mosel-Saar-Ruwer	4I	4I	4I	4I	4I	4I	5I	4I	4I	4I	5✓	3✓	4✓	3I	5I	3I	5I	4I	5I	4!
Austria																				
White	4I	4I	4I	3I	3✓	4✓	3I	3✓	4—	3✓	–	3I	4I	3I	5I	2I	4I	3I	4I	3I
Italy																				
Piedmonte	4I	4I	4I	4I	4I	4I	3✓	5✓	3✓	4—	5✓	2✓	4✓	5✓	5✓	4✓	4I	2I	3I	1I
Veneto	4I	4I	4I	4I	4I	4✓	4✓	4I	3✓	4I	4✓	4✓	4✓	3I	5I	3I	5I	3I	4I	–
Tuscany	4✓	5✓	5I	4I	4✓	4✓	4✓	4I	3I	5I	4✓	2✓	4✓	4I	4I	3I	4I	5I	2I	1I
Spain																				
Rioja	4I	4I	4I	3I	3I	4I	4I	3I	3I	5I	4✓	2✓	3✓	4✓	2I	4I	4I	5I	1I	2I
Penedes Red	4I	4I	3✓	3✓	3I	3I	4I	4I	3I	3I	4I	3✓	3✓	4✓	3I	4I	3I	4I	3I	3I
Ribera del Duero	4I	4I	3✓	3✓	3✓	4✓	4I	3I	3I	4I	3✓	2✓	3✓	4✓	4✓	5✓	4I	5I	1I	2I
Penedes White	3✓	5✓	5✓	4✓	3✓	3—	4✓	5✓	4I	3I	5✓	3✓	4I	3I	3I	4I	3I	3I	2I	2I

Key:
0 = Poor 1 = OK 2 = Above average 3 = Good 4 = Very good 5 = Excellent
✓ = Can drink, but will improve with keeping — = Keep a little longer ! = Probably past it
! = Ready to drink

YEAR	11	10	09	08	07	06	05	04	03	02	01	00	99	98	97	96	95	94	93	92
Portugal																				
Alentejo	4—	4✓	4✓	3—	3—	3—	3✓	3✓	3✓	4✓	4!	4!	3!	2!	4!	2!	4!	3!	1!	2!
Dão	4—	5—	4—	4—	3—	4—	5—	4—	4—	3—	4!	4!	3!	2!	4!	4!	4!	4!	4!	3!
Vintage Port	5—	n/a	4—	3✓	4—	n/a	n/a	n/a	4—	n/a	3✓	4✓	2✓	3!	4!	4✓	4✓	5✓	–	4✓
Australia																				
South Australia Red	4—	5—	4—	3—	3—	4!	5!	4!	3!	3!	4✓	4✓	3!	4!	4!	4!	3!	4!	2!	3!
South Australia White	4—	5—	4—	3!	4!	4!	3!	3!	4!	3!	3✓	3✓	4!	5!	5!	4!	4!	4!	2!	3!
New South Wales Red	4—	4—	4—	3—	3—	4—	4—	4!	3!	3!	4✓	3✓	3✓	5!	3!	5!	3!	3!	3!	1!
New South Wales White	4—	4—	3—	3—	3—	4!	3!	4!	3!	3!	3!	3!	4!	5!	1!	4!	4!	3!	3!	1!
Victoria Red	4—	3—	3!	3—	4!	4!	4!	3!	3!	4!	4✓	3✓	4!	5!	2!	3!	4!	3!	3!	5!
Victoria White	3—	4—	3✓	4✓	3!	4!	4!	3!	4!	4!	4✓	4✓	3!	5!	5!	3!	3!	4!	4!	3!
Western Australia Red	4—	5—	4—	4—	5!	3!	4!	4!	3!	4!	4✓	4✓	4!	2!	5!	5!	4!	4!	5!	2!
Western Australia White	4—	4—	3✓	3✓	4✓	3!	4!	3!	3!	4!	3✓	4!	2!	4!	4!	4!	5!	2!	4!	2!
Tasmania Red	4—	4—	3—	3—	4—	4!	4!	3!	4!	4!	3✓	4✓	4!	4!	4!	0!	3!	4!	4!	2!
Tasmania White	3—	4—	3✓	4✓	3!	1!	4!	3!	4!	4!	3✓	3!	4!	5!	5!	1!	2!	4!	3!	4!

Key:

0 = Poor 1 = OK 2 = Above average 3 = Good 4 = Very good 5 = Excellent
✓ = Ready to drink ✓ = Can drink, but will improve with keeping ▬ = Keep a little longer ▮ = Probably past it

YEAR	11	10	09	08	07	06	05	04	03	02	01	00	99	98	97	96	95	94	93	92
New Zealand																				
Red	5▬	4▬	3✓	4▬	3✓	4▮	4▮	3▮	4▮	3▮	5▮	4▮	5▮	3▮	4▮	2▮	5▮	4▮	2▮	5▮
White	4▮	4▮	3▮	4▮	3▮	4▮	4▮	4▮	4▮	4▮	4✓	4✓	4▮	4▮	4▮	4▮	2▮	4▮	3▮	2▮
South Africa																				
Red	4✓	5✓	5✓	3✓	4✓	4✓	3✓	4▮	5▮	3▮	4▮	4✓	3✓	3▮	4▮	1▮	5▮	4▮	2▮	4▮
White	4✓	4✓	4▮	3✓	3✓	4▮	3▮	3▮	5▮	3▮	3▮	5▮	3▮	3▮	4▮	3▮	3▮	3▮	4▮	3▮
Argentina																				
Red	4✓	3✓	4✓	4▮	3▮	4▮	3▮	3▮	4▮	4▮	4✓	4✓	4▮	1▮	4▮	4▮	4▮	3▮	2▮	3▮
White	4✓	4▮	4▮	4▮	4▮	3▮	3▮	4▮	3▮	4▮	–	2▮	2▮	1▮	3▮	3▮	2▮	4▮	2▮	3▮
Chile																				
Red	5▬	3✓	3✓	4✓	5✓	3▮	4▮	4▮	4▮	3▮	4▮	4▮	4▮	3▮	3▮	4▮	4▮	3▮	3▮	3▮
White	4▮	4▮	3▮	3▮	4▮	4▮	4▮	4▮	3▮	4▮	–	2▮	4▮	3▮	4▮	4▮	4▮	3▮	3▮	–

Key:

0 = Poor 1 = OK 2 = Above average 3 = Good 4 = Very good 5 = Excellent

I = Ready to drink ✔ = Can drink, but will improve with keeping ▬ = Keep a little longer I = Probably past it

YEAR	11	10	09	08	07	06	05	04	03	02	01	00	99	98	97	96	95	94	93	92
U.S.A.																				
California Red	4▬	4▬	3▬	4▬	5▬	4✔	5✔	4▬	4I	4I	4I	4I	4I	4I	4I	5I	5I	3I	4I	4I
California White	4I	3I	3✔	4I	4I	3I	4I	4I	4I	5I	4I	4I	4I	2I	3I	4I	4I	5I	3I	4I
New York State Red	4✔	4✔	3✔	3✔	3I	3I	4I	3I	3I	3I	4✔	3✔	2I	4I	4I	3I	4I	2I	4I	5I
New York State White	4✔	4✔	3I	4I	4I	3I	4I	4I	3I	3I	4✔	4I	3I	4I	4I	3I	5I	4I	4I	0I
Oregon Red	4▬	3▬	4✔	3I	4✔	3✔	4I	3I	3I	3I	—	4✔	4I	4I	3I	3I	1I	4I	3I	4I
Oregon White	3✔	3✔	4✔	4I	3I	4I	4I	4I	3I	3I	3✔	4I	4I	4I	2I	3I	2I	4I	3I	4I
Washington Red	4▬	4▬	4▬	3▬	4✔	4✔	5I	3I	4I	4I	3✔	5✔	4✔	4✔	4I	4I	3I	4I	4I	4I
Washington White	4I	4I	3I	4I	3I	4I	4I	3I	4I	4I	3✔	4I	4I	3I	4I	3I	4I	3I	2I	4I
Canada																				
Canada Red	4✔	5▬	4✔	4✔	5▬	4I	3I	4I	4I	3I	3✔	3✔	4I	4I	3I	3I	4I	3I	3I	2I
Canada White	4✔	5✔	4✔	4✔	5✔	4I	3I	4I	4I	3I	4✔	4I	4I	5I	4I	2I	5I	3I	4I	3I

GLOSSARY

The following list of words is by no means exhaustive, but it will help the new wine lover come to grips with the terminology commonly used in the wine industry and related fields. Where necessary the derivation of the word – that is, its language of origin – is shown immediately after it, followed by a guide to its pronunciation.

Key: Fr. = French; Ger. = German; It. = Italian; Lat. = Latin; Pt. = Portuguese; Sp. = Spanish

Abboccato (It.) (ab-boc-cah-toh) – medium sweet

Abocado (Sp.) (ab-oh-cah-doh) – medium sweet

Acid/Acidity – basic component of wine, either as malic acid or tartaric, that gives it an edge. Malic acid converts naturally to lactic acid which happens after the alcoholic fermentation

Adamado (Pt.) (ad-ah-mah-doh) – sweet

Adega (Pt.) (ah-day-gah) – cellar or winery

Amabile (It.) (ah-mah-bi-lay) – medium sweet, sweeter than abboccato (see above)

Amarone (It.) (ah-mah-row-nay) – bitter

American Viticultural Area (AVA) – wine-growing region designated by U.S. Government Agency TTB

Amontillado (Sp.) (am-on-tee-yah-doh) – a fino sherry that has been aged

Amtliche Prüfüngsnummer (A.P.) (Ger.) (amt-leekh-er proo-foongz-noom-eh) – official code given

to a quantity of German wine that has passed statutory tests in the region of origin

Anbaugebiet (Ger.) (an-bow-guh-beet) – a wine region

Añejado (Sp.) (an-yeh-hah-doh) – aged

Annato (It.) (an-nah-toh) – year

Año (Sp.) (an-yoh) – year

Anthocyanin – the tannin in grape skins which gives colour and flavour to red wines

Appellation d'Origine Contrôlée (A.O.C./A.C.) (Fr.) – (ap-pel-lass-ee-on d'orri-zheen con-troh-lay) – the designation awarded to French wines denoting a certain level of quality. It governs such things as the area of production, alcohol levels, grape varieties, and yields

Appellation d'Origine Protégée (A.O.P.) (Fr.) – (ap-pel-lass-ee-on d'orri-zheen proh-tay-jay) – the new term for Appellation d'Origine Contrôlée wines

Aroma – smell of the wine

Asciutto (It.) (ash-ee-oo-toh) – very dry

Assemblage (Fr.) (ass-som-blazh) – a blending of basic wines to create a cuvée, especially in Champagne and Bordeaux

Auslese (Ger) (ouse-lay-zeh) – sweet-tasting white wine produced in Germany made from late-picked grapes

Autolysis (oh-toll-ee-sis) – the interaction between wine and dead yeast cells

Azienda/Azienda Agricola (It.) (az-ee-en-dah ah-gree-coh-lah) – an estate or winery in Italy

Azienda vitivinicola (It.) (az-ee-en-dah vit-ee-vi-nee-coh-lah) – a specialist wine estate in Italy

Back-blending – the addition of sweet, unfermented grape juice to a wine to sweeten it

Ban de vendange (Fr.) (ban duh von-donzh) – the officially declared regional date for the beginning of grape picking

Barbaresco (It.) (bar-bar-ess-coh) – red wine made from Nebbiolo grapes produced in Piedmont in Italy

Bardolino (It.) (bar-doh-lee-noh) – a red wine made from Corvino Rondinella grapes in the Veneto region of Italy

Barolo (It.) (ba-roh-loh) – a D.O.C.G. wine made from Nebbiolo grapes in Piedmont, Italy

Barrel-ageing – maturing wine in oak barrels

Barrel-fermented – wine fermented in a barrel to give it stronger oak and vanilla flavours

Barrique (Fr.) (ba-reek) – a wooden barrel that can hold 225 litres

Baumé (Fr.) (boh-may) – the scale used in France which measures the amount of sugar in grape must

Bead(s) – bubble(s) found in sparkling wine

Beaujolais (Fr.) (bo-zho-lay) – a red wine produced from Gamay grapes in Burgundy, France

Beaujolais Nouveau (Fr.) (bo-zho-lay noo-voh) – the Beaujolais that is produced and released for sale to retailers only weeks after the harvest

Beaujolais Villages (Fr.) (bo-zho-lay vih-lahzh) – Beaujolais wine that is made from a blend of grapes from designated villages in the region and is slightly better in quality than ordinary Beaujolais

Beaune (Fr.) (bone) – city in the centre of the Côte d'Or in Burgundy

Beerenauslese (Ger.) (beer-en-ouse-lay-zeh) – white German wine made from ripe grapes affected by botrytis

Bentonite – the clay used for "fining" a wine

Bereich (Ger.) (beh-rike) – a group of villages within an Anbaugebiet

Bianco (It.) (bee-an-coh) – white

Blanc de Blancs (Fr.) (blonk-duh-blonk) – white wine made from white grapes

Blanc de Noirs (Fr.) (blonk-duh-nwahr) – white wine made from red grapes

Blanco (Sp.) (blank-oh) – white

Blending – the mixing of several wines to obtain a balanced blend

Bodega (Sp.) (boh-day-gah) – a cellar, wine shop or firm selling wine

Bordeaux (Fr.) (bore-doh) – the name of a city and wine producing region in western France

Bordeaux Barrique (Fr.) (bore-doh bah-reek) – standard barrel used in Bordeaux and elsewhere, it holds 225 lt of wine as opposed to the English hogshead which holds 300 lt

Botrytis cinerea (Lat.) (bow-try-tiss sin-eh-ray-ah) – mould that forms on the grapes, known also as "noble rot" which is necessary to make such wines as Sauternes, Beerenauslese and Trockenbeerenauslese

Bouquet – the smell of a wine

Branco (Pt.) – white

Bric (It.) (brick) – term used in the Piedmont region of Italy meaning hill

Brix (bricks) – scale that measures the level of sugar of unfermented grape juice (must)

Brut (Fr.) (brute) – one of the driest types of Champagne

Bual/Boal (Pt.) (boo-al/boh-ahl) – type of Madeira wine

Bundesweinprämierung (Ger.) (buhn-dez-vine-prah-my-run) – a German state wine award

Cabernet Franc (Fr.) (ka-bear-nay fronk) – red grape variety grown in France, mainly to blend with other grapes

Cabernet Sauvignon (Fr.) (ka-bear-nay sow-vee-nyohn) – red grape variety, one of the most popular worldwide

Cantina (It.) (can-teen-ah) – cellar

Cantina sociale (It.) (can-tee-nah soh-shar-lay) – a co-operative winery

Cap – floating skins in red wine must

Capsule – the foil or plastic coating over the top and neck of a bottle to protect the cork (wax may also be used to help)

Carbon dioxide – a by-product of fermentation, which is kept in Champagne and added to other sparkling wines

Carbonic maceration – uncrushed grapes fermented under CO_2 to increase the fruit flavours

Carvalho (Pt.) – (car-val-yoh) – oak

Cascina (It.) (ka-shee-nah) – a farm or esate, especially in northern Italy

Cava (Sp.) (cah-va) – a sparkling wine produced mainly in the Catalonia region of Spain

Cave (Fr.) (cahv) – cellar

Centrifuge – a machine which uses centrifugal force to separate particles and sediment from the wine

Cepa (Sp.) (thay-pa) – vine

Cepage (Fr.) (say-pazh) – grape variety

Cérasuolo (It.) (chay-rah-swoh-loh) – cherry-red

Chablis (Fr.) (shab-lee) – white wine produced from Chardonnay grapes in Burgundy, France

Chai (Fr.) (shy) – a cellar or winery

Chambolle-Musigny (Fr.) (shahm-boll moo-seen-yee) – village in the Côtes de Nuits area of Burgundy region in France

Chaptalisation – addition of sugar to grape juice (must) before fermentation

Chardonnay (shahr-dun-nay) – one of the most well-known and prolific white grapes grown around the world

Charta (Ger.) (khar-ta) – association of estate wine producers that promote quality in the Rheingau, Germany

Chassagne-Montrachet (shas-san-ya mon-trah-shay) – village in the Côte de Beaune in Burgundy, France

Château (Fr.) (shah-toh) – an estate in France

Chianti (It.) (key-ahn-tee) – a red wine produced from Sangiovese grapes in the Tuscany region of Italy

Chianti Classico (It.) (key-ahn-tee class-ee-ko) – the best area producing Chianti

Chiaretto (It.) – the colour of wine that is deeper than rosé, but not a full red

Cinsault (Fr.) (san-soh) – red grape variety grown in France's Rhône Valley

Clairet (Fr.) (clair-ray) – a pale red wine

Clarete (Pt.) (clah-ray-tay) – a light, red wine

Classic (Ger.) – in principle, this is a dry *Qualitätswein* that is intended to be food friendly. It needs to be made from classical grape varieties of the region and have a minimum of 12% alcohol by volume (Mosel has a lower limit of 11.5%)

Classico (It.) (class-ee-coh) – denotes a wine from a certain area within a D.O.C. region in Italy, usually the source of the best wines in that region

Climat (Fr.) (klee-mat) – Burgundian term for vineyard

Clos (Fr.) (cloh) – piece of land enclosed or once enclosed by a wall

Cognac (Fr.) (con-yak)– brandy

Cold soak – process of soaking red wine skins in grape juice before fermentation begins. Holding the mix at a low temperature allows extra colour extraction before the fermentation begins

Colheita (Pt.) (coal-ay-ta) – vintage

Collage (Fr.) (coll-azh) – "fining" of a wine

Colli (It.) (coll-ee) – hilly region

Commune (Fr.) (com-mewne) – an administrative district within a French département

Concentrated grape must – grape juice which is reduced to approximately 20 percent of its original volume

Concord – hybrid red grape variety grown in New York

Confrérie (Fr.) (con-frair-ree) – a "brotherhood" or association

Congeners – colouring and flavouring matter in wines

Consejo Regulador (Sp.) (con-say-ho ray-goo-la-door) – the organisation that controls each D.O.C. region in Spain

Consorzio (It.) (con-sortz-ee-oh) – a group of wine producers who control the wine of their region

Cool fermentation – fermentation conducted under temperatures of 18°C (64°F)

Corked – wine spoiled by an infected cork and which has a musty smell and flavour

Cosecha (Sp.) (coh-say-cha) –harvest

Côte/Coteaux (Fr.) (coat/coat-oh) – hillside(s)

Côte de Beaune (Fr.) (coat duh bone) – southern section of the Côte d'Or in Burgundy

Côte de Nuits (Fr.) (coat duh nwee) – northern section of the Côte d'Or in Burgundy, France

Côte d'Or (Fr.) (coat door) – area of Burgundy in France that produces some of the finest wines in the world

Côte Rôtie (Fr.) (coat row-tee) – a red wine from the northern section of the Rhône Valley in France

Côtes-du-Rhône (Fr.) – the Rhône Valley in France and also used to describe the wines themselves from that area

Courtier (Fr.) (coor-tee-ay) – a broker who is a liaison between a producer and buyer

Cream sherry (Sp.) – a sweet sherry made from a mixture of Pedro Ximénez and Oloroso

Crémant (Fr.) (cray-mon) – sparkling wine

Criada por (Sp.) (cree-ar-dah pour) – matured by

Crianza (Sp.) (cree-ahn-za) – wine aged for six months in oak followed by a second in the bottle; the least expensive of Rioja wines

Crozes-Hermitage (Fr.) (crows

air-mee-tahzh) – red wine from the northern section of the Rhône Valley

Cru (Fr.) (crew) – a growth of grapes (it will always refer to a particular wine)

Cru (It.) (crew) – vineyard

Cru Beaujolais (Fr.) (crew bo-zho-lay) – the highest level of Beaujolais wine which comes from one of ten villages in the region

Cru Bourgeois (Fr.) (crew bour-zhwah) – the quality level applied to over three hundred châteaux in Bordeaux, France

Cru Classé (Fr.) (crew class-ay) – an officially classified growth or vineyard

Crushing – the breaking of the grapes before fermentation begins

Crust – a deposit formed by a mature port

Cryoextraction – a techinique where grapes are partially frozen before they are crushed to help separate the sweet juice from the water

Cuvaison (Fr.) (coo-vay-zon) – a period of time in which a red wine is in contact with the grapes' skins

Cuve (Fr.) (coo-vay) – vat

Cuve close (Fr.) (coo-vay clohz) – the tank production method of making a sparkling wine

Cuvée (Fr.) – (coo-vay) – the contents of a vat, or a special batch of wine

Dão (Pt.) (dow) – a D.O.C. region of Portugal

Débourbage (Fr.) (day-bore-bahzh) – period between crushing and fermentation in which solids are allowed to separate from the must

Decanting – the process of pouring wine from its bottle into a larger glass receptacle, either to leave any sediment behind and/or to let it breathe (it can also be filtered through a cloth)

Dégorgement (Fr.) (day-gorzh-mon) – the stage in production of sparkling wine where sediment is removed

Demi-sec (Fr.) (deh-mee seck) – medium sweet

Denominação de Origem Controlada (D.O.C.) (Pt.) (day-nom-ee-na-sow day oh-ri-zhem con-troh-lah-da) – Portuguese appellation system

Denominación de Origen (D.O.) (Sp.) (day-nom-ee-nah-thee-on day oh-ree-zhen) – Spanish appellation system (basic level)

Denominación de Origen Calificada (D.O.C.) (Sp.) (day-nom-ee-nah-thee-on day oh-ree-zhen cal-if-ee-car-dah) – a superior level in the Spanish appellation system

Denominazione di Origine Controllata (D.O.C.) (It.) (day-nom-ee-nazi-oh-nay dee oh-ridge-ee-nay con-troh-lah-ta) – Italian appellation system (basic level)

Denominazione di Origine Controllata e Garantita (DOCG) (It.) (day-nom-ee-nazi-oh-nay dee oh-ridge-ee-nay con-troh-lah-ta y gah-ran-tee-tah) – slightly higher quality level than a designated D.O.C. wine in Italy

Département (Fr.) (day-part-er-mon) – a French administrative region

Depth – extent to which the flavour of a wine lingers in the mouth

Deutscher sekt (Ger.) (doy-tcher sekt) – sparkling wine made totally from German grapes

Deutscher tafelwein (Ger.) (doy-tcher tah-fell-vine) – lowest grade of German wine

Deutscher weinsiegel (Ger.) (doy-tcher vine-see-ghel) – quality seal around the neck of a bottle of German wine that has passed various tests

Doble pasta (Sp.) (doh-blay pah-sta) – wine macerated with twice the amount of grape skins to juice

Dolce (It.) (dol-chay) – sweet

Domäne (Ger.) (doh-main) – estate

Dosage (Fr.) (doh-sahzh) – the addition of a mixture of sugar syrup and reserve wine to sparkling to correct the sweetness

Doux (Fr.) (doo) – sweet

Dried out – term for a wine which has lost its fruit flavours as it has aged

Dulce (Sp.) (doll-thay) – sweet

Edelfäule (Ger.) (ay-del-foil-eh) – German term for the botrytis fungus

Egrappoir (Fr.) (egg-rap-pwahr) – a machine which removes the stalks from the grapes before they are crushed

Einzellage (Ger.) (ine-zel-larg-eh) – a specific vineyard

Eiswein (Ger.) (ice-vine) – wine made from Auslese-quality grapes picked while frozen (very expensive!)

Elaborado por (Sp.) (ay-la-bore-ah-doh pour) – made by

Elevage (Fr.) (eh-lay-vahzh) – the maturing of wines before they are bottled

Embotellado (Sp.) (em-bot-el-lah-doh) – bottled

Encépagement (Fr.) (on-say-pahzh-mon) – a varietal blend

Engarrafado na Origem (Pt.) (en garra-fah-doh na or-ee-zhem) – estate-bottled

En primeur (Fr.) (on pree-mer) – description of wines sold before they have been bottled

Enology – U.S. var. of Oenology, the study of wine

Enoteca (It.) (ay-no-tay-cah) – wine shop

Erstes Gewächs (Ger.) (erst-es guh-vex)– this is a "first class growth" wine from the Rheingau used for top-class wines from specific vineyards

Erzeugerabfüllung (Ger.) (air-zoy-geeer-ab-foo-lung) – estate-bottled

Espumante (Pt.) (ess-pew-mahn-tay) – sparkling

Espumoso (Sp.) (ess-pew-moh-soh) – sparkling

Estate-bottled – a wine made, produced, and bottled by the owner of the vineyard

Esters – sweet-smelling, fruity compounds in a wine

Extra dry – very dry

Fattoria (It.) (fat-or-ree-ya) – farm

Fermentation – process by which the sugars in the wine are converted into alcohol by the action of yeasts

Fermentazione Naturale (It.) (fair-men-taz-ee-oh-nay nat-ur-rah-lay) – natural fermentation

Filtration – passing of wine through some medium to extract yeast cells and solids

Fining – the clarification of wine, which usually uses a natural agent such as egg white, gelatine, or isinglass

Fino (Sp.) (fee-noh) – the driest type of sherry

First growth – the highest-quality wine in the Bordeaux region as designated by the Médoc classification of 1855

Flor (Sp.) (floor) – yeast peculiar to sherry, vital for fino sherry

Flore (It.) (floor-ray) – first pressing of grapes

Fortification – the addition of alcohol to some wines (e.g. sherry or port) before, during, or after fermentation

Fortified wine – wine that has had extra alcohol added

Foudre (Fr.) (food-ruh) – large, wooden barrel

Fouloir (Fr.) (fool-whahr) – revolving tube which crushes red grapes

Free-run juice – clear juice which comes from grapes before they are pressed

Frizzante (It.) (fritz-ahn-tay) – sparkling

Frizzantino (It.) (fritz-ahn-teen-oh) – slightly sparkling

Fût (Fr.) (foot) – barrel

Gamay (Fr.) (Gah-may) – red grape variety used for Beaujolais wine

Garantia de Origen (Sp.) (gha-ran-tee-ah day or-ee-gen) – basic wine produced in Spain

Garrafeira (Pt.) (ga-raf-air-ah) – wine made from grapes from more than one area and matured for three years, including one in the bottle, if

red, or eighteen months, including six months in the bottle, if white

Gemeinde (Ger.) (ghe-mine-deh) – commune or parish

Generoso (Sp.) (jen-air-oh-soh) – fortified

Gevrey Chambertin (Fr.) (zhev-ray sham-burr-tan) – village in the Côtes de Nuits in Burgundy in France

Gewürztraminer (Ger.) (ge-vertz-tra-mee-ner) – white grape variety, mostly grown in Alsace in France, California, Chile and Germany

Goût de terroir (Fr.) (goo duh tair-whahr) – taste of wine that reflects the soil and climate of the area where the grapes were grown

Gradi (It.) (grah-dee) – percentage of alcohol by volume in the wine

Gran Reserva (Sp.) (gran ray-zair-vah) – Spanish wines that have been aged for at least five years in cask and bottle before release

Grand cru (Fr.) (gron crew) – top quality vineyard

Grand cru classé (Fr.) (gron crew clas-say) – highest level of the Burgundy vineyard classification

Granvas (Sp.) (gran-vass) – sparkling wine

Graves (Fr.) (grahv) – dry red or white wine from Bordeaux in France

Grosslage (Ger.) (grohss-larg-eh) – a group of neighboring vineyards producing wines of similar style

Gutsabüllung (Ger.) (goots-ah-boo-lung) – estate-bottled

Gyropalette (Fr.) (jee-roh-pa-let) – machine used to automate "remuage" in Champagne and sparkling wine production

Halbtrocken (Ger.) (halb-trow-ken) – medium dry

Hectare – metric measurement of area (the equivalent of 2.47 acres)

Hectolitre – metric measurement of volume (100 litres, the equivalent of 22 gallons)

Herb (Ger.) (hairb) – dry

Hermitage (Fr.) (air-mee-tahzh) – red wine from the northern section of the Rhône Valley

Hock (Ger.) (hock) – British term for a wine from the Rhine

Imbottigliato (It.) (im-bot-tee-lee-ah-toh) – bottled

Institut Nationale des Appellations Contrôlées (I.N.A.O.) (Fr.) (an-stee-tew nass-ee-oh-nahl day ap-pel-lass-ee-on con-troh-lay) – governing body of the appellation system in France

Indicação de Proviência Regulamentada (I.P.R.) (Pt.) (in-dee-ca-sow day prov-ee-en-thee-ah reg-oo-lah-men-tah-da) – second level of Portugal's appellation system

Indication Géographique Protégée (I.G.P.) (Fr.) (an-dee-cah-sion jay-oh-grah-feek proh-tay-jay) – a quality level above vin de France which has a recognisable regional character

Indicazione Geografica Protetta (I.G.P.) (It.) (in-deecatz-ee-oh-nay gee-oh-graf-ee-cah proh-teh-tah) level of quality below Italy's D.O.C., but above Vino da Tavola

Isinglass – agent used for "fining" wine

Jerez de la Frontera (Sp.) (hair-eth day lah fron-tair-ah) – town in Spain where sherry is produced

Jeunes vignes (Fr.) (zhown veen) – young wines

Joven (Sp.) (hove-en) – young wine

Jug wine – basic drinking wine produced in California, sold in jug-style bottles

Kabinett (Ger.) (kah-bee-net) – first level of German "Prädikat" wine

Kellerei (Ger.) (kell-ur-rye) – winery

Landwein (Ger.) (land-vine) – German equivalent of France's I.G.P.

Lees – yeasts left after fermentation

Legs – the trails of wine that run down a glass after the wine has been swirled around it

Licoroso (Pt.) (lick-or-oh-soh) – a sweet, fortified wine

Liebfraumilch (Ger.) (leeb-frow-milk/milsh) – a bulk, off-dry white wine from Germany

Lieblich (Ger.) (leeb-lick/sh) – medium-sweet wine

Lie (Fr.) (lee) – (see Lees)

Liqueur de tirage (Fr.) (lee-kerr duh teer-ahzh) – a blend of sugar and yeast added to Champagne to begin its second fermentation

Liquoreux (Fr.) (lick-or-ruh) – sweet and rich

Liquoroso (It.) (lee-kwor-oh-soh) – sweet, fortified wine

Località (It.) (loh-cal-ee-ta) – single vineyard

Long-vatted – wine macerated with grape skins for a longer than normal period to increase the red colour

Maceration – the period of contact between wine and grape skins

Mâcon (Fr.) (ma-con) – area of the Burgundy region in France

Mâcon Blanc (Fr.) (ma-con blonk)

Mâcon-Villages (ma-con-vee-lahzh) – white wine from designated villages in the Mâcon area

Maderisation – heat-induced oxidation

Made wine – wine made from concentrated grape must

Maduro (Pt.) (ma-dhur-roh) – matured

Malmsey (Pt.) (malm-zee) – a rich form of Madeira wine made frm the grape of the same name

Malolactic fermentation – conversion (natural or induced) of malic acid to lactic acid

Manzanilla (Sp.) (man-than-nee-ya) – a dry, pale sherry

Marc (Fr.) (mark) – residue left after pressing grape skins, or the brandy made from it

Margaux (Fr.) (mar-go) – village and district in the Bordeaux region of France

Médoc (Fr.) (may-doc) – district of the Bordeaux region in France

Merlot (Fr.) (mare-loh) – red grape variety

Méthode champenoise (rurale, gaillaçoise, dioise) (Fr.) (may-tod shom-pen-wahz roor-ahl, guy-a-swharz, dee-wharz) – former term for the method used to make Champagne

Méthode classique (Fr.) (may-tod class-eek) – method used in Champagne, and other top sparkling wines, to cause a second fermentaion in the bottle in which the wine is sold

Metodo Classico (It.) (may-toh-doh class-ee-koh) – the méthode classique

Meursault (Fr.) (mehr-soh) – village in the Côte de Beaune in Burgundy in France

Microclimate – the climate of an individual vineyard or group of vineyards

Millésime (Fr.) (mill-ay-seem) – vintage

Mis en bouteilles (Fr.) (meez on boo-tie) – bottled

Mistelle (Fr.) (meess-tell) – fresh grape juice to which alcohol has been added prior to fermentation

Moëlleux (Fr.) (moh-ell-uh) – medium sweet

Mosel-Saar-Ruwer (Ger.) (mosel-sahr-roo-ver) – region of Germany that produces white wine

Mousseux (Fr.) (moose-oh) – sparkling

Moût (Fr.) (moot) – must

Müller-Thurgau (Ger.) (mew-lurr turr-gow) – white grape variety widely grown in Germany

Muscadet (Fr.) (moose-cah-day) – white wine produced in the Loire Valley, France

Muscat de Beaumes de Venise (Fr.) (Mus-cat duh bome duh ven-ease) – sweet, fortified wine produced in the Rhône Valley, France

Must – grape juice

Must concentrators – machines which remove water from the grape juice picked in the rain

Must weight – amount of sugar in the must

Mûtage (Fr.) (moo-tahzh) – addition of alcohol to must to stop it fermenting

Nebbiolo (It.) (neb-bee-oh-lo) – red grape variety mainly grown in Italy

Négociant (Fr.) (neg-oh-see-on) – merchant

Négociant-éleveur (Fr.) (neg-oh-see-on-ay-lev-uhr) – merchant who buys wine after fermentation and blends and bottles it him/herself

Noble rot – another name for botrytis cinerea

Nonvintage – Champagne made from a blend of vintages

Nose – the aroma of a wine

Nouveau (Fr.) (noo-voh) – new, or young, as in Beaujolais Nouveau

Nuevo (It.) (nway-voh) – new, as in Beaujolais Nouveau

Nuits-St-Georges (Fr.) (nwee-san-zhorzh) – town in the Côte de Nuits in Burgundy

Oechsle (Ger.) (oak-sleh) – measure of grape ripeness in Germany

Oenology (oh-nol-oh-jee) – the study of wine

Official Classification of 1855 – a classification of the best Médoc Chateaux of that era

Oloroso (Sp.) (o-loh-roh-so) – Lit. "scented". A style of sherry matured without "flor" yeast resulting in a nutty character. May be sweetened (dulce)

Oxidation – the result of the contact of air with wine

Palate – flavour of a wine

Passerillage (Fr.) (pass-seh-ree-larzh) – process of allowing grapes

to overripen on the vine. This term can also be used for grapes dried on straw mats

Passito (It.) (pass-eetoh) – strong, sweet wine made from semidried grapes

Pasteurisation – sterilisation of wine by heating

Pastoso (It.) (pass-toh-so) – medium sweet

Pauillac (Fr.) (poh-ee-yak) – village and district in the Bordeaux region of France

Pedro Ximénez (Sp.) (ped-roh him-eh-neth) – sweet, white grape variety grown mainly in Spain to produce sweet sherry

Perlant (Fr.) (pair-lon) – slightly sparkling

Perlwein (Ger.) (pearl-vine) – medium-sparkling wine

Pétillant (Fr.) (pet-ee-on) – slightly sparkling

Petite Sirah (pu-teet si-rah) – red grape variety grown mainly in California

Pfalz (Ger.) (p-falz) – wine region of Germany

pH (number) – measure of acidity or alkalinity

Phylloxera (Lat.) (fil-lox-air-ah) – parasite which attacks the roots of vitis vinifera

Pièce (Fr.) (pee-ess) – cask

Piedmonte (It.) (pee-ed-mon-tay) – region of northern Italy

Pinot Blanc (Fr.) (pee-noh blonk) – white grape variety

Pinot Gris/Grigio (Fr./It.) (pee-noh gree/gree-jee-o) – white grape variety

Pinot Meunier (Fr.) (pee-noh muhn-ee-ay) – red grape variety

Pinot Noir (pee-noh nwahr) – red grape variety

Pipe (Pt.) (peep) – Portuguese wine barrel of about 600 lt volume

Podere (It.) (ph-dair-ay) – small farm or estate

Pomerol (Fr.) (pom-uh-rol) – district of the Bordeaux region in France

Pommard (Fr.) (pom-mar) – village in Côte de Beaune in Burgundy in France

Pouilly Fuissé (Fr.) (pooh-yee fwee-say) – highest quality white wine of the Mâcon district in Burgundy

Pouilly-Fumé (Fr.) (poo-yee fooh-may) – white wine produced in the Loire Valley, France

Pourriture noble (Fr.) (pour-ee-tur noblh) – French equivalent of noble rot

Prädikatswein (Qm.P.) (Ger.) (pred-ee-cats-vine) – wines made from grapes ripe enough not to need more sugar, a quality wine which also has further categories.

Premier Cru (Fr.) (prem-ee-air crew) – highest level of the 1855 Bordeaux classification, the second level in Burgundy

Press – machine used to squeeze out the juice from the grapes

Press wine – a blending wine obtained from pressing grape skins after maceration

Pressoir (Fr.) (press-whahr) – grape press

Primeur (Fr.) (preem-uhr) – new wine

Proprietary wine – wine with a brand name

Puligny-Montrachet (Fr.) (pooh-lean-yee mown-tra-shay) – village in Côte de Beaune in Burgundy, France

Pupitre (Fr.) (poo-peet-ruh) – rack used for tilting sparkling wine bottles during rémuage

Qualitätswein (Ger.) (kval-ee-tates-vine) – quality wine

Qualitätswein (Qb.A.) (Ger.) (kval-ee-tates-vine) – the quality level below Prädikatswein (see above)

Quinta (Pt.) (kwin-tah) – vineyard/farm

Racking – decanting of wine from one vat or barrel to another, leaving the lees behind

Ratafia (Fr.) (rat-ah-fee-ah) – liqueur made from marc and grape juice in the Champagne region of France

Recioto (It.) (retch-ee-oh-toh) – special styles of sweet wines, principally Valpolicello and Soave, from the Veneto region in Italy, made from semi-dried grapes

Récolte (Fr.) (ray-colt) – harvest

Região Demarcada (Pt.) – (rej-ee-ow day-mar-cah-dah) – the former appellation system of Portugal

Remontage (Fr.) (rem-on-tahzh) – pumping of must over its skins to extract colour and flavour

Rémuage (Fr.) (rem-oo-ahzh) – manipulation of sparkling wine bottles so the sediment collects at the neck of the bottle

Rendement (Fr.) (ron-duh-mon) – allowed yield from a given area/appellation

Reserva (Pt.) (ray-zehr-vah) – wine from one or more areas from an outstanding vintage, which must

have a half percent alcohol above the minimum level

Reserve – used to indicate a better quality wine, specially selected by the winemaker

Residual sugar – amount of sugar left in the wine after fermentation is complete

Rheingau (Ger.) (rhine-gow) – wine-producing area of Germany

Rheinhessen (Ger.) (rhine-hess-en) – wine-producing area of Germany

Riesling (Ger.) (rees-ling) – white grape variety mostly grown in Germany

Rioja (Sp.) (ree-ock-ha) – red wine from Spain made from Tempranillo grapes

Ripasso (It.) (ree-pass-oh) – wine fermented on the lees of a recioto or amarone wine

Riserva/Riserva Speciale (It.) (ree-sair-va/speh-shahl-ay) – wine matured for a statutory number of years in a barrel

Rosado (Pt.) (rho-sah-doh) – rosé

Rosato (It.) (rho-sah-toh) – rosé

Rosé (Fr.) – pale pink wine

Rosso (It.) (ross-oh) – red

Rotling (Ger.) (roht-ling) – rosé

Rotwein (Ger.) (rote-vine) – red wine

Ruby port – young style of port

Sancerre (Fr.) (son-sair) – white wine produced in Loire Valley, France

Sangiovese (It.) (san jo-vay-zay) – red grape variety used to make Chianti in Tuscany, Italy

Sauternes (Fr.) (soh-tairn) – sweet, white wine from the Bordeaux region of France

Sauvignon Blanc (Fr.) (soh-vee-nyon blonk) – white grape variety

Schaumwein (Ger.) (shaum-vine) – sparkling wine

Sec (Fr.) – dry

Secco (It.) (seck-oh) – dry

Seco (Pt.) (say-koh) – dry

Sediment – precipitation of tannins and coloring matter in red wine due to aging

Sekt (Ger.) (sect) – sparkling wine

Selection (Ger.) (sel-ecs-yawn) – this is a *Spätlese* grade wine that is fermented dry (trocken) and from a specific vineyard

Sémillon (say-mee-yon) – white grape variety mainly grown in the Bordeaux region of France and Hunter Valley in Australia

Semi-seco (Sp.) (sem-ee-say-coh) – medium dry

Semi-secco (It.) (sem-ee seck-oh) – medium dry

Sercial (Pt.) (sehr-she-ahl) – driest form of Madeira wine

Shiraz (sheer-az) – red grape variety (see Syrah)

Silvaner/Sylvaner (Ger.) (sil-vahn-er) – white grape variety, grown a lot in Germany and Austria

Sin Crianza (Sp.) (sin cree-an-zah) – not aged in wood

Solera (Sp.) (soh-lair-ah) – system by which various vintages of sherry are systematically blended

Sommelier (Fr.) (som-mell-ee-ay) – a cellar master or wine steward in a restaurant

Sous-marque (Fr.) (soo-mark) – a secondary brand name of a producer

Soutirage (Fr.) (soo-tear-ahzh) – racking

Spätlese (Ger.) (shpate-lay-zeh) – the second level of German quality wine above Kabinett

Spritz/spritzig (Ger.) (pronounced as it looks) – lightly sparkling

Spumante (It.) (spew-man-tay) sparkling wine

Stainless-steel tank – container used to ferment and age wines

Stravecchio (It.) (stra-veck-ee-oh) – very old

Sugar – present naturally in grape juice, it is measured before fermentation to determine alcohol content and the style of wine

Sulphur dioxide (SO$_2$) – an antioxidant and preservative

Supérieur (Fr.) (soo-peri-er) – denotes a higher level of alcohol

Superiore (It.) (soo-peri-or-ray) – Italian D.O.C. wines carry this term to denote that they meet certain extra standards

Sur lie (Fr.) (seur lee) – aged on the wine's lees

Süss (Ger.) (zoos) – sweet

Süssreserve (Ger.) (zooss-reserve) – the addition of sweet, unfermented grape juice

Syrah/Shiraz (si-rah/sheer-raz) – red grape variety popular in northern Rhône and many New World countries, e.g., Australia

Tafelwein (Ger.) (tah-fel-vine) – table wine

Tannins – extracts from the skins of red grapes and oak which give a backbone to the wine

Tartrates – the potassium bitartrate naturally present in all wine, though most is removed before bottling

Tastevin (Fr.) (tast-van) – shallow cup used for tasting wine

Tawny port – port aged in pipes for average ten, twenty, thirty or forty years before bottling

Tempranillo (Sp.) (tem-prah-nee-yoh) – red grape grown in Spain

Terroir (Fr.) (tair-whahr) – literally means "earth", but refers to the effect of the soil and climate on a vine and the resultant taste of the wine it produces

Tête de cuvée (Fr.) (tet duh coo-vay) – the first and best flow of juice from crushed grapes

Tintillo (Sp.) (tin-tee-yoh) – light red

Tinto (Pt.) (tin-toh) – red

Traditional method (Fr.) – the method used to produce Champagne in France and applied to other sparkling wines

Trocken (Ger.) (trock-en) – dry

Trockenbeerenauslese (T.B.A.) (Ger.) (trock-en-beer-en-owz-lay-zeh) – the highest (fifth) level of German quality wine made from noble rot grapes

TTB – American government agency responsible for wine legislation – Alcohol and Tobacco Tax and trade Bureau

Tuscany – area of central Italy

Ullage (Fr.) (oo-lhazh) – air space between the wine and the cork in a bottle or the top of a barrel

Uvaggio (It.) (oo-vaj-jee-oh) – wine blended from a number of grapes

Uve (It.) (oo-vay) – grapes

Varietal – wine labelled with the predominant grape in its makeup (at least 85 percent)

Vecchio (It.) (veck-ee-oh) – old

Velho (Pt.) (vail-yoh) – old

Vendange (Fr.) (von-donzh) – harvest

Vendange tardive (Fr.) (von-donzh tar-deev) – a late harvest

Vendemmia (It.) (ven-dem-mee-ah) – harvest

Vendimia (Sp.) (ven-dim-ee-ah) – harvest

Verde (Pt.) (vair-day) – young, literally "green"

Viejo (Sp.) (vee-ay-ho) – old

Vieilles vignes (Fr.) (vee-yay veen) – the oldest and best vines

Vigna (It.) (veen-ya) – vineyard

Vignes (Fr.) (veen) – vines

Vigneron (Fr.) (veen-yeh-ron) – vineyard worker

Vignoble (Fr.) (veen-ohbl) – vineyard

Vin de France/Vin Ordinaire (Fr.) (van duh France/van ord-in-air) – basic or table wine

Vin de presse (Fr.) (van duh press) – press wine

Vin doux naturel (Fr.) (van doo nat-ur-rel) – wine fortified before all the sugar has been fermented (mutage)

Vin gris (Fr.) (van gree) – pale rosé

Viña/Viñedo (Sp.) (veen-ya/veen-yay-doh) – vineyard

Vin(o) santo (It.) (vin/veen-oh san-toh) – sweet, dry, white wine made from dry grapes

Vinho generoso (Pt.) (veen-yoh jen-air-oh-soh) – fortified, or dessert, wine

Vinho de mesa (Pt.) (veen-yoh day may-sah) – table wine

Vinhos Regionãos (Pt.) (veen-yos re-ji-o-nowsh) – Portuguese equivalent of French I.G.P.

Vino da arrosto (It.) (veen-oh da ah-rohs-toh) – robust red wine

Vino da tavola (It.) (veen-oh da tah-voh-la) – table wine

Vino de aguja (Sp.) (veen-oh day ah-goo-yah) – semi-sparkling, tank method wine

Vino de mesa (Sp.) (veen-oh day may-sah) – table wine

Vino de la Tierra (Sp.) (veen-oh day la tee-air-ah) – Spanish equivalent of French I.G.P.

Vino novello (It.) (veen-oh no-vel-lo) – new wine, as in Beaujolais Nouveau

Vintage – year of a wine's harvest

Viognier (Fr.) (vee-own-yay) – white grape variety grown in the Rhône Valley, France

Vitis labrusca (Lat.) (vit-iss lab-roos-cah) – species of vine native to America

Vitis vinifera (Lat.) (vit-iss vin-if-air-rah) – species of grape from Europe used to make wine in most countries

Volatile – an unstable wine where acids evaporate to give a vinegary smell

Volnay (vohl-nay) – a village in the Côte de Beaune region of Burgundy, France

Vosne Romanée (Fr.) (vone roh-mah-nay) – village in the Côte de Nuits area of Burgundy

Vougeot (Fr.) (voo-zhoh) – village in the Côte de Nuits area of Burgundy

Vouvray (Fr.) (voo vray) – white wine produced in the Loire Valley, France

Weingut (Ger.) (vine-goot) – an estate (the term can only be used on bottles where all the grapes are grown on the estate)

Weinkellerei (Ger.) (vine-kell-er-aye) – cellar or winery

Weissherbst (Ger.) (vice-hairbst) – rosé wine of the basic Germany quality level

Weisswein (Ger.) (vice-vine) – white wine

Winzergenossenschaft (Ger.) (veentz-er-ghen-ossen-shahft) – a wine-growers' co-operative

Yeast – micro-organism that causes the fermentation process of wine

Zero dosage (Fr.) (zhe-ro doh-sahzh) – very dry style of Champagne or traditional method sparkling wine made with no sugar in the dosage added after dégorgement

Zinfandel – red grape variety popular in California in the U.S.A.

FURTHER INFORMATION

The thirst for wine knowledge can be all consuming and there is a lot of information available to the enthusiast. If I have sparked that drive, here are some suggestions which I hope will begin to satisfy your quest for further wisdom.

Books

Bordeaux: A New Look at the World's Most Famous Wine Region, 3rd Edition Oz Clarke, Pavilion Books, London, 2012

Exploring Wine: The Culinary Institute's Complete Guide to Wines of the World Steve Kolpan, Brian H. Smith and Michael A. Weiss, John Wiley & Sons, Inc., New York, 2010

Grapes and Wines Oz Clarke and Margaret Rand, Pavilion Books, 2008

Hugh Johnson's Pocket Wine Book Hugh Johnson, Mitchell Beazley, London, (published annually)

The Oxford Companion to Wine, 3rd Edition Jancis Robinson, Oxford University Press, 2006

Parker's Wine Buyer's Guide Robert M. Parker, Jr., Simon & Schuster, London and New York, 2008 (updated regularly)

Phylloxera: How Wine was Saved for the World Christy Campbell, Harper Perennial, 2010

The Sotheby's Wine Encyclopedia: The Classic Guide to the Wines of the World Tim Stevenson, DK Publishing, London, 2011

World Atlas of Wine, 6th Edition Hugh Johnson and Jancis Robinson, Mitchell Beazley, London, 2007

Magazines

Decanter (12 issues per year)

Food & Wine (12 issues per year)

Wine Enthusiast (14 issues per year)

Wine Spectator (17 issues per year)

Websites

www.bbr.com (*The Independent's* top ten list of online wine shops 2012), this comes from the U.K.-based wine merchants, Berry Bros & Rudd, who have traded from the same shop in London for over 300 years. Good general information, info on wine courses and will ship around the world)

www.decanter.com (based on *Decanter* magazine, a good site for news and general information)

www.eRobertParker.com (based on the expertise of the respected American wine author, Robert Parker, this has lots of information, including vintage charts for the enthusiast)

www.vinopolis.co.uk (visitor attraction and events venue dedicated to the world of wine)

www.vino.com (carries features and articles on wine, plus recipes)

www.winespectator.com (based on the Wine Spectator Magazine. Good general site for information)

Apps

AG Wine Guide for IPad – a wine guide that looks at a region's grapes and wines

BB&R (Berry's Wine List) – the wine list of Berry Bros & Rudd, Britain's oldest wine merchant

Bordeaux Wine Trip – all you need to plan your visit to Bordeaux's vineyards

Christie's for IPad – lists upcoming wine auctions at the world-famous auction house

International Wine Challenge – all the results from one of the world's biggest blind wine competitions

When Wine Tastes Best – shows the best time to drink wines according to the Biodynamic calendar

Wine Maps – detailed maps of wine regions

INDEX

Note: bold page numbers indicate
illustrations.

Abbruzzo 233-4
A.C. *see* Appellation Contrôlée
acid levels 23, 58, 62, 83, 124, 206
    and food 342-3
Aconagua Valley region 272, **272**
Adolf, Awie 303, **303**
adulteration of wine 305-6, 307
aging *see* barrels
Aglianico del Vulture 234
Airén grape 248
Albariño grape 248
alcohol 367-9
    levels 22, 71, 96, 102, 124,
        202, 345-6
    laws for 154-5, 176
    "legs" indicate 31-2
Algeria 313
Aligoté 64, 136
Aloxe Corton (vineyard) 189, **190-1**,
    191-2
Alsace 67, 69, 71-2, 124, 136,
    174-5, **174-5**, 262
    Sélection de Grains Nobles 139,
        175, 345, 348, 377
Alsace Pinot Gris 337
Alsace Riesling 337
Alto Adige 82, **82-3**
Amarone 224-5
Anjou Rosé 176
Anjou-Saumur 61, 76, 176-8, **176**
Appellation Contrôlée/Protégée
    (A.C./A.P.) 33, **151**, 153-5, 168,
    170, 176, 185, 187, 363
Argentina 90, 101, 135, **268**,
    274-5, 380
    vintage chart 382
Arinto grape 253
aroma 32-4
Asti (region) 222, **222-3**
Asti Spumanti 71, 222, 349
Avignon **152–3**
Australia 96, 98, 101, 118, 121,
    278-91, **278**
    Canberra 283
    New South Wales 58, 59, 89,
        279-80, 281, 282-3
        Hunter Valley 67, 279, 282,

282-3
    noble rot in 139
    Northern Territory 281
    Queensland 281
    South Australia 62, 124, **278**,
        287-9
        Barossa Valley 89-90, **90**,
        124, 286, 288
        McLaren Vale 67, 91, 93
    Tasmania 115, **278**, 279,
        286-7
    varieties grown in 58, 59, 62,
        64, 66-7, 71, 79, 83, 103
    Victoria 71, 279, 281, 284-5
        Yarra Valley 87, **284-5**, 285
    vintage chart 381
    Western Australia 278, 290-1,
        291
    wine laws 282, 322
Austria 64, 68, 102, 124, 202,
    304-7, **304**, 378
    influence on Hungarian wine 310
    noble rot in 139
    regions 307
    vintage chart 380
    wine laws 304-5

Bacchus grape 51, 68, 202, 317
Baden 214, **214-15**
Baga grape 252
Barbera grape 101, **101**, 231
Bardolino 224, 225, 343
Barolo 101, 220-1, 349
barrels, oak 16-17, **16-17**, 24-5,
    35, 54, 62, 68, 72, 182-3, 193,
    272, **274-5**, 288
    barriques 79, 90, 101-3,
        111-12, 116-18, 121,
        221, 239
    pipes **146**, 147
Barsac 56, 58, 164-6, 377
Basilicata region 234
Bâtard Montrachet Grand Cru 54
Beaujolais 23, 197, 336, 343, 377
Beaujolais (region) 94, **94-5**,
    196-7, **196-7**
Beaulieu Vineyards 258
biodynamic 370-5
Blanc de Noirs/Blanc wines 87,
    171-2

blended wines 56, 58, 64, 74, 76-7,
    90, 91, 93, 114
    cépage 158, 162, 164, 171-2,
        180, 184, 185
    frowned upon in Germany 62
    regional 130
    Rioja 242, 243
Bollinger 130, **130**
Bonarda grape 221, 231
Bordeaux 108-13, 271, 349, 377
Bordeaux (region) **47**, 56, 74, **77**,
    78-9, 80, 82, 91-3, 114, 157-69
Botrytis cinerea *see* noble rot
bottles 67, **172-3**, 174, 185,
    298, 359
    shapes 214, 229
bottling 27, 134, **134**, **135**
Bourgogne Aligoté 64, 187, 194
brandy 140, 142, 147, 248, 297
    in mutage process 71
    Pisco 272, 277
Brasil **268**, 276, **276-7**
Britain *see* UK
Brunello de Montalcino 98
Brunello grape 229-30
Bulgaria 309-10, **309**
Bull's Blood 310
Burgundies 54, 90, 349, 357
    red 84, 114-15, 377
    white 116-19, 291, 377
Burgundy (region) 64, 84-5, 90,
    136, 186-97, **186**
Busby, James 88, 279-80, 293

Cabernet Blanc grape 74, **78**, 80,
    157-8, 222
    blended 76, 90, 198
Cabernet Franc grape 91-3, 108,
    158, 166, 169, 176, 178
Cabernet Sauvignon grape 56,
    74-9, **75**, **76-7**, **78-9**, 93, 219,
    235, 309
    in Americas 112, 261, 262,
        263, 265, 272, 277
    in Australia & New Zealand 282,
        285, 286, 288, 293
    in Austria 306
    blended 91, 108, 156, 161,
        162, 164, 229, 314
    with food 346, 349

in South Africa 301
in Spain 243, 247
Cahors 198, 275
California 54, 56, 64, 71, 90, 96, 98, 101, 257-8, 259-63, 381
Carneros 262
Central Coast/Valley 66, 82, 262-3
Napa Valley **6-7**, 56, 79, 91, 93, 112, 118, 258, 262, 362
Russian River Valley **258**, 259, 262
Sonoma Valley 91, 93, 118, 262, **263**
Campania region 234
Canada 8, 63, **264**, 266-7, **266**, 381
vintage chart 383
carbon dioxide (CO$_2$) 31, 130-1, 197
Carmenère grape 80, 83, 93, **93**, 111, 158, 272-3
Cava 237-8, 246
cellars *see under* storage
Central Valley region 272
cépage *see under* blended wines
Chablis 54, 116-17, 187-8, 342, 377
Chambolle Musigny, Burgundy 189
Champagne 14, 54, 86, 126-35, **127**, **128-9**, 262, 376, 377
opening/storing bottles 331, 337
styles 172-3
Champagne (region) 87, 128, **129**, 170-3, 246
Chardonnay grape 14, 26, 54-5, **55**, 62, 116, **116-7**, 188, 235
in Americas 261, 262, 264, 267, 272, 275
in Australia & New Zealand 282, 283, 285-8, 293, 294
in Austria 306
blended 72, 130, 136, 178, 244, 247
in Burgundy 193, 194, 196
in Champagne 171-2
with food 342, 347, 349
in South Africa 301, 302
Chasselas grape 68, 120, 179, 315-16
château system described 158, 162
Châteauneuf-du-Pape 66, 90, 95-6, 184-5, **184-5**

Châteaux
Beychevelle **160**
d'Yquem 58, **136**, 137, 165
Figeac 166, **167**
Haut-Brion 108, 109, 161, 162, **163**, 164
Lafite-Rothschild 109, 162
Latour 109, **110-11**, 162
Margaux 91, **91**, 109, **109**, 162
La Mission-Haut-Brion 164
Mouton-Rothschild 74, 108, 112, 161, 162
Musar (Lebanon) 90, 314
Pétrus 82, **168**, 169
Pichon-Lalande **158**
Reynella 288, **289**
Tahbilk (Australia) **90**, 279, 284-5
cheese, wines with 337, 346-7, 349
Chenin Blanc grape 60-1, 136, 139, 176, 290, 302
Chianti 96, 98, 228-9, **228-9**
Chile 82-3, **86-7**, 87, 90, **92**, 93, **93**, 96, 269-73
regions 121, 272-3
vintage chart 382
wine laws 271-2
China 316-17
Cinsault grape 96, 298, 314
claret 108-13
Classic (classification) 207
Clicquot-Ponsardin, Veuve **132-3**, 133
cloned vines 50-1, 98, 298
Cognac 67
Colheita Port 147
Coombard grape 67
Condrieu, Rhône Valley 71-2, 182
cooking with wine 349
Coonawarra Cabernet Sauvignon 289
corked wine 32
corks & stoppers 330-1, **330**, 335, **336**
corkscrews 328-30, **328-9**
Cornas 183, **183-4**
Cortese grape 222
Corton, Burgundy **189-90**, 190-1
Corvina grape 224
Costers del Segre 246-7
Côte de Beaune, Burgundy 117, 190-1, 193
Côte d'Or, Burgundy 85, **84-5**, 117-18, 188, **361**

Côte Rotie 89, 180-2
Côtes Chalonnaise 194
Côtes de Nuits, Burgundy 188, 193
Côtes du Rhône wines 96, 180, 184
coulure 48, 80, 93, 98
Crémant wines 69, 136, 175, 178, 194
Croatia 102, 311
crossed varieties 50-1, 68-9, **69**
Crozes Hermitage 64, 182
Cru villages 78, 94, 161-2, 164, 168, 175, 187-8, 190, 196
cryoextraction 137-9
Cyprus 312

decanting **332-3**, 333-5
dessert wines 137, 234, 246, 310, 343-5
varieties producing 58, 59, 61, 62
Deutscher Tafelwein (classification) 205
DNA testing 68, 74, 80, 102, 311
Dolcetto grape 222
Dôle wines 95, 316
Douro Valley, Portugal **252**, 253

Eastern Europe 308-11
Eiswein 62, 206-7, 210, 267
Eleanor of Aquitane **156**, 157, 316
Elqui Valley region 272-3
Emilia-Romagna region 231
England 315-16, **316-17**
Entre-Deux-Mers, Bordeaux 169
Erstes Gewächs (classification) 207
European wine laws 263

fermentation 14, **14-15**, 21, **22-3**, 23-4, 73
Champagne 127-8, 130, 171
maceration **22-3**, 23-4, 197
malolactic 26, 116, 193
Fetzer vineyard 260-1, **260-1**
Fiano di Avellino 234
Fino wines 140, 141, 340
fish, wine with 342, 345, 346, 348
flor (yeast infection) 140-1
"flying winemakers" 135, 199, 244, 309
food, wine with 231, 242-3, 260, 338-49
cheese 337, 345
chocolate 345
desserts **342**

exotic **344**, 345
fish 344-5
fruit 343-4
matching 340-2
meat & poultry **340-1**, **343**,
344-5
vegetables 346
fortified wines 66, 140-7, 184, 237,
263, 288-9, 356
storage 356
France 150-99, **150**, 360
varieties in 54-9, 67, 69, 71,
74-7
vintage chart 379
wine laws 49, 50, 79, 130, 136,
153-5, 322
Appellation Contrôlée 33,
151, 153-5
see also individual regions
Franken/Franconia 214
Friuli-Venezia-Giulia region 226-7
Fronsac/Canon Fronsac 169
frost 47, 188, 204, 262, 283, 315
varieties resistant to 63
varieties susceptible to 73,
77, 80
fungal diseases see pests

Galicia 47,
Gamay grape 94-5, **94-5**, 176,
197, 316
Garnacha grape see Grenache
Gascone, Vin de Pays de 67
Gattinara 221
Gavi 222
Georgia 311
Germany 139, 200-15, **201**, 262,
378
styles of wine in 122-4, 205
varieties grown in 62, 67,
68, 69
vintage chart 380
wine law 205, 213
see also individual regions
Gevery-Chambertin 189
Gewürztraminer grape 62, 72-3,
73, 174-5
glasses **30**, 31-2, 331-3, **331**
Graach **210**
Grande Cru see Cru
Grange 89, 288-9, 362
grapes 13-14, 36-51
growing see viticulture
harvesting 16-17, **18-19**, 48,

77, **204**, **308-9**, 309
"green" 61
late 69, 175
night 302
pressing **18**, 19-23, **20-1**, **115**
red wine 21
treading **20-1**, 144
skins 74-5, 82, 84, 103, 108,
114
see also maceration
varieties 52-102
aromatic 70-3
red 74-103
white 54-73
see also individual names
Graves, Bordeaux 158, 162-4
Grechetto grape 232
Greco di Bianco 234
Greco di Tufo 234
Greece 312
Grenache grape 95-6, **96-7**, 184,
242, 243, 244, 248, 288, 347
Grosslage wines 205, 209, 213
Grüner Vetliner grape 64, 306, 307,
310, 337
Guigal la Turque 89

harvest see under grapes
Hawkes Bay vineyards 293, **293**
health, wine and 368-73
Hermitage 64, **179-80**, 182-3
Hessische Bergstrasse 215
history of winemaking 71, 108,
150-2, 239, 256-8, 292,
316-17, 366-7
Hock 212
Howell Mountain wines 262
Hungary 139, 305, 310-11
HWB (Houghton's White Burgundy)
291
hybrid vines 42-3

ice wine see Eiswein
Inzolia grape 235
irrigation 38, **38**, 274-5, 281
Israel 313, **314**
Italy 216-35, **216**, 360, 378
varieties grown in 69, 71, 72,
79-80, 90, 96-101
vintage chart 380
wine laws 219, 229
see also individual regions

Jerez de la Frontera 249, **249**

Kir 64

labels 54, **151**, **154-5**, **158**, **162**,
318-25, **318-25**
examples 324-5, **324-5**
information on 130, 139, 174,
176, **207**, 271-2
proprietery 323
regional 321-3, **321**
varietal 262, 321
Lambrusco grape/wine 231
Landwein (classification) 205-6
Languedoc-Roussillion **4-5**, 76,
78-9, 82, 95-6, 198
Late Bottled Vintage Port 147
Lazio region 231
Lebanon 90, 313
legislation 360, 363
aging 101
grape varieties 50, 79
styles of wine 137
yields 49
see also individual countries
Leyda Valley region 273
Liebfraumilch 68, 201-2, 213, 214
Liguria region 223
Limari Valley region 273
Lirac, Rhône Valley 185
Loire Valley 56, 61, 76, 82, 92, 94,
120, 176-9
Crémant wines in 136
noble rot in 139
Lombardy 222-3

Mâcon 194, **195**
Mâconnaise 194-6
Madeira 66, 254-5, **254**, **255**
Madiran wines 198
Malbec grape 111, 158, 198, 247
Malvasia grape 228, 232, 233
manufacturing processes 10-26,
130-5
Marche region 231
Margaux
Château **108-9**
district, Bordeaux 162-4
Marlborough 294
Marsala 235
Marsanne grape 64, 90, 285
maturation 24-6
Mauzac grape 136, 198
Médoc region 91, 108, 137, 157,
158, 161-2
Premier Crus of 78-9, 161

Melon de Bourgogne grape 176
Mercurey 194
Merlot grape **37**, 80-3, **80-1**, 93,
    158, 166, 169, 222, 363
    in Americas 261, 265, 272, 277
    in Australia & New Zealand
        286, 293
    blended 76, 108, 156, 161,
        162, 164, 247
    in Switzerland 316
Mexico 277
Michelton 285
mildew 64, 67, 82, 84
millerendage 48, 80
Mittelrhein region 202-3, 209
Moët & Chandon 135, 172, 276, 285
Molinara grape 224
Molise region 234
Mondavi, Robert 112, 121, 362
Montagny 194
Montalcino 229-30
Montepulciano grape 231, 233, 234
Montepulciano (town) 230, **230-1**
Monthélie 192
Montrachet, Burgundy 116,
    116-17, 193
Morey-St-Denis, Burgundy 189
Morocco 313
Moscatel/Moscato 71, 222, 253
Moscato d'Asti 222
Mosel Valley 62, 122, **122-3**, 124,
    125, **137**, 204, **208**, **210**
Mosel-Saar-Ruwer **208**, 209-10,
    378
Mould **47**
Mount Veeder wines 262
Mourvèdre 96
Müller, Dr H. 51, 68
Müller-Thurgau grape 51, 68, 213,
    292, 316
Muscadelle grape 285
Muscadet 176, 345
Muscat grape 70-1, **70**, 174-5, 184,
    185, 312
    with food 349
    liqueur from 344
    in New World 269, 285

Nahe region, Germany 213
Nantaise, Loire 176
natural winemaking 370-5
Nebbiolo grape 98-100, **98-9**, **100**,
    220, 221, 275

Negroamaro grape 235
Nero d'Avola grape 235
New Zealand 56, 83, 87, 115, 120,
    120-1, 124, 179, 292-5, **292**
    Marlborough region 294, **295**
    vintage chart 382
Niersteiner Gutes Domtal 201-2
noble rot (botrytis cinerea) **46-7**, 56,
    58, 62, 68-9, 72, 123, 304, 310
    described 45-7
    effect of 137, 165
    regions affected by 139
North Africa 90, 96, 315
nose 32-4
Nuits-St-Georges 7, 190

oak
    barrels see barrels
    chips 118
Oechsle (classification) 207
Oloroso wines 140, 141
Opus One 108, 112, **113**, 362
organic wine production 260, 370-5
Ortega grape 51, 68, 202, 317
Orvieto 232, **232-3**

Palomino Fino grape 67, 140, **141**
Passetoutgrains 95
Pauillac 161-2
Penedés region 245-6, **245**, 378
Pérignon, Dom 128-30, **131**, 133,
    171, 198
Pessac-Léognan, Bordeaux 56,
    58, 164
pests & diseases 41-7, 50, 68, 72,
    89, 266
    fungal 45-7, 64, 67, 82, 83,
        139, 140-1
    in organic vineyards 260-1, 372
    see also noble rot; phylloxera
Petit Verdot grape 76, 91, 108,
    111, 158
Pfalz **212**, 213-14
phylloxera **42-3**, 74, 89, 93, 103,
    109, 157, 164, 239, 256-7
    described 41-2
    in New World 261-2, 271, 281,
        284, 297
Pias grape 269, 272
Piedmont 98-101, **98**, **100-101**,
    220-2, **220-1**, 378
Pierce's disease 45, 50
Pin, Le 362
Pinot Blanc grape 8, 69, 136, 222-3

Pinot Gris/Grigio grape 69, 136,
    174-5, 214, 222-3, 294, 348
Pinot Meunier grape 14, 130, 171
Pinot Noir grape 14, 55, 68, 84-7,
    84-5, 114-15, **128**, 174, 179
    in Americas 262, 263, 264,
        267, 272
    in Australia & New Zealand 285,
        286, 287, 293, 294
    in blending 95, 130, 136
    in Burgundy 189, 190, 194
    in Champagne 171-2
    in Chile **86-7**, 87
    with food 343, 346, 347, 349
    in Germany 209, 213, 214
    in Italy 222-3
    in South Africa 302
    in Switzerland 316
Pinotage grape 298, 302
Piper's Brook vineyard 286, **286-7**
Pomerol, Bordeaux 168-9, 362
Pommard, Burgundy 192
Port 103, 142-7, **145**, 253, 347
    Vintage 144, 334, 356, 378
Portugal 66, 103, 250-5, **256**, 379
    vintage chart 381
    wine laws 250-1
Pouilly Fumé 56, 120-1, 179
Pouilly-Fuissé 196, 197
Pouilly-Vinzelles/Pouilly-Loché 196
Prädikat Wein (classification) 206
Première Côtes de Bordeaux 169
Primitivo grape 234
Prohibition 257-8, 265
Prosecco 225
Provence 198-9, **198-9**
Puglia region 234-5
Puligny-Montrachet, Burgundy
    54, 193

Qualitätswein (classification) 206
Quinta port **142-3**, 144-6

Rasteau 184
Recioto wines 225
Reserva/Gran Reserva wine 240-1
Retsina 312
Rheingau region 203, 210-13, 378
Rheinhessen region **209**, 213
Rhine, River 62, 67, 203-4, 209,
    210, 213-15
Rhône Valley 64, 66, 71, 72, **88**, 89,
    90, 180-5
    Switzerland 316

Ribera del Duero region 247, 378
Riesling grape 51, 62-3, **63**, 174-5, 202, 203, 214
  laws concerning 213
  used in crossbreeds 68
Riesling wines 122-5, **122-3**, 209, 210, 215, 282
  Australian/New Zealand 287, 288, 294
  Spätlese Wehlener Sonnenuhr 62
  with food 344, 346, 348
Rioja 103, **103**
Roman winemaking 71, 157, 180, 203, 218, 316, 366
Romanée-Conti vineyard 190
Romania 311
Rothschild, Baron Philippe de 112, 161, **161**, 362
Roussanne grape 64-6, **65**, 90, 182
Roussillion *see* Languedoc
Ruby Port 147

Saale-Unstrut/Sachsen regions 215
St Emilion, Bordeaux 158, 166-8, **167**
St Estèphe 161
St Joseph 64, 66, 182
St Julien 162
St Peray 64, 66, 183
St Véran 194-6
San Gimignano 230
Sancerre 56, **119**, 120-1, 179
Sancerre Grande Cuvée Compte Lafond de Ladoucette 56
Sangiovese grape 79, 90, 96-9, 229-31, 233
  in Americas 261, 275
  blended 228-9
Sardinia **234-5**, 235
Saumur **60**, 61, 76, 176-8
Sauternes grape 56, 58, 137-9, 164-6, 377
  with food 344, 345, 347, 349
  noble rot and 46
Sauvignon Blanc grape 26, 56-7, **56**, 74, 120, **120-21**, 165, 179
  in Americas 261, 265, 272, 275
  in Australia & New Zealand 120, **120-21**, 287, 293, 294, 300
  in Austria 306
  blended 162, 164, 169, 178, 247

with food 342, 346, 347, 348
  in South Africa 301, 302
Savigny-les-Beaune,Burgundy 192
Scheurebe grape 68, **69**, 202
sediment 132-5, **134**, **334**
Selection (classification) 207
Sémillon grape **46**, 56, 58-9, **59**, 139, 165, 265
  in Australia 282, 288
  in blending 162, 164, 169
serving wine 326-37
  temperatures 334-5
sherry 67, 140-1, 237, 248-9, 330-1, 340, 376
Shiraz grape *see* Syrah/Shiraz
Sicily 235
Silvaner grape **66-7**, 67, 174, 213
  used in crossbreeds 68
Slovenia 311
smudge pots 47, **49**, 187
Soave 224, 225
soil 41, 62, 71-2, 85, 89, 93, 101, 103
  in Bordeaux 158, 162
  in Italy 219
  in Rhône Valley 185
solera system 67, 140-1
Somontano 244
South Africa 61, 83, 90, 121, 296-303, **296**, 360, 380
  regions **297-300**, 300-2
  vintage chart 382
  wine laws 298
South America 268-77, **268**, 360
Southern region (Chile) 273
Spain 67, 71, 95-6, 135, 236-49, **236**
  Aragon 244, **244**
  Cataluña 245-8
  Galicia 248
  Jerez 140-1, **141**, 237, 248-9, **249**
  La Mancha 248
  Navarra 243-4
  Rioja **102-3**, 103, 239, **240-1**, 242-3, **242-3**, 378
  vintage chart 380
  wine laws 240-1
sparkling wines 171, 183, 285, 286, 311
  Crémant 136, 175
  Italian 222, 223, 231
  opening/storing bottles 331, 337
  Spanish 237-8

varieties producing 61, 64, 176-8
  see also Champagne
Spätburgunder grape **201**, 209, 213
Spätlese wines 211
Spumanti wines 71, 222, 226
Stags Leap wines 259, 262
storage 346-57
  cellars **10-11**, **126-7**, 140, **302-4**, **310**, 348-51, 352-5, **356-7**
  kabinets **139**
styles of wine 104-47
Südtirol region 226, **226-7**
sulphur 21, 27, 32, 203, 261
sustainable agriculture 372-3
Switzerland 90, 95, 313-15
Sylvaner grape *see* Silvaner
Syrah/Shiraz grape 72, 79, **88**, 89-90, 180-2, **180**
  blended 183, 198, 314
  with food 345, 346, 347
  in New World 261, 272, 277, 282, 285, 287, 288

Tannat grape 76, 198, 276-7
tannin 35, 74, 76, 90, 98, 108, 112
  and food 246
tasting 28-35
Tavel, Rhône Valley 185
Tawny Port 147, **147**
Tempranillo grape 103, **103**, 242, 243, 247, 248
Teroldego grape 226
terroir 41, **94-5**, 117, 150, 153, 171, 186, 196-7, 360
  in Australia 281, 289
Tinto Fino grape 247
Tocai Fruliano grape 225
Tokaji wines 139
  Tokay Aszú 305, 310-11
Toro region 247-8
Torrontés grape 275
Touraine 61, 94, 176, 178, **178-9**
Traminer grape 72, 215
Trebbiano grape 224, 228, 232
Trentino region 226
Tunisia 313
Tuscany 79, 90, 96, 228-30, **228-9**, 378

Umbria 232-3
United Kingdom 127, 140, 249, 312, 316-17, **316-17**, 367-8
  varieties grown in 51, 68, 202

United States 256-65, **256**, 340,
  360, 367-8
  Oregon 87, 115, 258, 264,
    264, 381
  varieties grown in 80, 82, 87,
    90, 261
  Washington State 90, 115, 258,
    264-5, **264**, **265**, 381
  wine laws 258, 322-3
  see also California
Uruguay **268**, 276-7

Vacqueyras, Rhône Valley 185
Valdepeñas region 248
Valle d'Aosta region 223
Valle Central region see Central
  Valley region
Valpolicella 224-5
Valreas 184

Valtellina 101, 223
vats, stainless steel 15-16, 24,
  24-5, 62, 102, 111, 240, 243,
  358-9, 361
  temperature control in 245
Vega Sicilia 247
Veneto region 224-5, **224-5**, 378
Verdejo grape 247
Verdelho grape 66-7
Verdicchio grape 231
Vin de Pays described 82, 154-5,
  154-55, 199
Vin de Table described 155
Vin Doux Naturel 71
Vin Santo style 224
Vine training, Galicia **48**
Vinho Verde 252
Vino da Tavola (classification) 219
vintage charts 379-83

Vintage port 144, **145**
Viognier grape 71-2, 90, 180, 182,
  199, 261
Vosne-Romanée, Burgundy 115, 190
Vougeot, Burgundy **115**, 189-90
Vouvray 178-9

Wales 315-16
wine-making see manufacture
Winninger Uhlen, Mosel **124**
Württemberg 214-15

yeast 14, 21, 22, 33, 71, 139-40
  in Champagne 130, 131-3

Zinfandel 102, 261, 262, 263,
  277, 311

PICTURE CREDITS